Quantrill in Texas

CAPT. WILLIAM ANDERSON

CAPT. WILLIAM GREGG

CAPT. DICK YEAGER

COL. WILLIAM QUANTRILL

CAPT. DAVID POOLE

CAPT. JOHN JARRETTE

CAPT. GEORGE TODD

QUANTRILL'S STAFF

Quantrill in Texas

THE FORGOTTEN CAMPAIGN

PAUL R. PETERSEN

CUMBERLAND HOUSE

NASHVILLE, TENNESSEE

QUANTRILL IN TEXAS
PUBLISHED BY CUMBERLAND HOUSE PUBLISHING
431 Harding Industrial Dr.
Nashville, Tennessee 37211

Cover design by Gore Studio, Inc., Nashville, Tennessee

Library of Congress Cataloging-in-Publication Data
  Petersen, Paul R.
    Quantrill in Texas : the forgotten campaign / Paul R. Petersen.
        p.   cm.
    Includes bibliographical references and index.
    ISBN-13: 978-1-58182-582-4 (hardcover : alk. paper)
    ISBN-10: 1-58182-582-X (hardcover : alk. paper)
      1. Quantrill, William Clarke, 1837–1865. 2. Texas—History—Civil War, 1861–1865—Commando operations. 3. United States—History—Civil War, 1861–1865—Commando operations. 4. Texas—History—Civil War, 1861–1865—Underground movements. 5. United States—History—Civil War, 1861–1865—Underground movements. 6. Guerrillas—Texas—History—19th century. 7. Sherman (Tex.)—History—19th century. I. Title.
  E470.5.P48 2007
  973.7'42—dc22   2006100062

Printed in the United States of America
1 2 3 4 5 6 7 8 9 10—10 09 08 07

To my father,
Hans Jorgen Petersen,
a friend to his country and a believer in Christ

Contents

Maps

Acknowledgments

I WANT TO express my appreciation to Tony Swindell of Sherman, Texas, for his friendship and assistance in researching this relatively unknown part of William Clarke Quantrill's exploits in North Texas during this important time in Confederate history. Tony has discovered many previously unknown Quantrill sites in and around North Texas, and his newly discovered information about William Anderson and his wife, Bush Smith, has added a new chapter to Civil War guerrilla history.

I also want to thank Emory Cantey of Our Turn Antiques, Rick Mack, Patrick Marquis, Claiborne Scholl Nappier, Greg Walter, Byron Shutz, Robert C. Stevens, and James Pond III for the use of their Civil War photographs in this book.

Introduction

The Civil War is not ended: I question whether any serious Civil War ever does end.

—T. S. ELIOT

THE HISTORY of war is the history of warriors: few in number but mighty in influence. So it was with William Clarke Quantrill. Quantrill has gained a most noteworthy reputation for being the unsurpassed guerrilla leader of the Civil War. His daring exploits in protecting Southern interests in Missouri earned him accolades from Southern sympathizers not only in Jackson County but in almost every county as far east as Howard County, in the heart of Missouri, where he set the stage for Gen. Sterling Price's last raid in 1864. Many times Quantrill was able to strike at will in several counties north of the Missouri River, controlling the area by his reputation alone. His influence also extended south, through the western tier of Missouri counties, all the way to the border with Arkansas. Quantrill's reputation preceded him into Kentucky in 1865. His final foray into the Bluegrass State was known for hard riding and hard fighting against Federal forces either chasing the Missouri guerrillas or being chased during their efforts to bring him to bay. But his most unrecognized military accomplishment outside his adopted state of Missouri did not occur in Kansas, or even in Kentucky, but in the Lone Star State of Texas.

Quantrill's first experience in Texas, and his subsequent trips to and from the Lone Star State, show that he was familiar with the area as well as acquainted with many notable personalities there. His battles and skirmishes from Missouri to Texas only increased his reputation when word spread throughout the South of his victories. Quantrill's time in Texas shows us why he chose to take his men through Kentucky toward Virginia rather than return to Texas with hundreds of other Confederates at the end of the war.

11

While most fighting-aged men were absent from giving their full measure of courage and devotion to the cause, Texas did not remain peaceful. Armed desperados—mostly Union and Confederate deserters and conscription dodgers—hid in the impenetrable thickets and underbrush of North Texas and preyed on the citizens who remained behind. Quantrill's arrival with his men was welcomed when their presence proved to bring justice to the troubled area. While most historians interpret Quantrill's migration as a kind of self-imposed exile, he was actually catching cattle thieves, warding off Indian attacks, hunting down deserters and draft dodgers, and quelling riots. But his most beneficial and unheralded military accomplishments in Texas lay in the role he played of thwarting at least two Federal invasions of Texas.

Military dispatches preserved in the official records fail to tell the full story, but they are what many have used to study Quantrill's activities in Texas. Accounts of Quantrill's actions that are not a part of the official records are often given scant examination. Reconstruction of the story, however, has recently been pieced together from articles gleaned from local newspapers and church records in the small communities dotting the many counties bordering the Red River. Various accounts gathered from the memoirs of Quantrill's men, recalling their winter sojourns in Texas, comprise another angle on the story. Together these sources reveal the depth of Quantrill's participation in both civil and military affairs while he was away from Missouri.

Tales of Quantrill's exploits can also be found in county histories written after the war. Other descriptions can be found in the letters and diaries of Texans who interacted with the Missouri guerrillas. Consequently, Quantrill's exploits in North Texas must be mined from a wide variety of sources. His first experience came as a result of his escorting a Missouri farmer, Marcus Gill, and his family and property into Texas during the spring of 1861. Somewhere close to their destination, the party learned of the firing on Fort Sumter and war being declared. Endeavoring to fight for the South, Quantrill headed back north, joining the first organized military force he encountered. From here he made his way into the regular Confederate army commanded by Gen. Sterling Price and fought in every significant battle in Missouri during the first year of the war. After the battle of Lexington in the fall of 1861, Quantrill returned to Jackson County and gathered a small band that comprised the first organized force in Missouri to combat Jayhawker incursions from Kansas.

Whether in or out of Missouri, and with only a handful of trusted followers, Quantrill managed to achieve battlefield successes over numerically superior Union forces. Because his operations consisted mostly of small skirmishes, they were not given highly publicized notice, though given their frequency, Quantrill's military operations often accounted for more enemy casualties than a single well-publicized account of a large-scale battle. In comparison to David and Goliath, Quantrill's small band struck at Federal garrisons, patrols, and foraging parties at will. In addition to conducting small-unit operations by severing lines of communication, cutting telegraph wires, stopping stages, halting the mails, and establishing a cordon of spies to constantly relay intelligence information, Quantrill was able to gain national notoriety by winning victories in large-scale stand-up battles. The reaction of Federal forces in trying to negate Quantrill's operations never managed to achieve military success. From its inception, Quantrill's company gained a solid reputation as a formidable fighting force counterbalancing the Federal incursions into the Border State of Missouri. This reputation benefited him and his men wherever they traveled.

Outside of Missouri, little is actually known of Quantrill's guerrilla activities. As his original band expanded to a size that could not be easily hidden or supplied by Southern sympathizers once the harsh Missouri winters denuded the landscape, Quantrill took his command south, into Arkansas and Texas, for warmer climates and safety behind Southern lines. As he led his men out of Missouri, he continued to conduct offensive maneuvers. While traveling to and from Texas, his forces were often joined by other Southern commands. Together they conducted operations on targets of opportunity.

After returning from escorting Marcus Gill to Texas in early 1861, Quantrill remained in Missouri until the winter of 1862/63. He then took his band as far south as Arkansas. From there, Quantrill traveled with a single companion to Richmond to seek a colonel's commission from President Jefferson Davis. Verifiable accounts of Quantrill's movements during this period do not exist, except for a questionable verbal exchange he supposedly had with Secretary of War James Seddon. Even though there are no written accounts of Quantrill's experiences during his trip to the Confederate capital, other writings piece together what Quantrill must have experienced along his route. These accounts are important because they give credence to Quantrill's actions and decisions after his return to Missouri. During his absence, his men in Arkansas joined with the regular Confederate army and took part in several important battles. Some reports note that a handful of guerrillas ventured into North Texas before returning to Jackson County, Missouri, in the spring. And during the winter of 1863/64, after Quantrill's numerous victories along the Missouri-Kansas border, his trip into Texas was interrupted by a stunning victory over Union Gen. James Blunt's forces at the October 6, 1863, battle of Baxter Springs, Kansas. What is known is that, by mid-October, Quantrill and his band crossed the Red River at Colbert's Ferry and established a winter camp on Mineral Springs Creek, fifteen miles northwest of Sherman, Texas. Recent descriptions of the camp have been found in local history books and by actual explorations of the site. Due to the large void of research in this area, scant recognition has been given to Quantrill's military operations during this period. Also, the history surrounding his campsite and the descriptions of the local towns and personalities have only lately been discovered in local libraries throughout North Texas. As was his style in both Missouri and Texas, Quantrill became acquainted with the most powerful and wealthy citizens and was himself accepted by well-to-do society.

Descriptions of the North Texas area preceding Quantrill's stay and the guerrillas' living conditions while they were stationed there give us a more accurate picture of how the guerrillas spent their winters in the Lone Star State. What has been pieced together by deciphering the official records and local accounts is that the Missouri guerrillas successfully thwarted Federal invasions of the area on several occasions. The scale of fighting has been ascertained by in-depth research into local history and archaeological excavations. This volume about Quantrill's Texas activities helps debunk the myth that Quantrill's band was largely inactive and even disintegrating before returning to Missouri. Some have even said that his career as a guerrilla commander had ended; that is, until he gathered a few men and headed to Kentucky at the end of the war.

What we find in the history of North Texas is Quantrill's acting every part a guerrilla leader, continuing his mission until mortally wounded in Kentucky on May 10, 1865. While in Texas, he was given assignments to protect the state from Indian raids, to guard against cattle thieves, to break up illegal stills that were destroying the morale of Southern units, to quell riots, and round up deserters. In several instances he successfully defended Texas from Union invaders. All of this activity proves that he maintained a constant, active role in military operations that furthered the cause of the Confederacy.

Quantrill in Texas

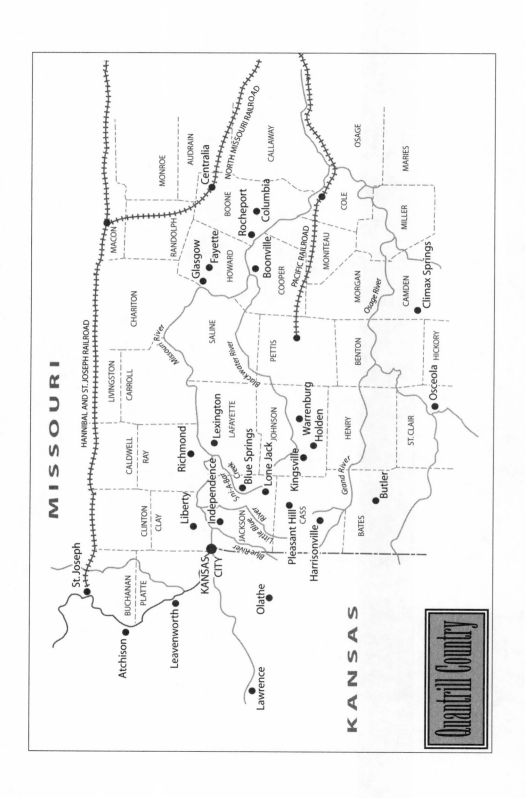

1

The Trip South

You may go to hell & I will go to Texas.

—DAVY CROCKETT (1786–1836)

THE ANCIENT PHILOSOPHER SOPHOCLES said, "Civilization hangs by a single thread," and in Kansas at the start of the Civil War, Jayhawkers were determined to cut that thread. Armed bands of plunderers bent on total destruction flooded across the Missouri border, wiping out all vestiges of normalcy. In Missouri, where once a thriving population lived and worked, there were now only a small number of people bravely clinging to their devastated surroundings. Few escaped the wanton carnage. In Jackson County, the population at the beginning of the war stood at more than fourteen thousand. At the climax of hostilities, only a third of that number carried on with their shattered lives. Bordering Jackson County on the south, where once ten thousand lived in Cass County in 1860, by 1863 only six hundred remained. To the south of Cass County, there were fewer people left in Bates County.

Even before war commenced, marauders from Kansas raided Missouri farms, causing great havoc. This history of violence and Missouri's avowed claim not to join Abraham Lincoln's military aggression against the South allowed Kansans to raid across the border to express their abolitionism. Finding few slaves to liberate, they plundered indiscriminately, so as not to return home empty-handed. In response, Missourians raided Kansas to recover their stolen property. The governor of Missouri offered a reward for any Jayhawkers caught in Missouri, and even the Federal government offered rewards for their capture. Only after a series of hostile incursions by both Kansas Jayhawkers and Federal forces did Missouri turn to the South for aid. It was not until November 28, 1861, that an act by the Confederate Congress admitted Missouri into the Confederacy.

When William Clarke Quantrill first immigrated to Kansas from Ohio, he became acquainted with some of the fanatical followers of the abolitionist John Brown. Mixing greed with their radical hatred of slavery, abolitionists executed armed incursions into Missouri. On December 10, 1860, Quantrill turned against his comrades when they planned a criminal enterprise on the Morgan Walker farm in Blue Springs, Missouri. His colleagues were surprised and several were shot and killed. They had planned to "liberate" Walker's slaves and rob him of his money and valuable thoroughbred horses. Writing to her sister, Ella Mercer described how the Jayhawkers "robbed Morgan Walker and Henry Chiles of everything that they had that could be moved."[1]

Henry Washington Younger, at the time an avowed Unionist, witnessed his property attacked and plundered by Jayhawkers early in the war. This forced his son Coleman to join Quantrill's forces, soon becoming one of his most noted officers. Younger owned three farms and thousands of acres. He also owned two stores and a livery stable in Harrisonville. Jayhawkers first stole several wagons and forty horses. Returning time and time again, the farm was soon stripped of everything of value. Everyone experienced depredation or saw their neighbors plundered. During May 1861, Kansas Jayhawkers attacked the farm of Solomon Young near Hickman's Mill. Young also owned a freighting business. He was robbed of twenty thousand dollars, and his home and farm were plundered. Jayhawkers burned his barns and fields. Throughout the war, they systematically returned to Young's farm, wreaking devastation with each new raid.

Another man forced into the ranks of the Confederates was Upton Hays. His father was Boone Hays, and his grandfather was the famous pioneer Daniel Boone. Before the war, Hays had formed a freight company, securing lucrative government contracts and equipping more than a hundred wagons for the venture. When one wagon train was returning to Jackson County, Jayhawker Charles Jennison attacked, seized the wagons, and stole more than twenty-five thousand dollars. Jennison then torched Hays's home and carried off his cattle, horses, carriages, and slaves. Jayhawkers also plundered and destroyed the home of Hays's brother, Samuel, who was mortally wounded while defending his property. Another Missourian, Larkin Maddox, and his sons, had played an active role in the Border Ruffian invasion of Kansas in

1855/56. For this, they were early victims of hatred and revenge. Jayhawkers under Jennison and James H. Lane made a raid on the Maddox farm, carrying off mules, horses, and other stock; burned their houses, barns, slave quarters, cribs, and outhouses of all descriptions; and stole their slaves. After this Maddox's sons—William, Richard, and George—joined Quantrill to protect what was left of their property and to seek retribution.[2]

From October 27 to November 27, 1861, Jayhawkers systematically marched through Jackson County. From Kansas City to Independence, they burned fields and sacked and destroyed homes. In the Crackerneck area of Jackson County, a short distance south of Independence, 12 homes were burned. Upon reaching Brooking Township, another 26 homes were put to the torch. In late November, Jennison's men swung south into Bates County and burned 30 homes in West Point and killed twelve Southern sympathizers. Some Jayhawker attacks in Missouri were so devastating that entire towns were wiped out. On January 1, 1862, Jayhawkers commanded by Charles Jennison burned all 47 houses in Dayton in Cass County. A week later, Jennison's men sacked and burned Columbus in Johnson County, Missouri, then ventured back into Cass County and plundered Pleasant Hill. In nearby Kingsville, eyewitnesses counted more than 160 houses on fire. Later that month, Jennison's men again struck Cass County, burning 150 homes in Chapel Hill. In July 1862, Jennison sacked Morristown in Cass County, killing several civilians. On September 17, Jayhawker James Montgomery returned and burned Morristown to the ground and killed three of the townspeople.

After the failed Jayhawker raid on his farm, Morgan Walker introduced Marcus Gill to Quantrill. Andrew Walker, Morgan's son, said that Gill was "a well-to-do farmer, a particular friend of my father's."[3] Gill had been born on April 9, 1814, in Bath County, Kentucky. He was a grandson of Thomas Gill, who served in the Revolutionary War. After migrating from Kentucky in 1854, Gill purchased a large farm in Jackson County, bordering the Kansas Territory, bringing his family and more than twenty slaves with him to start a new life. He settled ten miles south of Westport, Missouri, on land bordering the state line in New Santa Fe, a small hamlet and trading post consisting of a general store, post office, a church, and a stable. Gill's family included his thirty-eight-year-old wife, Mary Jane; twenty-year-old son Turner; five daughters; and one small son. An older son, twenty-two-year-old Enoch, was already living in Fayette County, Texas, and had appealed to his father to bring the family to a safer place until the approaching hostilities were over.

Shortly after the two men had been introduced, Quantrill saved Gill's life during a Jayhawker raid, earning a reputation as a brave man who knew how to handle a gun. John Newman Edwards, a fellow Confederate soldier, described Quantrill: "His eyes were very blue, soft and winning. Peculiar they were in this that they never were in rest. Looking at the face, one might say there is the face of a student. It was calm, serene, going oftener to pallor than to laughter. It may be that he liked to hear the birds sing, for hours and hours he would linger in the woods alone. His hands were small and perfectly molded. Who could tell in looking at them that they were the most deadly hands with a revolver in all the border? Perhaps no man ever had more complete mastery over a horse than Quantrell, and whether at a furious gallop or under the simple swing of the route step, he could lean from the saddle and snatch a pebble from the ground."[4]

Gill and Morgan Walker had a mutual friend, thirty-four-year-old Cass County farmer E. F. Slaughter. Gill and Slaughter were church members at the Bethlehem Church of Christ near Hickman's Mill in southern Jackson County. Before the war, Gill and many of his neighbors endured Jayhawker raids involving loss of their livestock and personal assaults. On one occasion, Gill's neighbor Jacob Teaford Palmer was driving a herd of hogs to Gill's farm when he encountered a gang of Jayhawkers. They drove off the hogs and stole several of his horses. The Jayhawkers then broke into a nearby home, smashed the furniture, and plundered what they pleased.[5] Another neighbor, thirty-year-old Emmett Goss, owned a farm near Hickman's Mill. When the war began, he quit farming and joined Jennison's dreaded Seventh Kansas Jayhawker Regiment. Local residents remembered: "From a peaceful thrifty citizen he became suddenly a terror to the border. He seemed to have a mania for killing. Twenty odd unoffending citizens probably died at his hand. He boasted of having kindled the fires in fifty-two houses, and having made fifty-two families homeless and shelterless, and of having killed, he declared, until he was tired of killing."[6]

Fearing further Jayhawker raids, Gill offered to hire Quantrill to escort his family and property south into Texas, behind Southern lines, where they would be safe. Andy Walker recounted: "He [Quantrill] stayed a part of the balance of the winter at Mark [Marcus] Gills. He went with Gill to Texas in the spring of 1861."[7] Also convincing Quantrill to leave the area until the situation quieted down was the rage of James Montgomery's Jayhawkers following the Morgan Walker raid, where several of his men had been killed. Gill loaded up his family and possessions, along with his slaves, and headed to Texas.[8] The Lone Star State had been an attractive spot for several years previously as rumors spread of its good climate and cheap, prolific soil. Many of the newcomers saw that "Texas was a big country to find a dollar in." Texas was also the birthplace of the Homestead Law, a gift to civilization, protecting families from the forced sale of their homes. Gill had several neighbors who were also anxious to get their slaves and belongings farther south. Among them was fellow church member Samuel Gregg and his wife, three children, and eight slaves. Gregg lived on a farm south of Hickman's Mill, near the Santa Fe Trail. He had recently seen one of his slaves with a Jayhawker and was certain there would soon be trouble. He decided to head south with Gill.

Early stories recall similar accounts of migration. One Texas newspaper recorded: "It is not an inferior order of citizens who come to Texas. Men of wealth, talent, and influence compose the more recent class of immigrants, who are well calculated to advance the interest of a new and growing state."[9] The area of Texas lured many like-minded Missouri farmers who saw the wide expanse of prairies and suitable climate as a haven for plantations and slavery. The land was very similar to northern Missouri land: generally level to gently rolling. Dark loamy alluvial soil was an inviting enticement to men wanting to escape the uncertainties of the upcoming conflict. In addition to the rich soil were milder temperatures, with an average high during the summer of 96°F in July to an average low of only 34°F in January. The rainfall was abundant and benefited the crops in a longer growing season. The majority of new immigrants were refugees from Missouri who settled near streams where water and wood were easily obtained. Their small farms generally produced wheat and corn.

Unlike some other immigrants, Gill purchased forty head of oxen to pull five wagons he had purchased for his trip. Each wagon weighed more than three tons when fully loaded. Wagons and other trail conveyances were as varied as the animals chosen to pull them. An expensive vehicle called a "rockaway" resembled an outsized schooner in full sail. Specially built of durable hardwood, it was equipped with bins, pockets, and drawers for storing items needed for the trail. In contrast, there were flimsy rigs that were little more than pushcarts. Hiram Young, a forty-six-year-old wagonmaker from Independence, sold many of these trail vehicles. One popular model was short and sturdy, stripped of excess baggage, and yoked to three oxen. Since Gill had eight oxen for each wagon, he must have relied on the larger "prairie schooner" type of vehicle. Extra oxen could have also been purchased as insurance against lameness or accident. Horses weren't especially popular, because they weren't good in mud: they got panicky. Oxen would be slower than horses or mules but less attractive to the Indians when they traveled through hostile territory. Further insurance was that Quantrill had experience as a bullwhacker on Henry Chiles's wagon train from his trip to Utah a couple of years before.

The merit of oxen over horses and mules was a never-ending debate on the trail. The controversy aroused arguments at every outfitting point. Oxen, although cheaper, were often sold, unbroken to the yoke, to the unwary purchaser. Half-broken animals, terrified of the yoke or halter, were hard to handle. If frightened, they could trample or drag and disable their wranglers. "Always count on splay-footed cattle to outhaul spike-hoofed mules in the mud," warned one authority. Oxen could survive on forage refused by mules, but mules could move a train faster. Indians bent on thievery would steal horses and mules rather than oxen, but should hunger trouble a beleaguered wagon train, oxen could be slaughtered for food.[10]

Gill's property included his household furnishings, bedding, a one-month food supply, water, farming implements, bales of hay, and other possessions. The women packed tools, knives, pots, and pans. Corn and salt were packed for the animals. A hide tied beneath the wagon bed cradled quantities of wood that were hoarded for use on a brushless prairie. Buffalo chips were used in emergencies, but like dry prairie hay, they burned too hot and too fast.

The 1861 trip was Quantrill's first to Texas. His pleasing personality reassured the nervous travelers. He said good-bye to the Walkers and the friends he had made in Blue Springs. "We had learned to like him," Andy Walker said, "and rather hated to see him go. Father made him a present of his fine saddle horse, bridle and saddle, and $100 in money, and I gave him a suit of clothes."[11]

Gill felt confident in having a man of Quantrill's ability guarding his family. The trip could have its dangers. Sickness or injury could strike at any time. Medical assistance on the trail was virtually nonexistent, and the women of the wagon trains were relied upon for treatment. Crude splints bound a broken leg or arm; slippery-elm poultices withdrew the poisons of infection; time was the healer. Guns in the hands of travelers unaccustomed to firearms accounted for accidental wounds and occasional agonizing deaths. When nearing steep banks leading to a stream or ford, the rear wheels were chained together to brake the wagon. Passengers had to guard against being thrown off balance. The danger was not from being thrown to the ground but being thrown under the grinding wheels, which could not be stopped.[12]

Quantrill led the Gill family down the easiest and most common road to Texas. From Jackson County, the line of travel headed due south, west of Pleasant Hill and Harrisonville in Cass County. The trains of oxen usually made around twelve miles a day. Campgrounds had already been established at intervals along the route. Camp routines were outlined for each night's stop on the trail. When the evening meal was over, clothes had to be washed, harnesses and ox chains had to be mended, wheels greased, animals doctored, and tents prepared for the night. Wagons were repacked for the next day's journey; left out were the few utensils necessary to make a quick breakfast before sunup. While some of the men hunted, the children scavenged for pecans around the trees. When traveling in an all-male caravan, travelers usually made "sowbelly and biscuit"—bacon and hot baked bread prepared in a Dutch oven. More palatable food was available if women were in a company of travelers. Eggs were safely packed in jars of corn meal. Wild onions were gathered along the trail to be used as seasoning. The "pantries" stocked potatoes, squash, rice, preserves, pickles, and other delectables. If time allowed, the women would roll out dough on the leather wagon seat and place it in greased pie tins, filling the crust with stewed fruit made from dried apples, peaches, or prunes, then baked in a Dutch oven. Sometimes, if a wild plum thicket or a gooseberry patch were encountered, a fruit cobbler would be served at dinner that night. After the meal, the travelers tried to get some sleep amid the howling of wild wolves.

Quantrill's small caravan continued down along the Missouri border, past Carthage and Lamar, before skirting the border south of Fort Scott in southern Kansas, taking the old military road through the Indian Territory. Moving as a column, he took the wagon train past the old frontier military posts through the old Seneca country known as the Texas Road, connecting Indian Territory with Arkansas, Kansas, Missouri, and Texas. There was plenty of grass and a multitude of streams along the way, which most years could keep the cattle well fed and watered. The streams were forded mostly across rickety bridges and on ferries where tolls were paid. The roads traveled were rough, often steep and rocky, and there was always the danger of quicksand. The territory had no towns at all. Many years before, the Federal government unwisely decided to relocate the Five Civilized Tribes—Cherokees, Chickasaws, Choctaws, Creeks, and Seminoles—from Alabama, Florida, and Mississippi farther west to Indian Territory in present-day Oklahoma. The area was considered undesirable land. These fifty thousand Indians were considered self-governing nations within their own allotted lands. Their new territory covered an immense wilderness of prairies and mountains bounded by Arkansas on the east, Kansas on the north, a strip of no man's land on the northwest, and Texas on the west and south. No one seemed to question the wisdom of what to do with the Indian tribes already settled there. What transpired was open hostility between the various tribes. Caddo, Delaware, Kanchanti, Kickapoo, Shawnee, and Uchee had lived and used this area for hunting grounds for years. Even though the plains Indians agreed to withdraw farther west, they continued to use their former hunting grounds to harvest buffalo and lived in close proximity to the resettled tribes. The Chickasaw and Choctaw tribes built schools and established law and order in their resettled territory, but lightning raids from the plains Indians farther west soon threatened their way of life.

In 1834, Congress passed what was called the Intercourse Act, excluding white settlers from Indian Territory and permitting the presence of white traders only under Federal license. In those days there were two laws. If an Indian killed another Indian, Indian law addressed the matter. But if a white man killed an Indian or an Indian killed a white man, the white man's law applied. Several deputy marshals scoured the country all the time.[13]

By the early 1850s, Texas cattle herds bound for Kansas were crossing the territory in the thousands, and prospectors were streaming through on their way to the gold fields in California. A few years later, the routing of the east-west overland mail through the territory threatened to turn it into a gigantic thoroughfare.[14] To protect the newly relocated Indian tribes, the U.S. Army set up a line of military posts, the most significant ones being Fort Arbuckle, Fort Cobb, Fort Gibson, and Fort Washita.

The first military post Quantrill and the Gill family came to was Fort Gibson in northeastern Indian Territory. It was 138 miles southwest of their last major stop in Carthage, Missouri. Fort Gibson was one of the oldest military posts in Indian Territory, having been established in 1824 when the increasing tensions between the Cherokee and Osage nations led the army to relocate its westernmost presence from Fort Smith, Arkansas, farther west. The establishment of the fort encouraged the newly relocated eastern Indian tribes to resettle nearby, which provided protection against the more hostile Indians of the western plains. These hostile Indians made incursions upon the relocated tribes as well as white settlers. As late as 1858, Maj. Earl Van Dorn had been fighting raiding Comanches. When the Civil War began, the U.S. Army vacated Fort Gibson (just before Quantrill's arrival), knowing it did not have the resources to keep large numbers of troops in the territory. Confederate troops immediately occupied the fort, since it was important to establish control both over the Indian Territory and the Texas Road.

Farther south, another fort had been established shortly after Fort Gibson was built. In 1841, Gen. Zachary Taylor and a troop of mounted cavalry rode into Indian Territory to scout the best site for a new post that could guard the Choctaws and Chickasaws. Taylor soon found an ideal position eighteen miles north of the Red River, along the banks of the Washita River. The Red River formed the boundary between Texas and Indian Territory. Its early

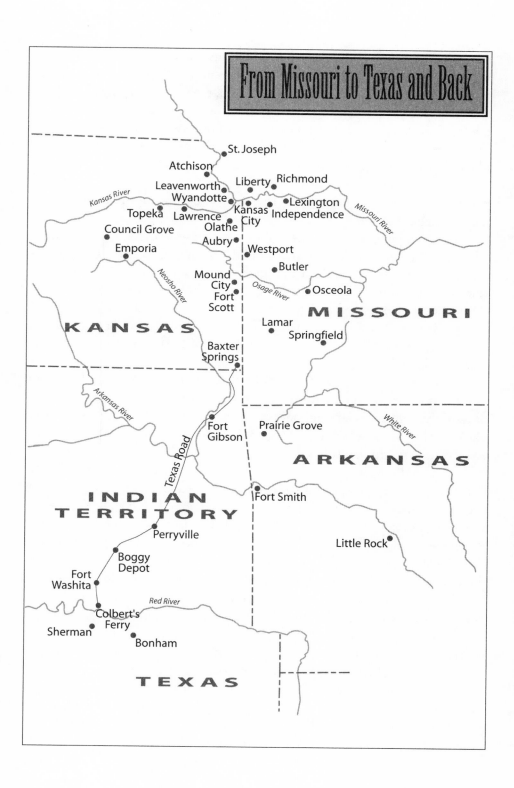

From Missouri to Texas and Back

tributaries and main bed are dry most of the time, consisting of a sandy valley, which holds a raging torrent during excessive rainfall, when a sandy red sediment rich in minerals is carried downstream, creating the color from which the river derives its name. The new fort was occupied in April 1842 and named Fort Washita, twenty miles north of Preston, Texas. Because this fort mainly served to run patrols and skirmish with the lightning attacks of the plains Indians, it contained an extensive corral and stable area, as well as shops for blacksmiths and farriers. The fort covered a large area consisting of barracks and quarters. Included in the enclosure were a hospital, a commissary, and a guardhouse.

Seventy-five miles southeast of Fort Washita was Fort Arbuckle, built in 1851 and remotely nestled in the middle of Indian Territory. The government needed to have a military presence in the southeastern Indian Territory to protect the Civilized Tribes from the Kiowa and Comanche. Assistance was also needed to protect the heavy stream of immigrants heading south into Texas and west into California. The new fort was on the Canadian River, along the trail leading out of Fort Smith, Arkansas, to Santa Fe, New Mexico.

Farther west of Fort Washita was Fort Cobb, the smallest and last of the military outposts in Indian Territory. It was in the Caddo country in present-day southwestern Oklahoma, along the junction of Pond Creek and the banks of the Washita River. It was established in October 1859 to maintain order among the Indian tribes.

Most of the military forts were constructed in the same manner. The buildings were one story within a rectangular stockade, with blockhouses on the corners. A line of barracks was constructed on either side, with commissary and quartermaster's quarters at one end and officers quarters at the other. A separate building for a kitchen, dispensary, and hospital and sometimes a sutler's cabin for the soldiers comprised the other structures, all made with puncheon floors (floors made from logs split in half and laid as flooring) and wood-shingled roofs. The buildings were usually made of logs, hewn and chinked with wood and clay and outfitted with stone chimneys or chimneys made with sticks and mud. More elaborate dwellings had plaster interior walls finished in black walnut. The middle of the encampment was used for a parade ground. The forts were usually constructed alongside a river or stream so a never-ending water supply could easily run a mill and furnish water for troops and weary travelers.[15]

Shortly before Quantrill traveled with Gill to Texas, Comanches and other hostile plains Indians began raiding the area where the relocated Indians had settled and stole a large number of horses. Not many Federal troops were kept in the southwestern posts, and most of them were in Texas. The Indian agent for the territory was Douglas Hancock Cooper, who, with the aid of troops, tried to keep peace between the various tribes. Cooper was influential in organizing a group of Indians as mounted rangers to patrol their own territory, an experience he soon put to use as a Confederate general. He had served in the Mexican War in the Mississippi regiment commanded by Jefferson Davis, and he and Davis were good friends.

The trip to Texas must have seemed like a pleasant outing for Gill and his family, even though there was great political uncertainty. The threat from the Indians was minimal compared to the fear of Jayhawker attacks back home. There was an abundance of wild game along the way, and Quantrill's marksmanship provided meat for the travelers. Game included bear, buffalo, duck, goose, pigeon, prairie hen, quail, venison, wild turkey, and fish in addition to the fare the women cooked up from their own provisions.

After getting forage for their animals and a fresh supply of water at Fort Gibson, Quantrill's group continued south on the Texas Road. Their next stop was north of the Red River, at a place known as Boggy Depot, early capital of the Chickasaw and Choctaw tribes at a point where the Fort Gibson and the Fort Smith roads forked. Boggy Depot, situated in a fertile valley, was dubbed thus by traders who used the area to bargain with the Indians, and it later became the main Confederate commissary and ordnance supply depot. The Confederate government purchased most of the wheat produced in North Texas, paying fifty cents a bushel.

After leaving Boggy Depot, Quantrill's party headed southwesterly, crossing the Blue River and heading for Fort Washita, their last major stop before entering Texas. Many travelers remarked that this part of Indian Territory was the most beautiful part of the Indian nation.[16]

Texas differed from the rest of the Confederate states in one respect: Texas was only partially settled. To newcomers, the sheer size of the state was intimidating, and the terrain could be as frightening as it was beautiful. One prominent individual said: "If I owned both Texas and hell, I'd rent out Texas and live in hell."[17] On the whole, survival was a daily challenge, especially so for traveling families. Roads were littered with bleached ox skulls and charred wagon parts, testifying to the wretched luck of earlier ill-starred trains. A Texas frontier education was quick and hard, and novices often paid for ignorance with their lives. Heading west, newcomers were certain to encounter Comanches, arguably the finest cavalry in history, and they made travel across western Texas extraordinarily perilous. An Indian attack, expected at any time, came from any direction. The shouted trail halloo, "Men in the distance!" sent chills of anxiousness through a wagon company until it could be determined if the approaching party was whites or Indians, and if Indians, friendly or hostile. One traveler remarked about his experiences: "It required nerve to come to Texas but more nerve to live here among privations and dangers that surrounded us. Wild Indians were burning the land and homes often within a few miles of town. On every road as we came in, we met hundreds who told us to go back to Tennessee, that we could not get a good drink or a square meal in the whole state." There was a succinct old saying: "Texas ain't fer amateurs."[18]

The most favorable crossing on the Red River was Chickasaw Ben Colbert's place, commonly known as Colbert's Ferry. Benjamin Franklin Colbert was a half-breed Chickasaw, and he established his Red River ferry crossing in 1847, leading from the main trail into North Texas, first mapped out in the 1853 Whipple Survey. From Indian Territory, one could see three hills, the highest points in Grayson County, which served as landmarks for travelers entering Texas. Ten log cabins and a post office at the crossing furnished accommodations for weary settlers. Colbert was a shrewd ferryman and also a tribal chief. He solemnly told how he had secured from the Chickasaw tribal council permission to establish the ferry and how the venture had prospered from the very beginning, besides raising cattle and farming his eight-hundred-acre farm. White men and Indians approved of Ben Colbert. Doctor Alex Acheson remembered him as a "quiet gentleman, wealthy and kind, generous to a fault." One of his employees, John Malcolm, said that he was "strictly honest and a perfect gentleman, and expected everyone else to be the same."[19] Colbert's home, which he named Riverside, was on a bluff overlooking the crossing on the Oklahoma side. It was a gathering place for white and Indian friends of the area, which was settled by only a few families. The house was a white cottage divided in the center by an open hallway, called a "dog alley." A small town soon sprung up on the south bank about two hundred yards from the ferry landing. From the north, long wagon trains loaded with freight and newly arriving families made their way across the Red River. From the south, wild-looking longhorn cattle were driven across the shallows, making their way to the railroads farther north.

Across the river from Colbert's Ferry, Grayson County had been created the year before, being carved out of a western portion of Fannin County. The county was named for Peter W. Grayson, who had immigrated to Texas in 1830. Grayson served Texas in the revolution and was attorney general of the republic. In 1846, the county was organized, and Sherman was made the county seat. The town was named for Capt. Sidney Sherman; he had commanded the left wing of the little army of Texas in the battle of San Jacinto on April 21, 1836. Sherman was said to be the first man to raise the battle cry, "Remember the Alamo!"

Consisting of 942 square miles, the county was divided into two distinct geographical regions. The upper level to the west was covered with timber, running south from the Red River and known as the Cross Timbers. The area to the east was rolling prairie, inundated with numerous springs and brooks. By 1850 the county had a population of 2,008, primarily from the South. Most of the migration came from the Upper South: Arkansas, Kentucky, Missouri, Tennessee, and Virginia. By 1860 Grayson County's population had grown to 8,184—20 percent of whom came from Missouri—a significant part of the increase having occurred after 1858. The county was thirty miles wide from east to west, but its northern border was longer because of the meandering Red River. In 1859, one thousand wagons crossed the Red River into Grayson County.

Before Quantrill's arrival, Texas riders used a communication network among the settlers to establish paths and lanes. In 1847, Texas state legislators ordered a road from Preston to Sherman, and another road was requested in 1853 by the Grayson County court from Colbert's Ferry to the county seat. Indian and cattle trails, as well as wagon ruts that traversed the area, became roads.

There was also a persistent desire for improved mail service between the eastern states and the states and territories in the West. Responding to pressure for more dependable and speedier service, Congress in 1857 authorized the postmaster general to contract for a new overland mail route. John Butterfield won the contract, and by September 1858 the Butterfield Overland Mail enterprise was launched. It was the greatest stage line in American history, covering 2,759 miles. Sherman's city fathers secured routing of the Butterfield Line through the town by entertaining Butterfield and his associates, who were surveying potential routes, with a champagne supper. Colbert's Ferry was then adopted as the line's Red River crossing. When the population more than doubled in the district during 1858/59, the people of Grayson County thought so much of the Butterfield line, they bridged all the streams in the county, and Colbert agreed to ferry Butterfield's coaches across the Red River free of charge.

The initial Butterfield stage arrival was a time of celebration. The stage was destined for San Francisco, coming from St. Louis through Fort Smith. It crossed the Red River at Colbert's Ferry, veered west of Denison, crossed Iron Ore Creek, and entered Sherman west of Austin College. The vehicle headed south on Travis Street to the town square, where it stopped for ten minutes in front of N. Byrd Anderson's hotel, time enough to hitch up a fresh team at the Jones Livery Stable, which was on the southeast side of the square. The next stop would be El Paso, where a fresh driver and fresh team waited. One newspaper reported, "The big stable of the establishment, also a general livery stable, is the most imposing public institution in Sherman, not, of course, the handsomest building, but large, with wide doors always open and having a look of night and day work unceasing."[20]

The horses had scarcely halted when they were unfastened from the traces, while others were held in check long enough to be fastened. The driver threw the mail from the boot of his stage to another with little slackening of speed. On the road ahead, wells had been sunk at intervals along the long dry stretches, and stations were provided every ten to twenty miles, where mail could be collected or deposited and where fresh horses and drivers could be secured. The stations included a keeper's house, stables, and a blacksmith shop. During times of Indian hostility, guards of four or five men defended the stage posts.[21]

Each coach had two men on it, one to drive and one to whip. The first coaches were Concord spring wagons, carrying four passengers and their baggage and five to six hundred pounds of mail. The leather springs of Concord coaches gave a swaying, easy motion. Later, more commodious coaches carried six to nine passengers inside and one to ten outside. Hauling teams consisted of four horses or mules, but on the more difficult stretches, additional animals were attached and kept in a seven-mile-per-hour trot.

Passengers noted that the coach drivers were a peculiar "breed." Drivers were constantly watchful while holding a tight rein or flourishing their whip. They kept a finger on the trigger of at least one of the two six-shooters or shotgun they carried, and they talked constantly, mainly pointing out places where stages had been robbed or passengers killed.[22]

The dangers of Indian and bandit attacks were so great that every stage passenger was well armed and prepared to fight. A San Diego newspaper recommended the following equipment for overland passengers: "One Sharp's rifle and a hundred cartridges; a Colt's Navy revolver and two pounds of balls; a knife and sheath; a pair of thick boots and woolen pants; a half dozen pair of thick woolen socks; six undershirts; three woolen overshirts; a wide awake hat; a cheap sack coat; a soldier's overcoat; one pair of blankets in summer and two in winter; a piece of India-rubber cloth for blankets; a pair of gauntlets; a small bag of needles, pins, a sponge, hairbrush, comb, soap, etc., in an oil silk bag; two pairs of thick drawers, and three or four towels.[23]

One of the first Butterfield passengers described his arrival in Texas: "We crossed the wide, shallow, and muddy Red River on one of Mr. Colbert's boats and saw quite a number of his slaves busily engaged in lowering the present steep grade up the banks. . . . On our way to Sherman in Texas, we passed several large gullies, or beds of creeks, which are being bridged at the expense of Grayson County."[24]

Another passenger described the scene of the stage's approach and departure from Sherman: "Sherman is a pleasant little village of about six hundred inhabitants. We found Mr. Bates, the superintendent of this part of the line, ready with a team of mules to carry the mail on without a moment's delay. . . . Our course lay across a fine rolling prairie, covered with fine grass, but with no trees and scarcely a scrub for eighteen miles, crossing a number of beds of little brooks which were now dry, but whose banks in winter afford plentiful grazing for cattle. . . . The first station after leaving Sherman was twenty-miles distant, and our team traveled it in three hours, so that before we reached there the beautiful moonlight lit up the vast prairie, making its sameness appear like the boundless sea and its hills like the rolling waves."[25]

Mail delivery was semiweekly. In Sherman, a public mailbag was hung on a branch of an old pecan tree. The cost of delivery was ten cents per letter. Outgoing mail was dropped in the bag and left unattended until the stage picked it up. By necessity, the pecan-tree post office gave way to space in a log house on the south side of the square. The stage-line business boomed, but the war put an end to the line on March 21, 1861, when the final passengers arrived in Missouri. While it was in service, the Butterfield Line gave prospectors and immigrants the opportunity for a home in the golden West and linked squatters' homes with civilization.[26]

North Texas, at the edge of the frontier, was a combination of the Old South and the New West. Although only one family in four owned slaves in Texas, most Texans opposed any interference with the practice of slavery, which they believed necessary for the continued growth of the state. The new white settlers found resettled southern Indian tribes in Indian Territory to their north and hostile Indian tribes to the west. Even though Marcus Gill was leaving the Missouri border area and the ravages of the Jayhawkers behind him, Texas had its own set of problems.

During the fifteen years that Texas had been in the Union, the state's population had quadrupled and the people had prospered. But by 1860 the approaching political crisis generated no little uneasiness. When separation from the United States was debated in the Lone Star State, the eight counties in the Red River region narrowly voted against secession. Stories circulated of an underground Unionist conspiracy, said to have the support of Jayhawkers and Kansas cutthroats, aimed at overthrowing Confederate authority in North Texas. Reports of slave uprisings and poisonings prevailed. Fires occurred almost simultaneously at Dallas, Denton, Pilot Point, Black Jack Grove, Waxahachie, Kaufman, and Gainesville.[27] On July 3, 1860, a three-hundred-thousand-dollar fire destroyed the Dallas town square. Local historians noted:

> The plot was conceived, (according to a Dallas correspondent) by certain abolition preachers who had been expelled from the county. It was charged that the plan was to demoralize by fire and assassinate the whole of North Texas, and then a general revolt of the slaves, aided by the North, was to take place on election day in August. Military companies were organized, in most cases for general protection against the Negroes and abolition enemies both in the state and out of it. Many of the problems were caused by Kansas settlers coming to North Texas to foment unrest. There seems to have been no overt acts by abolitionists in Grayson County, though accounts exist of murder in the Choctaw Nation by slaves and poisonings in Fannin County.[28]

Texans expressed increasing concern over attacks upon Southern institutions by Northern political leaders. At the beginning of the hostilities, Texan James G. Bourland was sent into Indian Territory to ascertain their sympathies. In April 1861, he encountered 120 wagons filled with people "from Grayson, Johnson, Collin, and Denton counties [who] were returning to Kansas after failing to sway the vote against secession, and they told Bourland they had even campaigned for the northern tier of counties to form a new state. . . . Having failed in that effort, about 500 voters were returning from whence they had come."[29]

Bourland had been born in 1801 in North Carolina before moving to Kentucky. He owned a large plantation on the Red River at what was known as Bourland's Bend. He traded principally with the Chickasaws across the river. At one time he led a volunteer force against marauding Indians in 1841, and during the Mexican War, he was second-in-command of the Third Regiment of the Texas Mounted Rifles. At the beginning of the Civil War, the sixty-year-old Bourland was made a colonel and given command of all Confederate troops along the northwestern frontier. His battalion was stationed at Fort Washita in Indian Territory.

Just before the war, political fervor abounded in North Texas. In April 1859 a meeting in Grayson County adopted a resolution declaring the county in favor of the Union "while it can be preserved without dishonor."[30] In the summer of 1860 several slaves and a northern Methodist minister were lynched in North Texas for antislavery sentiments. In early 1861, in the county seat of Bonham in adjacent Fannin County, citizens issued a warning to some church members and "other organizations of similar feelings on the slavery question to desist from talking their doctrine either in public or in private," and "anyone feeling themselves aggravated by this action [was] given sixty days to depart from the country forever, and that a vigilance committee be organized to enforce the above regulations."[31]

During the spring of 1861, in the early days of the war, one Sherman citizen threatened to slap the face of any Secessionist he found. Another citizen accepted his threat and called the man out on Travis Street for a fight. When the fight ended, the man who had made the threats and two of his friends were dead. About the same time, a Union sympathizer tore down the Confederate flag over the courthouse. Prominent attorney and ardent secessionist Thomas C. Bass raised another Confederate flag over the courthouse, and then he kept guard over it with a shotgun, daring anyone to try to haul the flag down again. Needless to say, the flag remained flying. Shortly afterward, the townspeople organized a Home Guard company of "at least 100 men ready and willing at any time and on short notice to defend Southern interests and Southern equality in the Union or out of it."[32]

During the war, Confederate Col. Thomas C. Bass organized and commanded the Twentieth Texas Cavalry and served in Indian Territory and later in Mississippi. During the 1872 yellow-fever epidemic in Memphis, while volunteering as a nurse, Bass fell victim to the disease himself.

As was noted above, several North Texas counties voted against secession. Rumors of Unionist alliances with Kansas Jayhawkers and Indians along the Red River—together with the petition of editor E. Junius Foster of the *Sherman Patriot* to separate North Texas as a free state—brought emotions to a fever pitch. In 1862 after Foster had published an editorial praising the murder of Confederate Col. William C. Young by Union men, Foster was confronted by the victim's son. When he refused to recant his criticism of the colonel and the Confederacy, Foster was shot and killed and his newspaper office and archives were burned.

When Quantrill entered Texas, he learned of the bombardment of Fort Sumter and the subsequent Federal surrender on April 13. During late February and March 1861, Texas had already begun recruiting troops. In May in

Indian Territory, the newly formed Confederate government dispatched Albert Pike of Arkansas, already well known to the Indians, to negotiate alliance treaties. Pike convinced many Indian leaders to support the Confederacy; many tribes had a deep enmity for the Federal government after their forced relocation. Confederate president Jefferson Davis was well aware of the importance of securing an alliance with the Five Civilized Tribes. He believed such an alliance would protect Texas from Kansas and that the Indians had sufficient cattle to feed the armies of the South. Also the tribes could render valuable service as scouts and cavalry operations along the border. Pike's purpose in negotiating with the tribes was not to secure military support for the Confederacy, since the Indians were not numerous enough to be of substantial help, but to act as a buffer between Texas and Kansas once Texans left their homes to serve in the Confederate army. Since many bands of Indians had been raiding in Texas, Pike hoped that an alliance would redirect the focus of these attacks to the north, to Kansas.

Many Indians owned slaves and thus had a stake in the Southern cause. To win their support, the Confederate government made several promises. These included protection from invasion, continued annuities payments, a measure of tribal self-government, and guarantees of the Indians' right to their lands. In return, the Indians agreed to provide troops to fight only in Indian Territory.[33]

In Arkansas, Federal troops under Capt. Samuel Sturgis were garrisoned at Fort Smith. For almost two decades Fort Smith had been a funnel through which pioneers, military caravans, Indian supplies, and gold seekers had proceeded on the Texas Road through Indian Territory. Fearing that Arkansas would secede and that his men would not be able to defend the post, Sturgis evacuated Fort Smith on April 23, 1861. Within hours, state militia from Little Rock took control of the facility. A month later, Arkansas officially joined the Confederacy, and the garrison at Fort Smith became a Confederate outpost. Confederate troops from Arkansas, Louisiana, Texas, and even Indian Territory drilled at the newly acquired stronghold.

Gen. Benjamin McCulloch was put in command of the several thousand troops at Fort Smith. Famed as a leader of the Texas Rangers during the Mexican War, the fifty-year-old McCulloch was tall, spare, and slightly stooped. His long black hair fell over his ears, he had a short but full beard, and his deep-set gray eyes were shaded by heavy brows that "gave an expression of almost suspicious scrutiny to his countenance." In manner, he was cool, serious, and taciturn. He wore no uniform, and instead of a saber, he carried a hunting rifle.[34] McCulloch was naturally a favorite in Texas. Originally from Tennessee, McCulloch had known Davy Crockett and had followed him to Texas, arriving in time to be part of the Texas army that defeated Antonio López de Santa Anna at the battle of San Jacinto. McCulloch had been elected to the second congress of the republic and later to the first legislature of the newly formed state. With the outbreak of the Civil War, McCulloch and his brother Henry participated in the takeover of Federal garrisons in San Antonio.

In San Antonio on February 16, 1861, Bvt. Maj. Gen. David E. Twiggs surrendered all Federal government and military property in Texas to the Confederacy. Twiggs, however, was not happy with the manner that McCulloch forced his surrender and complained that he was not treated as a gentleman or given the respect his rank required. He charged, "General McCulloch, you have treated me shamefully, ruining my reputation as a military man and now I am too old to reestablish it."[35] Also in San Antonio at the time was Lt. Col. Robert E. Lee, who had stopped en route from Fort Macon to Washington, D.C., to report to General in Chief Winfield Scott. Fort Macon stood on the northern edge of the Texas hill country, overlooking the Llano River.

Reaction in Texas to the surrender of Fort Sumter was much the same as it was throughout the South. Cautious politicians tried to calm excitable spirits. Radical Northern abolitionists incited the nation with their rhetoric, while Southern "fire-eaters" called for immediate secession. Former Texas president Sam Houston now represented the state in the U.S. Senate. Though a slaveholder himself, Houston often voted against the expansion of slavery in the new territories. He ardently opposed any threats of disunity, whether from Northern or Southern agitators. The Texas legislature officially condemned his position the year after his vote against the 1854 Kansas-Nebraska Act. This virtually ended his career, though in 1859 he ran for governor a second time and won. During the all-important presidential election of 1860, Houston might have been the one man who could have prevented sectional strife and kept the country together, but by a narrow vote at the Constitutional Unionist Party's convention, he lost the nomination to John Bell.

After Abraham Lincoln won the subsequent election, the country was in an uproar. Anxiously trying to keep Texas in the Union, Houston called a special session of the state legislature. He warned that civil war would result in a Northern victory and a defeat for the South. But passions were too high for any to heed his warning. Ignoring his pleas, Texans clamored for an ordinance of secession. Houston acquiesced to these demands. When he refused to take a loyalty oath to the newly formed Confederate States of America, Texas legislators removed him from office.

News of Fort Sumter arrived at Austin on April 17, 1861. Governor Edward Clark immediately provided for the organization, equipment, and instruction of volunteer companies in every county in the state. Texas troops of the Eleventh Texas Calvary recruited in North Texas under Col. William C. Young moved quickly to occupy Forts Arbuckle, Cobb, Gibson, and Washita. Young's men started from Sherman, gathering forces as they went. His force was not trained and many were poorly armed, some men having only pikes and Bowie knives. They numbered fewer than 300 men when they reached their first objective, Fort Arbuckle.

Meanwhile, Federal leaders in Washington realized that they did not have enough troops to defend these forts, and three days after the surrender of Fort Sumter, they ordered the forts abandoned. In May 1861, 530 Texans found Fort Washita deserted but stocked with a considerable amount of corn and oats. Texans also rushed to occupy the other abandoned forts. Two companies from Cooke County were stationed at Fort Cobb, three companies at Fort Arbuckle, and four companies at Fort Washita. The men drilled twice daily and acquired "great proficiency in the evolutions."[36] The Confederate "conscript law" passed on April 1, 1861, called out men between the ages of eighteen and thirty-five for three years' service or the duration of the war. By September 1862, the upper age limit was raised to forty-five, and in February 1864 the age limits were extended to seventeen and fifty until the country was gradually drained of its men.

Feeling that he would soon be called on to face the Federals pouring into Missouri, McCulloch sent the following dispatch on June 30, 1861, from his headquarters at Fort Smith: "Men of Texas. Look to your arms and be ready for any emergency! The state of Missouri is almost subjugated. The small force she has in the field is being driven back upon Arkansas. We march today to help and aid them. The Black Republicans boastingly say that they have conquered Missouri and will now overrun Arkansas and Texas. Will you permit it?"[37]

Texans were horsemen, and the call to arms found no self-respecting Texan interested in joining the infantry. An easterner remarked that a Texan wouldn't go ten paces without riding his horse. British Lt. Col. Arthur Fremantle of the Coldstream Guards traveled through Texas during the war and observed firsthand the fondness for cavalry service: "It was found very difficult to raise infantry in Texas, as no Texan walks a yard if he can help it." Most Texans signed up exclusively in the cavalry with the requirement that every recruit furnish his own horse and weapons. Texans joined many independent commands. They elected their own leaders as well as the colonels of their regiments. Displeasure was shown whenever a regular army officer was put in control of a local unit. It was usually a strained combination, and appeals to patriotism were often the only way to keep commands together.

Many North Texas units gained notoriety during the war. One of the most notable regiments was the Fifth Texas Partisan Cavalry Regiment organized in 1863 by consolidating the Ninth Partisan Ranger Battalion and the Tenth Cavalry Battalion; the Fifth Texas Cavalry fought in numerous skirmishes in Indian Territory. Another famous unit was the First Texas Cavalry, also known as the First Texas Mounted Rifles, comprising approximately fifteen hundred men. They participated in more than a dozen campaigns, including the Red River campaign with Quantrill's company. Camp Rusk, situated in North Texas in Delta County, just a few miles east of Bonham, was established in the fall of 1861 as a training site for the Ninth Texas Infantry.

In addition to the troops recruited by Benjamin McCulloch, his brother Henry Eustace McCulloch and veteran Texas Ranger John S. Ford were responsible for enrolling much-needed cavalry regiments. Henry McCulloch assumed command of the posts on the northwestern frontier, from Camp Colorado, 250 miles southwest of Sherman, to the Red River. During the war, Henry McCulloch never led troops in battle or took part in any combat operations other than an ill-fated attempt to relieve the siege of Vicksburg with Maj. Gen. John G. Walker's division. Though he did not share his brother's fighting abilities, Henry did have a strong character and personality. Both men were known to be arrogant, brash, egotistical, and insecure. A Texan said, "The featherbed general of the northern sub-district of Texas, and brother of the gallant Ben McCulloch was a general who had nothing to recommend him but the name of his gallant brother."[38] Given the rank of colonel by the Confederate Congress, Henry McCulloch organized the First Regiment, Texas Mounted Riflemen in 1861. After promotion to brigadier general, McCulloch commanded approximately one thousand men in the Northern Subdistrict of Texas from 1863 to the end of the war.

The Confederate government authorized three Indian regiments for military service. Col. Douglas Hancock Cooper commanded the Choctaw-Chickasaw regiment; Col. John Drew commanded the Cherokee regiment; and Col. Stand Watie formed a regiment of Cherokee tribesmen who were staunchly devoted to the Confederacy. Together the three regiments numbered more than five thousand men and involved approximately ten thousand men before the war ended. Albert Pike was made a general and placed in command of all Indian Territorial forces.[39]

In Texas, Grayson County authorized the formation of three companies of Home Guards "for the protection of our homes and the northern frontier." The commander, Capt. Michael Pittman, organized one company at Sherman, another at Kentuckytown, and another at Pilot Grove. Fear of invasion was great in North Texas since the region was only separated from the Federals in Kansas and Missouri by the undeveloped and largely undefended Indian Territory of present-day Oklahoma.

All the wartime Texas governors were zealous in their efforts to aid the Confederacy. Edward Clark was succeeded by Francis R. Lubbock, who governed from November 7, 1861, until November 5, 1863. Pendleton Murrah succeeded Lubbock and served until June 1865. Even though Texas was considered safe against Federal invasion, Murrah believed that every able-bodied man in the state should serve in the armies of the South. He succeeded in this effort; within fifteen months, more than sixty-eight thousand Texans were under arms.

Meanwhile, in Missouri after the surrender of Fort Sumter, Governor Claiborne Jackson desperately tried to keep his state neutral, but Northern radicals would not allow it. North of the Missouri River, in Liberty, citizens were quick to act in defense of their state. On April 20, 1861, a group of one hundred to two hundred men rode to the Federal arsenal in Liberty and seized it. They removed all the arms and ammunition and sent them south of the river, where they were secured by trustworthy citizens. As the stores in the arsenal were considered public property for the state's use in protecting its citizens, the seizure was seen as essential in keeping the arms from being confiscated by the Federal government. Over the next three days, a party of men removed all the military property and supplies, including cannon, gun carriages, caissons, battery wagons, forges, arms, accouterments, implements, and gunsmith tools and machines.[40]

Even though Missouri was closely aligned to the Southern states through commerce and ancestry, the governor's initial motive was to maintain a state of armed neutrality. With this in mind, Jackson appointed Sterling Price as a major general in command of all state forces and activated the state militia into the Missouri State Guard. The fifty-one-year-old Price had seen two decades of service to the state. He was a popular hero in the South and held the esteem and confidence of pro-Confederate Missourians. He had been Speaker of the Missouri House, U.S. representative, and governor. He had put down an Indian uprising in New Mexico and won fame during the Mexican War when he captured the city of Chihuahua. Missourian Col. Thomas Lowndes Snead described Price as "well born and well bred, courteous and dignified, well educated, and richly endowed with that highest of all mental faculties: common sense."

Radical Republicans had a key hold in the city of St. Louis, and from there they fomented agitation that set the wheels of war in motion. Seeking political control over Missouri politics, the Radicals indulged in political intrigue. With Lincoln in power and the Southern states quickly seceding, Jackson's move toward armed neutrality was not agreeable with the Radicals' political agenda. They wanted Missouri to fully support the Union, and they were intent on achieving that goal at any cost.

For a long time, the Republicans in St. Louis organized military units not affiliated with the state militia. These paramilitary groups drilled for the express purpose of coercing others to accept their political will. Missourians hotly contested these paramilitary units since most were comprised of German immigrants who hadn't yet become American citizens or learned English. Furthermore, they were led by agitators who had fled to this country after an unsuccessful revolt in Germany, where as revolutionaries their lives were forfeit. With strong German support of the Union, these units were quickly absorbed into the political machinations of the Missouri Republican Party led by Francis P. Blair.

Blair's brother Montgomery was postmaster general in Lincoln's cabinet, and he asked his brother to influence the president to help the Radicals gain control of Missouri. The first step was to gain both political and military control. Political control was sought with the armed backing of Blair's German mercenaries. Next he needed to remove two highly placed military leaders who opposed his scheme: Gen. William S. Harney, commander of the Department of the West, and Daniel M. Frost, commander of the Missouri State Guard for the district that included St. Louis and the nearby arsenal.

Blair sought to have Capt. Nathaniel Lyon, a radical abolitionist stationed at Fort Leavenworth, Kansas, transferred to St. Louis. Lyon was the worst possible choice for maintaining peace. He never understood how much Missourians detested Federal interference. Lyon wanted a free hand in Missouri. After scheming to have Harney removed, Blair hoped to have Lyon promoted to brigadier general of volunteers and then use his military force to seize power.

Sterling Price had an agreement with Harney that he would use the state militia only to maintain the peace, blocking potential invaders from the new Confederacy and restricting movement of Federal forces throughout the state, while Harney would maintain control of St. Louis. Both Harney and Price agreed to make no military movements in the state. The Harney-Price agreement prevented the Radicals from claiming the state for the Union and the fire-eaters from calling on Missouri to join the seceding Southern states.

In violation of the Harney-Price agreement, Unionists in Kansas City called for Federal troops from outside Missouri to garrison the city. On June 14, 1861, the *Kansas City Journal* printed articles from the *Independence (MO) Messenger* expressing outrage at the government's attempt at subjugation:

> Will the people of Jackson County submit to the occupation of their territory by the hireling in Kansas City? In plain violation of the agreement of General Price and General Harney, this thing is done. Two companies of cavalry and one of infantry, besides more to follow, are at or will be in our county. Who asked their aid, and by what authority are they sent here? We are a peaceful, law-abiding people, and we want no hired soldiers quartered in our midst. We denounce it as a gross usurpation right, beyond all precedent, and like our fathers of old time, when men were honest and meant what they said, we say, "Burn, harrow, and destroy every vestige of a tyrant's footstep." We are able to take care of ourselves, and we ask no aid from foreign states to help ourselves in this unnatural war, which is forced upon us. Our people are engaged in raising their crops. The season is propitious; everything in nature smiles upon us; the genial rain and sunshine are blessing the labor of the farmers, and now, to have them trampled down and the crops ruined by the hirelings of Lincoln's soldiery is too bad. Will the citizens of Missouri submit to it?

Missourians in Jackson County were so aroused that a unit of six hundred Home Guardsmen quickly assembled in Independence. Twelve miles to the east, a large Federal force occupied Kansas City with infantry, cavalry, and artillery from Kansas and Iowa. On June 13, 1861, the Federals rode toward Independence, seeking to strike the first blow. Halfway between Kansas City and Independence, the two forces came face to face. Officers rode out to speak to each other, and then a nervous volley from the Southern troops startled both sides. The Southerners lost two of their officers, and the Federals retreated to Kansas City. After being reinforced with additional troops, the Federals marched back toward Independence, only to find the Southerners gone. This was considered the first military operation of armed troops against each other in the state and was afterward known as the battle of Rock Creek.

Francis P. Blair continued his political machinations at gaining control of the state government by deception and intrigue. He was as much opposed to the recent violent actions that had upset the citizenry as was Governor Claiborne Jackson. Realizing that Missouri was on the brink of losing its sovereignty, Jackson and Price requested a meeting with Blair and Lyon in St. Louis. The meeting began amicably enough with the governor saying that he still wished to maintain neutrality and use his state forces only to maintain the peace. Price added that he could maintain order but insisted that the Federal government make no military movements in the state that would create excitement and jealousies. Blair stated the Radicals' wishes to have the state give its full backing to the Federal government and support Lincoln's call for volunteers to fight against the seceding states. After three hours of courteous discussion, Lyon exclaimed: "Before I will concede to the State of Missouri for one single instant the right to dictate to my government in any matter, however unimportant, I would see you, and you, and you, and you, and every man, woman and child in the State, dead and buried."[41] After this, Lyon stalked out of the room, leaving a stunned Jackson, Price, and Blair speechless. His brash statement led to only one conclusion: he would be moving quickly to seize the state capital at Jefferson City.

Jackson and Price immediately left for the capital on a waiting train. They hurriedly sent dispatches to the various units of the state guard to muster and defend the state against invasion. On their way to the capital, they burned the bridges behind them, hoping to slow the expected pursuit of Lyon's forces. Lyon, however, was slow in advancing his army; his assembled forces moved by riverboat on Jefferson City. Missouri's elected leaders met in special session prior to Lyon's arrival and voted to defend the state against this unwarranted Federal coercion and outright subjugation.

The Missouri government abandoned the defenseless capital, moving south and setting up temporary governmental offices in Neosho in southwest Missouri. Here Price gathered all loyal state forces and organized the scattered militia units into one army, but he knew he needed more experienced men. Pressed on all sides by huge numbers of troops invading his state, Price fought as best he could. Many recruits showed up without arms. Price appealed to the Confederate government.

Confederate Gen. Benjamin McCulloch commanded all Southern forces in nearby Arkansas, Louisiana, and Texas. He responded to Price's plea for help. Missourians impressed by his reputation saw him as the man who would help them to redeem their state.[42] McCulloch joined Price at Cassville, south of Springfield, Missouri, on July 29. He brought with him an army of fifty-seven hundred, consisting of a brigade of Louisiana and Texas and a "division" of Arkansas militia commanded by Brig. Gen. N. Bart Pearce.

As the Southern states began seceding, many men raced to join local commands. Realizing that his duty lay with his Southern compatriots, Quantrill made sure the Gill family was across the Red River at Colbert's Ferry and safely into Texas before he turned back north. It had been slow going with the oxen, taking more than a month to make the journey from Jackson County. Gill continued on to Sherman, parking his vehicles in the wagon yard before traveling on to his destination. With his mission accomplished, Quantrill said good-bye to Gill and his family. The Gills remained in Texas until the end of the war. Traveling back through Indian Territory, Quantrill encountered and joined Capt. Joel Bryan Mayes's First Cherokee Regiment of the Confederate army in April.[43]

Mayes had been born near Carterville, Georgia, on October 2, 1833. As a Cherokee, his family traveled to Indian Territory in 1838, where he attended the tribal schools from 1855 to 1857 and then became engaged in the cattle business. His grandfather was Samuel Mayes, a descendant of the first Scottish settlers in Indian Territory who married into the Cherokee tribe. As one of the first families among the Cherokees, Mayes exerted significant influence among the Cherokees though he had a white man's name, spoke English, and bore little physical resemblance to his fellow tribesmen.

Mayes was described as a rugged character. He was known for his integrity and executive ability. He stood six feet tall and weighed more than two hundred pounds. In society he was a practicing Methodist and a Mason. As the war progressed, the Cherokee nation divided. Those with Northern sympathies moved their families into the northern Indian Territory and southern Kansas, while those like Mayes with Confederate leanings moved their families southward. Mayes settled in Rusk County in North Texas. His regiment was eventually assigned to Gen. Douglas H. Cooper and later incorporated into the First Indian Brigade.

After the surrender of Fort Sumter, Indian leader Stand Watie immediately began recruiting a troop of both Cherokees and whites to protect Indian Territory from Federal forces. Watie was made a general after organizing a large number of tribesmen into militia units. His command became known as the Cherokee Mounted Rifles, of which Quantrill, under Mayes's command, was shortly attached. Fifty-five-year-old Watie became a superb commander of Indian forces during the war. He never ordered a charge that he did not lead, and he never received a wound in battle. Watie was small in stature but had great physical strength and endurance, and while not a great orator, he was a good writer. Later, on May 10, 1864, Jefferson Davis appointed Watie as a brigadier general in the Confederate army. He was the only Indian of this rank on either side during the Civil War.[44] When the war began, Watie reported to Gen. Benjamin McCulloch.

Quantrill was only with Mayes's Cherokees a short while. He traveled north with them until he could find a Missouri unit to join. Once he found Gen. Sterling Price's Missouri State Guard, Quantrill transferred to the partisan ranger company commanded by Col. Jeremiah Vardeman Cockrell attached to the First Brigade, Eighth Division under Gen. James Spencer Rains. His company commander was Capt. William Steward, whose men were settlers from southern Kansas who had joined Watie's Cherokee Mounted Rifles. Quantrill had already become a well-known personality among the early Southern volunteers. He was easily recognized by the four Colt Navy revolvers stuck into his belt and his Sharp's carbine.

After seizing the state offices in Jefferson City and setting up a provisional government supporting the Federal cause, Lyon moved south to attack Price's army.

McCulloch was willing but not eager to aid Missouri, believing that the Missouri forces were not as experienced as his own. He wrote to the Confederate War Department on July 18, claiming "[Price's] force of 8,000 or 9,000 men is badly organized, badly armed, and now almost entirely out of ammunition. This force was made by the concentration of different commands under their own generals. The consequence is that there is no concert of action among them, and will not be until a competent military man is put in command of the entire force."[45] McCulloch's additional statements about Price's being "nothing but an old militia general" did not endear him to Price or the Missourians.

Price had a simple design in mind: he knew that his men would fight to the death before they would be driven from their homes. But nearly two thousand of his seven thousand men had no weapons. Those who had rifles were prepared for battle by drilling and marksmanship training. Price planned to place all his unarmed men directly behind his army, so they could pick up the weapons of their wounded and dead comrades and those of the enemy after the battle. McCulloch disagreed with this and issued an order that all unarmed men should stay at least one day's march behind the army.[46]

Price was confident that he could defeat Lyon's fifty-four hundred men with the help of McCulloch's forces, but McCulloch's reluctance only exacerbated the affair. Putting his rank and pride behind him, Price went to McCulloch's headquarters and pleaded:

> I am an older man than you, General McCulloch, and I am not only your senior in rank now, but I was a brigadier-general in the Mexican War, with an independent command when you were only a captain; I have fought and

won more battles than you have ever witnessed; my force is twice as great as yours; and some of my officers rank, and have seen more service than you, and we are also upon the soil of our own State; but General McCulloch, if you will consent to help us to whip Lyon and to repossess Missouri, I will put myself and all my forces under your command, and we will obey you as faithfully as the humblest of your own men. We can whip Lyon, and we will whip him and drive the enemy out of Missouri, and all the honor and all the glory shall be yours. All that we want is to regain our homes and to establish the independence of Missouri and the South. If you refuse to accept this offer, I will move with the Missourians alone, against Lyon. For it is better that they and I should all perish than Missouri be abandoned without a struggle. You must either fight beside us, or look on at a safe distance, and see us fight all alone the army, which you dare not attack even with our aid. I must have your answer before dark, for I intend to attack Lyon tomorrow.[47]

Even though McCulloch had no confidence in Price's army, he was slow to act on two other accounts. First, he appeared to want total control of the army but often vacillated during his conversations with Price, and second, if he were in total control, he was afraid of the responsibility of ordering a retreat if it was necessary.[48]

Lyon's forces at this time had been marching south in pursuit of Price's army. On August 9, Lyon found the Missourians twelve miles southwest of Springfield at a place called Wilson's Creek. At 5:00 a.m. the next morning, Lyon split his command into two columns commanded by himself and Col. Franz Sigel and attacked Price and McCulloch's forces. Half of the Federals under Sigel were German immigrants, many of whom could not speak or understand English. The first blow by Sigel fell on the Confederate cavalry, to which Quantrill was assigned. The horsemen fell back under the onslaught of Federal artillery, but the advance slowed to a halt as Sigel's soldiers stopped to pillage the Southern campsite. Confederates were soon rushed up to stabilize the position. As Quantrill rode along the front lines closest to the enemy, he made a dashing figure on a splendid black horse. With much bravado he wore a red shirt so no enemy would see any blood from his wounds.[49] In the counterattack, Sigel's forces were routed, driving them pell-mell across the prairie. Quantrill's company suffered twenty-eight casualties as they routed the fleeing Federals and chased the excited Germans as they ran or hid in the timber. Most all of Sigel's men were either killed or captured, but Sigel escaped by disguising himself in the uniform of one of the Texas troopers. Meanwhile, not realizing that Sigel had fled the battle, Lyon continued the fight.

The Confederates attacked Lyon's line three times but failed to break through. On the last heroic charge, at around 11:00 a.m., the Missourians poured a devastating volley into the Federals. Lyon was killed, becoming the first Union general to be killed in battle, and Maj. Samuel D. Sturgis took over the command. With Lyon dead and Sigel routed, Sturgis knew the day was lost and ordered a retreat, falling back toward Springfield.

As soon as Price realized the Federals were withdrawing, he called for an immediate pursuit, but McCulloch refuse to order it, thus losing the opportunity to completely destroy Sturgis's army. Meanwhile, not all of McCulloch's men had been involved in the fighting. The Confederates had twenty-seven hundred cavalry and two thousand infantry who had seen little or no action or scarcely fired a shot.[50]

The ensuing victory gave the Confederates control of southwestern Missouri. Immediately afterward, not only did McCulloch want all the military glory for being the commander in charge of this victory, he also wanted any spoils of war that were taken during the battle. He took possession of the rifles the Missouri State Guardsmen had gleaned from the dead on the battlefield for his own men, and when he discovered the Guardsmen had captured four cannon, he ordered them to be turned over to his command. In obeying the letter of the law, the Guardsmen relinquished the guns but kept the harnesses, implements, caissons, and ammunition that came with the cannon.

The battered remnants of Lyon's army retreated more than one hundred miles to Rolla, where there was a direct rail link with St. Louis. The Federals had casualties of 1,317 killed, wounded, or missing, while the Confederates suffered 1,230 killed, wounded, or missing.

On August 12, two days after the battle, the Confederates moved to occupy Springfield. Price urged McCulloch to advance to the Missouri River with him, meeting with McCulloch three times in fifteen days and trying to persuade the reluctant Texan to join him. His vast experience told him that it was imperative to follow up a defeated foe to keep him from rallying, reorganizing, regrouping, and counterattacking. An opportunity like this would not present itself again. It was inexcusable for McCulloch not to maximize this stunning victory. But McCulloch told Price that his troops lacked ammunition and the dead and wounded needed attention; he also claimed that his men were needed to protect Arkansas and Indian Territory. His thinking was horribly flawed, for any invading Federal army would have to advance through Missouri to get to his areas of responsibility. Yet Richmond may have been reluctant to aid Missouri, because the state had not yet seceded from the Union, and the Federal onslaught at Wilson's

Creek had unsettled the Confederate government, which was hastily re-thinking its priorities.

In urging Missouri to secede, McCulloch proclaimed after the battle: "I have driven the enemy from among you. The time has now arrived for the people of the State to act; you cannot longer procrastinate. Missouri must now take her position, be it North or South." In late October the duly-elected Missouri government in exile met at the relocated capital in Neosho and passed an ordinance of secession. But McCulloch, ever cautious, pulled his Texas troops back into Arkansas.

Feelings were running high against McCulloch among the Missourians. Where at first they saw McCulloch as a hero, whispered words were making their way into official reports. McCulloch sent dispatches that bruised the once-friendly feelings he enjoyed among the Missourians. He remarked in a letter to Gen. William J. Hardee, commander of the Upper District of Arkansas, that he would find a more favorable environment in Boston than in Missouri. This remark cut deeply when it reached the Missouri troops. At Wilson's Creek it was the Missourians who had stood for five hours and with-stood a murderous fire from Lyon's crack troops on Bloody Hill. Yet McCul-loch displayed contempt for his Missouri allies by writing: "We have little to hope or expect from the people of this State. . . . The force now in the field is undisciplined and led by men who are mere politicians; not a soldier among them to control and organize this mass of humanity. The Missouri forces are in no condition to meet an organized army, nor will they ever be whilst under the present leaders. I dare not join them in my present condition, for fear of having my men completely demoralized."[51]

With McCulloch adamant on returning to Arkansas, Price moved his six thousand State Guardsmen westward out of Springfield on August 25, then north toward the Missouri River. Even humbly placing himself under McCul-loch at the recent battle did not keep Price from gaining a great reputation himself; his accolades were printed and discussed all the way back to Rich-mond. Subsequently, a newspaper correspondent of the *Mobile Advertiser* at Corinth, Mississippi, wrote on July 12, 1862, about the esteem in which Price's men held their commander:

> Early this morning, General Price reviewed his troops. His men greeted him with tremendous cheers. I never witnessed before such demonstrations of wild enthusiasm as the Missouri troops entertain for their general. They fairly worship him and most worthy and deserving is he of their devotion. I had the pleasure of calling on him the other evening and must confess that

he is one of the most prepossessing men I ever saw. He is about six feet in stature, full-rounded, commanding form, and fleshy, without disposition to corpulence. Is about fifty-five years of age, has short grey hair, bright blue eyes, high broad forehead, is smooth shaved, has regular features a mouth showing great firmness, decision and concentration of character, and a face beaming all over with intelligence and benevolence. He is extremely affable, has an easy graceful carriage, while his manner is highly dignified, courteous and polished, commanding the greatest respect. He looks every inch the general, and such are his noble qualities that no one can approach him without an involuntary love and respect for the man.

With or without McCulloch's help, Price kept his focus on defending his state from Union control. He needed to enlarge his small army, but he could not afford to wait in Springfield for recruits to trickle in. In a bold maneuver, Price decided to march north toward Lexington and gain control of that section of the Missouri River. Robert E. Lee used similar tactics later in the war when he said: "I was too weak to defend, so I attacked."

As Price proceeded toward Lexington, he received reports of Jayhawker raids led by James H. Lane from Fort Scott, Kansas. Price dispatched Gen. James S. Rains's cavalry—of which Quantrill was a member—to scout the area for Jayhawkers. On September 2, Rains encountered five hundred Jayhawkers at Drywood Creek, near the Missouri-Kansas border. In the tall grass of the prairie, the Kansans fired their two cannon at the advancing Confederates. One cannon directed by Col. Thomas Moonlight and Lt. John Rankin blew up a Confederate battery near Pvt. William C. Quantrill, sending it flying end over end and killing two of its gunners. The badly outnumbered Kansans fled back across the border. Rather than pursue them into what he considered a sovereign state, Price instead issued a warning that he would return and retaliate in kind for any further encroachment on Missouri soil by the Jayhawkers.

Southerners were concerned not only about the atrocities committed by the Kansas Jayhawkers but also with a wide range of atrocities perpetrated by Missouri Unionists. Sometime in September 1861, Sen. Joshua Chilton of Shannon County was seized by Federal soldiers at his home and imprisoned along with two nephews and another man. The four prisoners were taken first to Rolla and then to a lonely roadside, where they were shot. One of Chilton's nephews, realizing that death was imminent, escaped and returned home with the sad news. Local papers reported: "The bloodthirsty monsters, after perpetrating this diabolical act, as if to make their crime more hideous, if possible, cut off the head of Senator Chilton, hoisted it upon a pole, planted it by the roadside and there left it, 'a warning' as they were afterward heard to say, 'to all rebels and traitors!' The bodies of these unfortunate men were subsequently recovered by friends and interred. Senator Chilton had not taken any part in the war but his known sympathy for the South seems to have been a sufficient cause for his arrest and death."[52]

After Rains had chased Lane's Jayhawkers back into Kansas, Price continued his advance toward the Missouri River. He chose Lexington as his objective because the prosperous town was strategically situated on the bluffs overlooking the Missouri River, and the area was known for its pro-Southern sentiments. According to the latest intelligence, Lexington was held by a small contingent of Unionist immigrants. Once Price invested the town, he could blockade the river while recruits from north Missouri could cross the river to join him.

But there was also a monetary reason for Price to target Lexington. To fund the operations of the State Guard, the Missouri legislature in May had authorized the reappropriation of money formerly earmarked for public education and had required banks to loan additional funds to the state. Most of this money had not been collected. More than nine hundred thousand dollars was still in the Lexington bank; thirty-seven thousand dollars was due the state. Governor Jackson joined Price's advancing army, and as head of the state government, he could personally requisition the funds.

Price progressed slowly toward Lexington, turning back any Federal opposition along the way. It wasn't long before he had the Lexington garrison of Col. James Mulligan and his Irish Brigade surrounded and starving. While engaged here, Price sent former U.S. Sen. David Rice Atchison to northwest Missouri to hurry along the recruits from the Fourth and Fifth Districts of the Missouri State Guard who were marching from their camp in Andrew County, north of St. Joseph. Most managed to cross the river before being intercepted by the Union Third Iowa Infantry. Again, most recruits had no equipment of any kind.

On September 9, 1861, Mulligan was forced to surrender after a nine-day siege. He had asked for but not received reinforcements from Gen. John Charles Frémont, commander of the Department of the West, headquartered in St. Louis. In the battle for Lexington, the Federals lost 39 killed and 120 wounded out of 3,600 men. Confederate losses were 25 killed and 72 wounded out of a total force of 18,000, most of whom were unarmed camp followers. Price captured 7 cannon, 3,000 desperately needed rifles, 750 horses, and a large quantity of other supplies.

Mulligan seized the state funds from the Lexington bank and buried the money under his tent, intending to turn it over to Federal authorities in St. Louis. But Price's men found the cache of cash and reappropriated it, claiming only the portion that was legally due the state and returning the remainder to the bank managers. In nearby Fayette, Federals seized one hundred thousand dollars from the branch bank of the state of Missouri and planned to ship the money to New York. They were apprehended by Confederate Capt. John A. Poindexter, who returned the funds to the bank.[53]

But even after this second outstanding victory by his Missouri troops, Price realized he could not hold out indefinitely with his ragtag army so far north, and so he appealed once again to McCulloch for aid. He sent his adjutant, Col. Thomas Snead, to Arkansas to ask McCulloch to reinforce the Missouri forces at Lexington or at least supply percussion caps for the rifles he had captured. McCulloch rejected both pleas. Price afterward blamed two men for his failed campaign to repossess Missouri: McCulloch for not supporting him and Jefferson Davis for the general do-nothing policy regarding Missouri.[54] Even with his captured weapons, Price's army desperately needed more arms and ammunition.

Most of Price's men had volunteered for short enlistments. Quantrill, like many Southerners, had joined for six months, and this term was rapidly expiring. Price drew his army southward, allowing some of his soldiers to return home to harvest their crops and to get winter clothing. The easiest unit Price could release in its entirety was Col. Jeremiah Cockrell's Partisan Ranger Company in Rains's division. Without supplies or funds to support a large army, Price granted permission to Cockrell's command to return to their homes and engage in guerrilla warfare by disrupting the mails, cutting telegraph lines, attacking foraging parties, military garrisons, and Union strongholds, and generally disrupting Union activity whenever possible. Price subsequently commissioned Cockrell as a recruiting officer and sent him north to recruit. After Cockrell's unit was disbanded, Quantrill obtained permission to return home to Jackson County.

Soon after the battle of Wilson's Creek, many Texas military units were called upon to campaign in Missouri, Arkansas, and Louisiana. Whenever a Northern invasion was imminent and its direction known, Texas units were rushed into the neighboring states. One important city the South sought to protect was New Orleans. The Crescent City was the largest and richest metropolis in the entire Confederacy. In 1860, it had a population of nearly 170,000, while Richmond, Mobile, and Charleston together had less than two-thirds as many people. At the beginning of the war, ninety-two million dollars' worth of cotton was shipped from its ports. If this strategic port fell into enemy hands, many cities along the Mississippi would be effectively cut off and the Confederacy divided in half, which would stem the supply lines from Texas and Arkansas to the armies in Tennessee and Virginia. When the city surrendered in April 1862, the Federals turned their attention to controlling the river all the way to Cairo, Illinois. Lincoln gave the job of taking the Confederate stronghold of Vicksburg, Mississippi, to Gen. Ulysses S. Grant. After laying siege to the city, that city surrendered on July 4, 1863, one day after Lee's defeat at Gettysburg. Until the fall of Vicksburg, Southern morale was high. But when Vicksburg fell, control of the Mississippi River was in Federal hands.

With the Federals controlling the Mississippi and virtually cutting the Confederacy in half, Confederate Gen. Edmund Kirby Smith called for a convention on August 15, 1863, with representatives from Arkansas, Louisiana, Missouri, and Texas to discuss self-sustaining measures, "as they cannot look to the East."[55] After the fall of Vicksburg, the North executed several blows at different points west of the Mississippi River. One of these occurred on September 10, 1863, when Union Maj. Gen. Frederick Steele, commander of the Army of Arkansas, sent Brig. Gen. John W. Davidson's cavalry division across the Arkansas River to move on Little Rock from the south and attack Brig. Gen. John S. Marmaduke's Confederates entrenched in the Arkansas capital. Davidson encountered resistance from Marmaduke at Bayou Fourche, but he was aided by strong artillery fire from the north side of the river, thus forcing the Confederates out of their position and putting them to flight back to Little Rock, which fell to Union troops that evening. Bayou Fourche sealed Little Rock's fate, and the fall of Little Rock further contained the Confederate Trans-Mississippi Department, isolating it from the rest of the South. With these defeats, Texas began to endure a plague of stragglers, deserters, and paroled prisoners who preyed on civilians. Even some regular Texas soldiers began to vandalize their neighborhoods.[56]

2

Men of Valor

No better friend—No worse enemy.

—GEN. J. N. MATTIS, USMC

O N RETURNING TO BLUE SPRINGS after leaving Sterling Price's army, William C. Quantrill was supported by ten recruits who had personally experienced devastating Jayhawker attacks. They armed themselves for protection and to seek justice. One of Quantrill's first engagements occurred near his base camp in Blue Springs in early February 1862. Union Capt. William S. Oliver of the Seventh Missouri Cavalry, stationed in Independence, submitted a report on the incident to his commanding officer:

> I have just returned from an expedition which I was compelled to undertake in search of the notorious Quantrill and his gang of robbers in the vicinity of Blue Springs. Without mounted men at my disposal, despite numerous applications to various points, I have seen this infamous scoundrel rob mails, steal the coaches and horses, and commit other similar outrages upon society even within sight of this city. Mounted on the best horses of the country, he has defied pursuit, making his camp in the bottoms of the Sni and the Blue, and roving over a circuit of 30 miles. I mounted a company of my command and went to Blue Springs. . . . Quantrill will not leave this section unless he is chastised and driven from it. I hear of him tonight 15 miles from here, with new recruits, committing outrages on Union men, a large body of whom have come in tonight, driven out by him.[1]

It was fortuitous that Quantrill arrived back in Jackson County when he did. Kansans had been raiding constantly through the Blue Springs neighborhood. Upton Hays, another local guerrilla leader, had enlisted some men from Westport to guard against incursions by Charles Jennison's Seventh Kansas Jayhawker Regiment. The regiment organized on October 28, 1861, and immediately went into action against the Home Guard troops of Hays and Quantrill; Hays's command of thirty men had joined forces with Quantrill's ten. Their first combined action occurred at the farm of Charles Younger, four miles south of Independence. While the Federals were encamped, the guerrillas fired on their position, killing twelve and wounding twenty-eight.

Jennison withdrew, pausing only to bury his dead in the Pitcher Cemetery before deciding to turn back and make a raid on Independence. Earlier calls by Missouri's governor and other Southern generals to Missourians to rally for the state's protection brought eager young men into the ranks. Some headed south to join Sterling Price's Missouri State Guard, while others gathered whatever weapons they had and sought to join Quantrill in order to avenge the depredations carried out against their families and homes. Confederate Gen. Thomas C. Hindman, commander of the Trans-Mississippi Department, attempted to rouse the Missourians: "Remember that the enemy you engage has no feelings of mercy or kindness toward you. His ranks are made up of Pin Indians, free negroes, Southern tories, Kansas jayhawkers, and horrid Dutch cutthroats. These bloody ruffians invade your country; stolen and destroyed your property, murdered your neighbors; outraged your women; driven your children from their homes; and defiled the graves of your kindred."[2]

Hays's and Quantrill's guerrillas participated in another skirmish on February 22, 1862. Quantrill rode into Independence at dawn, his men close behind him. Riding down the fog-covered streets, he hoped to find a company of Ohio troops at a bakery, getting their daily bread ration. But instead of one company of Federals, he encountered two. Quantrill opened the engagement by firing at point-blank range before retreating eastward down the Spring Branch Road, closely pursued by the Ohioans. Two guerrillas, Gabriel George and Hop Wood, were killed trying to escape into the safety of the rock-covered bluffs overlooking the public spring. Quantrill was also wounded and his horse killed. The Federals emptied their pistols then pursued the guerrillas with sabers. Reaching the crest of the steep bluff, Quantrill held off his pursuers long enough to recover the bodies of his fallen comrades. Before scattering into the timber, he gave orders to rendezvous at the nine-hundred-acre farm of David C. George in Oak Grove. The guerrillas killed seventeen Federals and only suffered two dead and several wounded.

Days later, a funeral was held for Gabriel George in Oak Grove, no doubt officiated by Hiram Bowman, pastor of the local Baptist church. Quantrill attended, supported by a cane and accompanied by his men, who provided security during the funeral. One of those present recalled:

> Young Gabriel, at the age of a little over 19 years and ten months had laid down his life for the cause for which he fought, and for his convictions. His leader thought enough of him to risk his own personal safety to come to the funeral and pay a tribute to the fallen comrade. Quantrill had in that dangerous time taken his own time, and at great personal risk, to appear and be with them in the most trying hour of sorrow—the loss of a young soldier son in wartime. All the venomous writings . . . of the world can never serve to wipe out this impressive evidence of Quantrill as being a kind, considerate, sympathetic leader who commanded respect from all who knew him best.[3]

In later years, a relative of Gabriel George recounted:

> At the George Cemetery, Quantrill, the guerrilla chieftain, his head bared, stands at the head of the coffin by the open grave, "wearing" a cane because of his recent injury. He is speaking softly of the young soldier whose body rests in the coffin—one of the youngest men of his band. Quantrill, a man of about five feet nine inches in height, a small mustache and beard, a long, but shapely neck buried in the collar of a course coat, is now about twenty-five years of age. His penetrating blue eyes are moistened with tears; his light hair fluffs gently in the winter breeze. He speaks with the apt words of an ex-teacher, and with the clipping rate of an officer used to commanding men, but his voice is now tender. If we could but hear him, no doubt we would hear words of praise for the dead comrade, brave and devoted to duty. In well-chosen words he speaks comfort to the family and friends of young Gabriel. But no doubt he also asks, with added praise for the South and its cause, further volunteers and supplies. Softly at first, then with rising appeal, the leader throws out a challenge to the Southerners to furnish more men, horses, arms, and supplies for the Confederacy, in so doing, he recalls, perhaps with exaggeration, the cruel deeds of the Kansas and Federal leaders. No doubt he concludes with further tribute to his dead comrade, and with words of consolation to the family, giving assurance that Gabriel William George had not sacrificed in vain. Thus, Quantrill no doubt concluded. He says a few words privately to David C. George and other men of the civilian group, grasps the hand of Nancy Elizabeth George, the bereaving mother, in

silent sympathy, and bades them goodbye for the time being. He talks briefly and quietly to his men, and slips silently into the friendly timber, accompanied by one of his trusted lieutenants. His men scatter in three directions as silently as they had come but a short time before."[4]

Despite the small victories Quantrill was achieving for the Confederacy along the western border, elsewhere the South was not faring as well. In Tennessee, the loss of Forts Henry and Donelson to Gen. Ulysses S. Grant the previous month caused impending doom to hang like a cloud over Confederate efforts in the Trans-Mississippi area. Though the number of casualties was relatively low, the loss of both forts was a critical blow to the South. Situated on the Tennessee River and armed with obsolete guns, the fall of Fort Henry on February 6, 1862, and the fall of Fort Donelson ten days later opened the Tennessee River to Union gunboats. These Southern losses were the first major victory of the Civil War for the Union. The loss of these forts opened the gate for a Union invasion into the heartland of the Confederacy.

At this time, Gen. Sterling Price moved south and set up his headquarters in the southwestern portion of Missouri at Neosho. Constant pressure in March 1862 from the new Union commander in Missouri, Brig. Gen. Samuel R. Curtis, with soldiers from Illinois, Indiana, Iowa, Kansas, Missouri, and Ohio, pushed Price's small and badly supplied army farther south into northwest Arkansas.

Confederate forces combined in this area to form an army under Gen. Earl Van Dorn, and this force confronted Curtis's Federal army on March 6 at Pea Ridge, Arkansas. But the Confederate attack lost momentum in the initial confrontation with the battlefield deaths of two important generals: Benjamin McCulloch and James McIntosh. Added to these loses was the capture of Col. Louis Hebert of the Third Louisiana. McCulloch's death demoralized the Texas troops and halted their attack. Van Dorn, however, led another column to drive back the Federals on the high ground around Elkhorn Tavern. Missourians commanded by Price pushed the Federals farther back and then successfully held the ridge, the tavern, and the Telegraph road.

The next day, Curtis regrouped and attacked near the tavern, employing his artillery and forcing back the Confederates except the Missourians under Price. With his losses mounting, Van Dorn was concerned that he could not depend on half his army to hold their positions. Unable to resupply them with much-needed ammunition, he reluctantly ordered a withdrawal from the field. Price was thunderstruck by the order to retreat; he had never before left the field of battle as anything other than a victor. "Let me fight them," he implored, "and I'll wade through it." But Van Dorn had made up his mind.

The hope of all Missourians of taking back their state from Federal invasion and subjugation was effectively ended at the battle of Pea Ridge. When it became evident that the South could not hold Missouri, an exodus began of investors, businessmen, cattleman, and plantation owners into North Texas. They took with them their families and whatever goods they could carry through the Federal lines.

The Confederate retreat from Pea Ridge was as disastrous as the fighting itself. After the battle, late on the evening of March 8, most of the Confederate army re-formed at Van Winkle's Mill, on the east side of the White River. The men were famished. They devoured everything in sight, but the sparsely populated Ozark countryside provided only a fraction of the food needed to feed thousands of men and animals. For the next week, the pathetic column staggered south over primitive trails through almost uninhabited country. Hundreds of Rebels wandered away in search of food and never returned to the ranks. Many chose to fight as guerrillas after Pea Ridge to keep from being transferred to fight in Tennessee and elsewhere. Many former cavalrymen were to be used as infantry, and this did not please them. Some, like Matthew Houx, along with thirty members of the Fifth Texas Partisan Rangers and Capt. Kit Dalton and a number of Kentucky troops, headed north and eventually joined Quantrill's company in Jackson County.

A newspaper quoted Dalton about these soldiers-turned-guerrillas after the battle of Pea Ridge. "Jackson, Cass and Clay counties at this time," said Dalton, "were hotbeds of Federal nondescripts, regulars, jayhawkers, marauders, pillagers, plunderers, Kansas red-legs and every description of vermin that ever were spawned in the infernal regions, and the joy of their existence was murder, rapine, loot and arson."[5]

Many of Quantrill's men had relatives in various Confederate units. Before going north and joining Confederate Gen. Jo Shelby's cavalry, Christopher Poole served with the Ninth Texas Partisan Ranger Battalion; his brother David was one of Quantrill's officers.

George T. Maddox said of his stint in the regular army: "That kind of warfare did not suit me. I wanted to get out where I could have it more lively; where I could fight if I wanted to, or run if I so desired: I wanted to be my own general."[6]

At the same time, men who had completed their three- and six-month enlistments in the regular army returned to their homes to fight as guerrillas and avenge the Jayhawker raids that had occurred during their absence.

Allen Parmer described joining the guerrillas: "I was only sixteen years old when I joined up. There were very few at that first muster roll that were over twenty. Most of Quantrill's recruits came from Jackson County, young farm boys, wild, reckless, dare devil fellows, all of them aching for adventure."[7] They were "bearded men and boys of various ages, wearing coarse, dark clothing, a few carrying squirrel rifles and shotguns, all with two or more revolvers—Colts and Whitneys. The armed ones are fully equipped, with caps and balls, powder horns and shot bags at their waist, some wear revolvers in holsters, others with one holstered and extra revolvers stuck in their belts, along with knives."[8]

Their only hope for success in thwarting the Jayhawker raids in their neighborhoods was to band together and employ guerrilla tactics. They utilized ambushes and hit-and-run tactics.

Almost daily, either singly or in small groups, Southern soldiers drifted back to their homes defeated but defiant. Quantrill gathered these former soldiers and joined them to his own band of guerrillas and immediately put them into action. Rather than the usual pyramidal command structure used by the regular army, Quantrill's command structure was like a spider web, a tug at any point had an impact throughout the structure. Quantrill could direct small-unit patrols away from Jackson County or call in his entire command for a large-unit operation if necessary. One Union officer commented: "[Quantrill's] men were braver and more dangerous than the Apache or Comanche Indians and were better riders. They were industrious, blood-thirsty devils, who apparently never slept; today they would attack with a mad rush of twenty or forty men against a hundred, if they could see a chance of surprise, and in one night's ride they would be fifty miles away. They were familiar with every cow path, knew every farmer, ninety-five percent of whom would give his all to help a bushwhacker fighting the Northern invader." The guerrilla ranks grew so rapidly that Union Gen. Henry W. Halleck, military commander in Missouri, issued General Orders No. 2: "All persons are hereby warned that if they join any guerrilla band they will not, if captured, be treated as ordinary prisoners-of-war, but will be hung as robbers and murderers."[9] Halleck's order raised the black flag of "no quarter" during combat, and he would soon regret his rash and ill-advised decision.

On March 7, 1862, Quantrill and forty men attacked a Union outpost in Aubry, Kansas. At least three Federals were killed, while Quantrill did not lose a man. On March 18, Quantrill took his men north, across the Missouri River, and attacked Liberty. After killing one soldier in a brief skirmish, he paroled the remainder of the Federal garrison. Quantrill marched back into

Jackson County, and twenty new recruits from Cass County rode in to join his command. Now with sixty men, a raid was planned on the three-hundred-man garrison at Independence. As he was riding toward the city, intelligence reports reached him that another three hundred Federals had arrived at Independence the day before, forcing him to change his plans. Skirting Independence to the south, Quantrill attacked a Federal detachment of thirteen men at the Twenty-seventh Street Bridge over the Big Blue River. From there he rode another ten miles, quartering his men at sympathizers' homes near Little Santa Fe.

On March 22, Quantrill and about thirty men were staying at the farm of David Tate. They were surrounded during the night. A newspaper reported the encounter: "On the 28th utl. a party of Feds marching from Independence to the Blue Springs neighborhood, were met by part of Quantrill's command, near the bridge on the Little Blue, at which place an engagement ensued, in which three Feds bit the dust and the remainder, sixteen, surrendered, unconditionally. Quantrill, at another time, with twelve men, successfully fought and drove back 200, who had surrounded the house he was in, and he left the house only after it had been set on fire. He killed and wounded thirty-seven and only lost one killed and wounded."[10]

Even though his encounters with Union troops were on a small scale, Quantrill received noteworthy recognition throughout the South. A few months later, the June 7, 1862, *Dallas Herald* reported on Quantrill's skirmish at the Tate House: "Quantrill, the betrayer of the Kansas Jayhawkers, at Walker's, Jackson County, Missouri has possession of Jackson and Cass Counties, and is fast avenging the death of the noble Southerners whom the Unionites have killed."

A Missouri woman wrote admiringly in her diary: "Quantrill has held his own. He is exemplifying what one desperate, fearless man can do."[11] When news of the Tate House fight reached nearby Federal outposts, they were immediately put on the trail of Quantrill and his men. A few days later, Capt. Albert P. Peabody and a sixty-five-man patrol of the First Missouri Cavalry found Quantrill's camp on the Samuel Clark farm in southeast Jackson County and brought on an engagement. Quantrill had only seventeen men with him, besides Clark and his young son. Quantrill arranged his men around the house and among the outbuildings and successfully held Peabody's men in check. The fighting went on for over an hour, and then a second Federal company rushed in to reinforce Peabody. The numerical advantage of the Federals forced the guerrillas to abandon their horses and take to the timber. Quantrill's decision was not an easy one. The guerrillas' horses were in the barn two hundred yards away. They could either risk their lives to get the horses or escape on foot. Quantrill chose the latter. When William Gregg remonstrated Quantrill for losing the horses, Quantrill replied, "I had rather lose a thousand horses than a single man like those who have fought with me this day. Heroes are scarce; horses are everywhere." Even with the loss of the horses and being on foot, Quantrill's next move was not simply to escape, he devised a cunning counterattack.

Though they had been fighting the Federals from a defensive position, it was not out of weakness. Rather Quantrill used his position to compel the enemy to attack the strength of his defense. Withdrawing into the timber, Quantrill rallied his men, and on foot they ran to a nearby ford, where Quantrill knew more Federal reinforcements were sure to come. Utilizing basic guerrilla tactics, Quantrill planned an ambush. He arranged his men around the cliffs surrounding the ford. When the Federals arrived, they instinctively bunched together in the middle of the stream to water their horses. On Quantrill's command, the guerrillas opened fire on the unwary soldiers. Those who tried to make a stand were shot down, while their comrades ran to escape the deadly trap. After collecting the enemy's weapons and mounting the captured horses, Quantrill's men rode away leisurely. They spent the night with the family of guerrilla Thomas Harris in the Valley of the Little Blue then moved the next night a mile away to the farm of Job Crabtree, a relative of two men in Quantrill's company. The guerrillas camped the remaining night just to the south of Crabtrees, at the abandoned farm of Jordon R. Lowe.

Fifty-three-year-old Lowe was an early settler of Brooking Township in Jackson County. At the outbreak of hostilities and because of recurring Jayhawker raids, he abandoned his four-hundred-acre farm and left the area until things returned to normal. His house was a small one-story log cabin that faced west, with the only opening being the front door. A loft had been built over the main portion of the living area for more room. After their recent narrow escapes, Quantrill kept his men constantly on the move, alternately attacking then moving to a new location. Rarely did they sleep more than one night in the same place. On April 15, 1862, Union Lt. G. W. Nash's two-hundred-man patrol was close on the Quantrill's heels. Several guerrillas wounded in previous engagements were recuperating in well-hidden camps, deep in the woods and hills of the Little Blue. Quantrill only had eight men with him: George Todd, Joseph Gilchrist, Andrew Blunt, William Kerr, and four others, including a young Irish boy who had just joined. They had been sleeping in the woods, but it had started to rain during the night, and the guerrillas moved into Lowe's abandoned log house. At first light, Nash surrounded the house and began pouring a deadly fire into the building. Despite being completely surrounded, Quantrill miraculously managed to escape toward the Little Blue. The young Irish boy fell at the first fire. Kerr was taken prisoner. After being captured, Blunt and Gilchrist were shot; Gilchrist was killed, and Blunt was wounded in the arm. The Federals then took the wounded Blunt back to Independence as a prisoner. Surgeon P. H. Henry had often served with Quantrill, and he was called in to care for Blunt; he later helped Blunt to escape.

In May, Quantrill and George Todd rode into the Federal headquarters in Hannibal, Missouri, disguised as Union officers who were buying arms and ammunition to replenish and refit their company. Todd had originally come to Kansas City from Scotland via Canada with his father, mother, sister, and older brother Tom. Those who knew the Todds described them as highly respected. Hired as stonemasons and engineers for the city of Kansas City, Tom married a woman in St. Louis sometime before 1859. While working on a bridge, Tom was struck and killed by a stone that rolled down an embankment. Before succumbing to his wounds, he asked George to take care of his wife and see that she was protected. George married his brother's widow on December 9, 1861, and moved to Kansas City.[12]

Returning to Jackson County, Quantrill found many new recruits eagerly waiting to join his command. Around June 16, 1862, the guerrillas waylaid a mail courier six miles east of Independence. The story was carried in the *St. Louis Republican* newspaper: "A two horse buggy was attacked by Quantrill's robber band, about six miles east of Independence, on the Little Blue. An escort of ten men accompanied the mail, which contained a quantity of military correspondence and other valuable matter. Quantrill's men, number not stated, were concealed on a bluff, and fired upon the party, killing one and wounding six. The mail was then seized and carried off."[13]

With Quantrill's command always facing superior forces, he was often forced to fight only when he had the advantage. From this perspective, he was able to exploit the enemy's vulnerabilities and avoid open battle. By the first of July, Quantrill had enough men to organize an independent partisan-ranger company structured with officers, orderly sergeants, scouts, quartermasters, and even surgeons.

On July 16, 1862, on a routine patrol south of Lee's Summit, Quantrill and his company clashed with a detachment of Company A, First Missouri Cavalry, commanded by Capt. Henry J. Stieslin. One of Quantrill's orderly sergeants was killed, and the Federals found on his body a muster roll of

Quantrill's command. This document informed the Federal authorities exactly who belonged to Quantrill's partisan company. Over the next few
weeks, the men listed on the muster roll were hunted down. The Federals
seized family Bibles, looking for names on the list. If they could not be found,
their relatives were murdered for being Southern sympathizers and their
homes destroyed. On July 30, 1862, Kansas militia stationed in Harrisonville
attacked, robbed, and murdered Henry Washington Younger, father of Cole
and James Younger, whose names were on Quantrill's muster roll. Old men
and boys as young as ten years old were shot down on their doorsteps. Homes
were burned by the dozens. Older women were abused, and younger women
were raped. Negro slaves were raped in front of their owners. Rather than
curtail guerrilla activity, these actions only caused more men to swarm into
the Southern ranks, many of them enlisting in Quantrill's company.

Sterling Price sent Col. Upton Hays into Jackson County to recruit soldiers for his Guardsmen. Hays knew he would need protection, so he consulted with Quantrill. They decided that Quantrill would lure the Federals out
of Jackson County so Hays could recruit unmolested. As a result, Quantrill assigned twenty men to act as Hays's bodyguard, and with forty men he moved
toward Pleasant Hill in Cass County, luring the enemy out of Jackson County.
Quantrill's decoy plan worked perfectly, and he was soon hotly engaged in battle. Guerrilla John Hicks George commented after the fighting, "[We] were
surrounded by 400 Federal soldiers and a hot fight ensued."[14] Seven of Quantrill's men were killed and two were taken prisoner; Federal losses were ninety-
two killed. George himself took a conspicuous part in the battle. His comrades
recounted that he "never fired a shot at the enemy without cursing them, either in a biting whisper or out loud, and that he was an excellent shot."[15]

While Quantrill was busy engaging the enemy in daily skirmishes, his
small tactical conflicts were building into a thoughtful plan. By August 1862
he had gathered enough intelligence to know that Col. James Buel, commander of the Federal garrison in Independence, was not prepared for an attack. Buel had stopped sending patrols into what was referred to as "Quantrill
country" because they had all previously been attacked and annihilated.
Quantrill discovered that Buel kept his headquarters in the Mechanic's Bank
building, a block from the courthouse and two blocks from the headquarters
of the provost guard. The remainder of Buel's command was spread throughout the town, and thus his control over them was fractured. Quantrill suggested that Confederate Col. John T. Hughes attack Buel's headquarters. If
the Union garrison could be defeated, recruits from north of the river could
safely travel south to join Price.

Buel was apprised that a large Confederate force was nearby, but he believed they were attempting to recruit in the community since he could plainly see their flag flying nine miles south of Independence on the Charles Coward farm. Buel sent a heavy patrol out the next day to round up arms from the neighborhood. Quantrill's spies alerted him to Buel's plans. Quantrill knew the advantage must be exploited quickly.

From the small town of Strother (modern-day Lee's Summit), south of Independence, to the small hamlet of Blue Springs to the east, the Confederates assembled a small army, successfully deceiving and confusing the enemy as to their real intentions.

Quantrill and his men were the most important component of the operation. When the actual blow came, Quantrill led the assault. Riding into Independence with sixty men in two platoons, Quantrill cut off Buel in his headquarters from the rest of his command. This enabled Confederate Col. Gideon W. Thompson to attack the Yankees camped outside town. Buel tried to hold out with some of his men. To force the Federals from the building, some of Quantrill's men attempted to set it on fire. Realizing his plight, Buel quickly surrendered. William Gregg obtained Buel's horse and overcoat. The Confederates captured 300 rifles, 170 pistols, 200,000 rounds of ammunition, 300 horses, 6 wagons, 1 ambulance, and all the tents and garrison equipment of Buel's command. Quantrill obtained the horse of Buel's quartermaster and named him Ol' Charley, riding him until the end of the war. The Confederates' bold maneuver stunned the Federal command. The Southerners captured about 150 of Buel's men then paroled them, the others having escaped, hidden, or been killed. The victors pulled their forces back to the tiny hamlet of Lone Jack, twenty-five miles east of Independence. After the victory at Independence, the Confederates remained in control of the border area for only a short while.[16]

Detailing William Haller and thirty men to make camp at the Ingraham farm, six miles west of Lone Jack, Quantrill supervised his remaining men in gathering up the military stores in Independence, loading them into wagons, and hiding them at various sympathizer's farms across the countryside.

At 9:00 p.m. on August 15, Union Maj. Emory Foster led eight hundred men from Lexington to Lone Jack in search of the enemy. Confederate Col. Sidney D. Jackman, a former Baptist preacher and a member of Col. John T. Coffee's command, informed his men, "They have come out from Lexington in search of Quantrell and his band of braves, and they know full well it will take men of extraordinary nerve to cope with Capt. Quantrell anywhere in

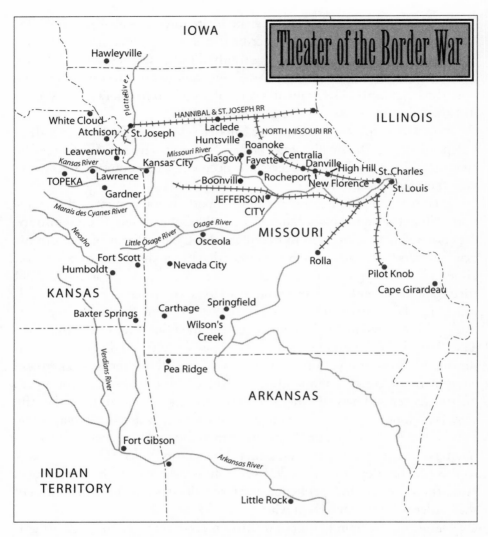

Jackson County, and especially in the Sny hills."[17] Foster discovered Coffee's large body of Confederates camped in an open field and drove them into the timber. During the night, troops under Cols. Jeremiah V. Cockrell, Gideon W. Thompson, and Upton Hays joined forces and made plans for an assault at daylight. The next morning Foster was attacked in force. The fighting raged for more than five hours, and the battle swung back and forth through the streets of the tiny hamlet. After being mortally wounded, Foster turned over command to Capt. M. H. Brawner. When Coffee heard the sound of the guns, he rode toward what he knew was Federals engaging Southern forces. When Coffee reappeared with his men, Brawner ordered a retreat to the safety of the buildings in town. The seesaw battle came to a standstill until Capt. William Haller arrived with a portion of Quantrill's company. Knowing they were up against Quantrill's company, the Federals surrendered. Soldiers fortunate enough to escape retreated to Lexington. The following day the Confederates were forced to pull back to the south after large Federal forces from Missouri and Kansas began converging on their flanks.

The last two Confederate victories within a week's time marked a potential turning point in the Missouri campaign. As the Southern officers pulled their men and new recruits to the south to join Price, Upton Hays continued his recruiting efforts in southern Jackson County along the banks of White Oak Creek in Brooking Township. Hays's camp was protected by Quantrill's newly bolstered force of 160 men. Enlistments were brisk. The men from nearby Brooking Township and other area villages flocked to join up. The officers noted that they found "the woods full of men" willing and ready to join the Southern fight. The recent Confederate triumphs had made the local men eager to enlist. Recruiting had been very rapid indeed for twenty-four hours; in fact, they came in from every direction. The woods seemed alive with men, all fleeing the wrath of what was known as the Gamble Order.

H. R. Gamble, provisional governor of Missouri, had recently issued an order that required all men subject to military duty in the state to enter Federal military service. The order caused a general stampede of Southern men into Confederate ranks rather than join the ranks of the enemy.[18]

While Hays and Quantrill's men were camped along the creek, they were attacked by two regiments belonging to Cols. Charles Jennison and William Penick. During three separate charges, the Southerners turned back the Federal attacks, eventually chasing them back into Kansas. One Missourian, H. T. Ritter, who joined Quantrill after being constantly harassed by Kansas Jayhawkers, described his part in the battle: "During the fight I saw a Jayhawker fall within twenty-five yards of where I stood. Another ran to pick him up and with my shotgun I piled him on top of his comrade. Another came and I piled them three deep. I was somewhat shielded by a rock and discovered one of the enemy shooting at me from behind a tree. I bided my time and finally got a reasonably fair shot at him. He immediately broke cover and ran, falling before he went far."[19]

QUANTRILL AND his men continued to engage the enemy throughout the summer and into the fall. So far it had been an eventful year. The guerrillas had been actively engaged in some sort of contact with the enemy almost

daily. Most noteworthy was the battle of the Ravines in July, near Pleasant
Hill in Cass County; the battles of Independence, Lone Jack, and White Oak
Creek in August in southern Jackson County; the battle of Wellington in
Lafayette County; a raid on Olathe, Kansas, in September; and a raid on
Shawneetown, Kansas, in October. These engagements proved that Quan-
trill was willing and able to fight stand-up battles against overpowering numbers. One guerrilla remarked, "It shows that Quantrill was a real military
leader and understood and used good military strategy."[20] But conditions in
Missouri were dramatically changing. Instead of just guarding against incursions of Kansas Jayhawkers, the Missouri guerrillas found themselves battling
Federal troops from Colorado, Illinois, Iowa, and Ohio. Quantrill knew that
the odds were simply too great to sustain continued action year round. Their
hiding places along the banks of the Sni and Little Blue would not conceal
them after the leaves had fallen. Tracks in the snow and the smoke from
mud-packed chimneys built into their improvised shelters would easily give
away their location to any passing Federal patrol.

The oncoming winter was already posing a special concern. Besides the
early evidence of changing leaves, the temperature had rapidly been falling,
and the guerrillas who were accustomed to sleeping under the open sky were
experiencing some bitterly cold nights accompanied with frost. It was mid-
October when Quantrill issued orders for his men to assemble. Some
wounded men from the numerous summer skirmishes were now recuperated
enough to be able to ride south, but the more seriously wounded guerrillas
and some who chose to remain behind to take care of family members decided to remain in Missouri. Guerrilla officers like Cole Younger, Joseph C.
Lea, and Dick Yeager remained behind, each with a small detachment. It
was barely daylight, a little after 6:00 a.m. on October 22, 1862, along the
banks of the Little Blue, eight miles south of Independence, when the scattered guerrilla bands came together for muster. Some came in companies,
some in small groups, and some rode in two by two. After an arduous summer campaign, they were still a dashing-looking company. Black plumes
adorned their hats. Most wore Federal coats buttoned over their elaborately
decorated guerrilla shirts, homespun or gray pants tucked into knee-high
black cavalry boots, and large Mexican spurs. A brace of revolvers hung
around their waists. Their horses were the best-blooded stock Missouri had
to offer, and a cavalry saddle completed the equipage. The Federal authorities felt somewhat relieved when they learned that Quantrill was leaving
Missouri, although one Union colonel advised his subordinate officers about
Quantrill's departure: "When the leaves are out, they'll be back."[21] Quantrill

passed the word to his men that they had two weeks to find serviceable mounts in which to make the difficult journey, plus they were to outfit themselves with enough cartridges for any action along the way.

After the allotted time, the guerrillas reassembled and formed two ranks for inspection. For almost fifty yards, Quantrill traversed the lines, counting each from front to rear and quickly observing each man as he passed. Most were old veterans with whom he had shared many a blanket and hardship during the past year, but there were also fresh faces driven into his ranks by some cruelty or offense by those with whom they fought. He counted seventy-eight men ready for service and gave them directions to split into small groups and get food for the day at some local homes and to meet the next morning ready to ride south.

On Sunday, November 3, thirty-three men of the Enrolled Missouri Militia from north of the Missouri River joined Quantrill's command. After the muster, along with the seventy-eight guerrillas, there were a number of civilians wishing to be escorted south. They were mostly part-time guerrillas and farmers with their families wanting to get behind Confederate lines and into Texas. As they started out, Quantrill put his best men in the lead, among them were George Todd, William Gregg, Boone Scholl, Fletcher Taylor, George Shepherd, John Koger, Simeon Whitsett, James Little, John McCorkle, and George Maddox. Riding past Harrisonville on the old road leading toward Warrensburg, they had been in the saddle only a short time when Quantrill's advance came upon a Federal wagon train close to the small town of Dayton. Dayton had been a prosperous town before Charles Jennison's Jayhawkers burned it to the ground along with the neighboring town of Columbus on January 3, 1862.[22] The Federal officer in charge of the wagon train was a lieutenant named Satterlee, who had thirty cavalrymen escorting fourteen wagons of provisions. Quantrill ordered a charge. The Federals immediately tried to circle the wagons after firing a few rounds, but after forty guerrillas charged them so quickly, they tried to escape in various directions across the prairie. Some with better horses managed to stay ahead of the pursuing guerrillas for up to four miles before they were overtaken and shot from their saddles. In the end, four soldiers and six teamsters were killed. Only a handful escaped. John McCorkle pursued one Federal for a quarter of a mile. The soldier, sensing he was about to be shot, stopped his horse, threw up his hands, and begged for mercy. After taking the man's rifle, pistol, and horse, McCorkle paroled him.[23] Satterlee and several privates were taken prisoner then paroled and set free. The guerrillas took what supplies they could carry and then torched the fourteen wagons. The cattle were unyoked and turned loose on the prairie. The

Federal parolees headed straight for Harrisonville to report the guerrillas' line
of march.

When Union Col. Edwin C. Catherwood, the commander at Harrisonville, received Satterlee's report, he moved quickly with 150 cavalrymen to
pick up Quantrill's trail. With the distraction of the sudden skirmish and
scavenging what was left after the battle, Quantrill decided to rest his command just a few miles beyond. The guerrillas encamped around 5:00 p.m.,
just after sundown, in a five-acre grove of timber, with prairie in all directions
for ten miles around.[24] Shortly after 9:00 p.m., Catherwood discovered the
camp of Quantrill's rear guard, commanded by Capt. Charles Harrison with a
sergeant and ten raw recruits. Harrison's pickets reported the approaching
Federals. As soon as he was within range, Catherwood's men fired into the
rear guard's ranks. The Federals easily drove them into the main body, where
Quantrill's veterans instinctively knew what to do. Capt. William Haller
shouted for the men to mount their horses and fall into line. After firing a
volley, the guerrillas slowly fell back, giving the civilians in the main column
time to get away. Haller employed this tactic for a half hour before finally
falling back himself. It was a running battle, and six different attacks were
made upon Quantrill's rear guard. Each time, Haller held the enemy in check
until the Federals started encircling him, causing him to withdraw to a more
advantageous position.[25]

Relying on a maneuver that had worked so well in the past, Haller gathered fellow guerrillas George Todd and William Gregg, and with their most
trusted men, they formed a line below the crest of a ridge the Federals were
sure to cross. With the enemy having superior numbers, the Confederates
employed proven guerrilla tactics: they waited in the darkness of the valley
below. When the enemy came into view, cresting the top of the ridge, the
guerrillas charged, surprising the Federals and hurling them back more than a
half mile. Three times the enemy regrouped and returned in ever increasing
numbers. Wishing to end the engagement, Quantrill ordered the third charge
to be so impetuous that the enemy scattered, calling off any further pursuit.
The guerrillas did not lose one man killed or wounded. The damage inflicted
on the Federals was never recorded.[26] Catherwood eventually lost the guerrillas' trail as Quantrill kept dividing his command and scattering the men in
the woods until the Federals' horses finally gave out. Catherwood claimed to
have killed six guerrillas and wounded as many as twenty-one, but it would
have been impossible to ascertain such information in the darkness. Official
records relate that Catherwood "managed as to let them all get away without
killing a single man."[27]

Continuing south at a brisk pace, the guerrillas rode all night until they crossed the Osage River at the former site of Papinsville—a once-prosperous community destroyed in a Jayhawker raid by Capt. John E. Stewart on December 12, 1861.

The landscape was starting to break up as the guerrillas left the dense brush and wooded areas and crossed the open prairie to the south. Quantrill's rear guard spied a Federal regiment on their trail five miles back, causing them to keep moving quickly. They rode all day, without stopping, until finally having to rest and feed the horses and get something to eat themselves. It was 10:00 p.m. before they could finally feel at ease. By 4:00 a.m. Quantrill had his command up and moving south again, approaching Lamar in Barton County. On November 5, guerrilla scouts discovered a nearby Confederate camp of forty men, also heading south. The unit was commanded by twenty-nine-year-old Col. Warner Lewis, a native of Dayton in Cass County who served as part of Gen. Jo Shelby's personal escort and had been paymaster in Rains's division of the Missouri State Guard. Lewis and Quantrill knew each other from Quantrill's service in Sterling Price's army; they had fought together at the battles of Wilson's Creek, Lexington, and Lone Jack. His home in Dayton had been destroyed by Jayhawkers early in the war, and he was presently assigned as a recruiting officer for Price. Quantrill told his scout to have Lewis join him in his camp so they could travel together.

Lewis was very familiar with Lamar. He informed Quantrill that only one Federal company held the town and suggested that, by joining forces, they could defeat them before heading out the next day. Quantrill was especially anxious to kill the Federal commander, Capt. Martin Breeden. Breeden had been a scout for Gen. Nathaniel Lyon at Wilson's Creek and had served under the noted Jayhawker James H. Lane at the skirmish at Drywood Creek. His cruelty was well known to the citizens of the area. Vengeful Lamar neighbors once placed dynamite under a corner of Breeden's house, but Breeden survived.[28]

Quantrill and Lewis decided to attack after dark, at 10:00 p.m. They would separate their commands in a pincer movement, with Quantrill attacking from the south, while Lewis would lead his forty men in an attack from the north. Somehow the Federals knew an attack was imminent, stockpiled their weapons, and barricaded themselves in the brick courthouse and a few defensible buildings.

The guerrillas charged down the main street, firing left and right before dismounting and trying to dislodge the Federals on foot. Quantrill's men were armed with only sidearms, and they quickly realized that these were useless against brick walls. Some guerrillas resorted to old tactics. They divided into small squads, maneuvered as close to the enemy as they could, hiding behind whatever protection was available. Unleashing a tremendous fusillade, they caused the defenders to hunker down and fire on the muzzle flashes in the dark.

The guerrillas lost James Donohue during the second attack. Peter Burton was also killed. John McCorkle and William Halloran advanced in tandem, covering each other as they leapfrogged forward to the protection of an old wood-frame building. Once there, they fired into the courthouse windows. The Federals quickly turned their fire on the two soldiers, and their bullets filled the wooden structure with flying splinters, which knocked both men down. Halloran was struck in the neck; another hit McCorkle above an eye.

The guerrillas battled the Federals for more than thirty minutes. They changed tactics. John Noland, a black soldier under Quantrill, crawled closer to the courthouse and began shouting commands as though a much larger Confederate force was present. He called for General Shelby to attack from the south side of the courthouse, for General Marmaduke to attack from the west, and all artillery batteries to concentrate on the courthouse. But the Federals either didn't believe the ruse or were willing to fight to the death.

After three failed attacks in two hours, and finding the Federals unwilling to surrender, Quantrill withdrew his men and resumed his march to Texas. An exaggerated account of the fighting declared that the dirt streets around the square were left red with the blood of the dead and wounded attackers. Some described the number of wounded as "many." A Southern account in the *Dallas Herald* claimed that Quantrill's assault at Lamar killed or wounded twenty-two enlisted men and three officers, adding that the guerrillas set fire to one-third of the town before departing.[29]

Guerrilla James Donohue's body was thrown across his horse and buried two miles south of town; the guerrillas erected a fence around the grave before they departed. Quantrill's and Lewis's commands moved south, into Newton County, where they separated: Lewis marched into Arkansas, while Quantrill headed into Indian Territory.

John McCorkle commented that it was a godsend that all of Quantrill's men wore Federal uniforms; Union militias were swarming all through Arkansas. Small groups of Federal militia even rode up to Quantrill's column and, believing they were comrades, initiated casual conversation before the guerrillas shot them down. It was a desperate but necessary practice; the guerrillas had no provisions for caring for prisoners along the way. Quantrill had told his men what to do whenever they encountered Union soldiers in this way. Each man was to ride next to each Federal, engage him in conversation, and wait for Quantrill's signal to shoot the man next him. Whenever this happened, every Federal was killed with a single shot; not one guerrilla was wounded.[30] McCorkle noted that the guerrillas lost track of the number of Federals they killed in this way. Guerrilla Harrison Trow added, "It will never be known how many isolated Federals, mistaking Quantrell's men for comrades of other regiments not on duty with them, fell into a trap that never gave up their victims alive."[31] On the road to Texas, near Cassville, Missouri, in Barry County, twenty-two Federals were shot after approaching Quantrill's column.

Because of his prior experience with the migration of the Marcus Gill family to Texas, Quantrill knew that the closest place that could afford rest and protection for his men and the accompanying civilians was Fort Gibson in northern Indian Territory. Once the civilian travelers were safely camped there, Quantrill marched seventy miles to Fort Smith, Arkansas, where Gen. Sterling Price presently had his headquarters. On November 17, Quantrill requisitioned twenty-four hundred pounds of corn and forage for the 211 animals in his company, which was authorized by Maj. W. H. Haynes, the quartermaster in Fort Smith, and approved by Col. Jonathan B. Clark, a former Missouri congressman. These records also show that other Confederate soldiers had attached themselves to Quantrill's command in addition to the original seventy-eight men who had mustered in Missouri at the start of the journey.[32] After the guerrillas crossed the river and entered Van Buren, Arkansas, part of Quantrill's command was attached to Gen. Joseph O. Shelby's division of Price's Missouri State Guards. Some of Quantrill's men continued south—including brothers Nathan, Hiram, and John George from Oak Grove and their neighbor Ezra Moore—to Kentuckytown, Texas, driving a herd of cattle to be traded for horses and food. When they returned, Nathan George joined Shelby's Brigade on February 12, becoming a captain; Hiram and John George and Moore rejoined Quantrill's command.

The Georges had reason enough to want to fight in Quantrill's guerrilla band. During the war, the home of their father, David C. George, was burned down seven times. A younger brother, Gabriel, joined Quantrill early in the war and was killed during a February 22, 1862, raid on Independence. But the Georges had a special relationship with Quantrill. David C. George owned a nine-hundred-acre farm in the Sni-A-Bar Township of Oak Grove that Quantrill used frequently as a campsite. The Georges remarked that Quantrill was "an admirer of many of a Sni-A-Bar Township's beautiful girls; and one in particular, a Miss Abindy Hudson, a sister of John and James Hudson."[33]

Two of Quantrill's men were reported ill and admitted to the Confederate Rock Hotel Hospital in Little Rock, Arkansas. Pvt. Richard P. Maddox, the company forage master, was diagnosed with diabetes and admitted to the hospital on December 31. C. D. Saunders was admitted on the same day with a case of typhus. Both men were discharged and returned to duty on March 9, 1863, in time to return to Missouri with Quantrill the following spring.[34]

About twenty-five guerrillas had relatives in North Texas and continued moving south to spend the winter. After getting supplies, some went to Sherman, and one group was reported to have established a camp in nearby Kentuckytown, fifteen miles southeast of Sherman.

Kentuckytown was described as a bustling hamlet, where it was said that a man might walk out on his front porch on any morning and kill a deer with his rifle. The village was first named after the founder's daughter, Ann Eliza, but with so many Kentuckians living there, it became known as the "Kentuckians' town," and the name stuck. Approximately one hundred families migrated there in 1852. Described as well educated and cultured, these early settlers hoped to find tillable land, "cheap in price and rich in promise." Dr. Joseph L. Hieston, the promoter and developer of Kentuckytown, remarked: "The Kentuckians moved in and took possession of the square, which was really rectangular in shape. Naturally, these industrious and thrifty people began to build their shops and stores around the square, a tavern, a blacksmith's shop, a mill and a stage stand followed quickly. By the start of the Civil War Kentuckytown had a post office, two schools, a church, a lodge, a lawyer and three doctors. It was located on the stage and freight lines from Shreveport and Jefferson."[35]

Sam and Ben Savage built the first store in town, a log house about twelve by eighteen feet situated just east of the square, near a well. A double log house built in 1852 became the first hotel. The town was a trade center and soon added four dry-goods stores, four groceries, a saddle shop, and two wagon factories, which also produced wooden parts for wagons, coffins, plows, and planters. The Kentuckians were religious people, and soon there was talk of a meetinghouse. A Baptist church was built because most of the settlers were Baptists from the "Old States"; during the war the church claimed to have between forty and fifty members.

Jacob and Joseph Weber, brothers from Ohio, came here in 1858 and established a steam-driven mill one and a half miles south of town, on the Thomas Dean track. Dean described the mill's success: "People would come for miles, even as far as Cooke and Wise Counties to have their wheat and corn ground, and to await their 'turn' to get their flour and meal. They came in wagons sometimes drawn by several yoke of oxen or four-mule teams, and camped until they could get their 'grinding' which would sometimes be a week or more owing to the great amount of work the mill had to do."[36]

Quantrill's men camped on the southwest corner of the Dean tract. The people living nearby were nearly all Southerners, and the guerrillas felt at home visiting and attending church services with them. One visitor to northeast Texas wrote: "I think that during my short visit there I saw as much practical living Christianity as I have at any time or in any place seen under like circumstances. [They] are as honorable, intelligent, hospitable and well disposed, so far as I saw, and am able to judge, as any people that I have ever seen in a newly settled country."[37]

One Kentuckytown record noted, "George Todd and his small detachment of around thirty stayed here only a few weeks before returning to Missouri to rejoin Younger's group. So far as is known, there were no severe incidents of trouble during this first winter of their stay here. It is not known why they selected Kentuckytown as the place for this first year's encampment."[38]

Residents commented on the changes in Kentuckytown after the arrival of Quantrill's men. It was common to see well-armed men cross the square dressed in Federal uniforms and overcoats, and there was little trouble regarding the guerrillas' social and economic needs. The number of saloons in town increased from three to seven, and on frozen days the town square clacked with the hoofbeats of the Missourians' horses, while the bars and gaming rooms resounded with their voices. The guerrillas billeted wherever they wanted, in barns for free or in hotels on credit. Rarely would a farmer or a hotel clerk refuse requests for such accommodations. Every road and street of every hamlet for miles around bore the hoof prints of the guerrillas' horses. Whether in Missouri or in Texas, mounted guerrillas moved as if beast and rider were a single fast-moving machine.[39]

While a handful of Quantrill's men spent the winter in Kentuckytown, citizens held a mass meeting in February 1862 and hanged five Unionists.[40] Another fifty Union sympathizers were hanged in Gillespie County several weeks later.

There is much confusion about which guerrilla units camped near Kentuckytown. Many claimed to belong to Quantrill's command. One of these was Capt. Henry Taylor, former sheriff of Vernon County, Missouri. At the beginning of the war, Taylor raised a company for the Confederacy, but he was captured and held at Fort Leavenworth. After Taylor was exchanged for another prisoner, he returned to Vernon County but found that his home had been destroyed by the Federals. He led a small guerrilla band and marched his men to Texas during the winter of 1862/63, where he stayed at a judge's house four miles from Kentuckytown.

Texas residents felt somewhat relieved to have the Missouri guerrillas taking up quarters among them. With so many Texans away from home in the regular Southern army, the only protection in the area was the local militia. Citizens with relatives in Missouri were unnerved by letters with news of the atrocities committed by the Kansas Jayhawkers back home. A November 21, 1862, letter from Liberty, Missouri, bestirred entire Texas neighborhoods: "[James H.] Lane has orders to leave Fort Leavenworth next Friday with thirty thousand troops for Arkansas and Texas. Often his force is in the neighborhood of the fort. His transportation is almost perfected, his stores ready and a little time for organization is all that hinders his advance. The probability is that he will sweep everything before him, Negroes and all, and will have possession of Western Texas in which there is a strong Union sentiment in a few days."

Meanwhile, as soon as he established a camp for his men near Price's headquarters, Quantrill intended to travel to Richmond to seek an independent commission as a partisan ranger colonel. He obtained a leave of absence from Shelby sometime before November 21 and left his command in charge of his adjutant, Lt. William Gregg. His command had enjoyed the most successful summer campaign of any Southern military unit west of the Mississippi River, and his exploits made headlines in newspapers across the South. His reputation preceded him as he made his way to Richmond with his orderly sergeant, Andrew Blunt. They traveled to Little Rock and caught an eastbound train to Memphis.

The South had nine thousand miles of track compared with the North's twenty thousand miles of railroads. Battles tended to be fought in proximity to major rail routes and intersections. Because of their significance in relocating troops and supplies efficiently, each side dispatched cavalry raids against the other's railroads, and the defense and attack of railroads became a major part of military strategy. Southern armies depended heavily on the railroads for food, clothing, and war supplies. Additionally, rail travel was an adventure in itself. Besides the threat of military attack, there was also concern for accidents. A few months before Quantrill's trip to Richmond, a Confederate division was bound by rail to Meridian, Mississippi, when a car jumped the track. The passengers leaped from the car and were strewn along the track.[41]

Quantrill's trip was anything but pleasant. The railroads used mostly narrow-gauge tracks, and the different companies seldom shared the same gauge as neighboring railroads, forcing passengers to disembark and reload many times in order to continue subsequent legs of their journeys. The Confederate government failed to connect the unconnected railroads in order to exploit the geographical advantage of its interior lines and to distribute food and military supplies where they were most needed. Often tracks were in very bad repair, and there was little progress in repairing them. A journey was usually made at the rate of fourteen to eighteen miles per hour, but travelers were lucky if their train progressed at five to eight miles per hour. Trains were always late and connections were missed. Often the trains had difficulty with graded track, and passengers would have to get off and push. Accidents, many of which were fatal, happened because of the unstable condition of the track and equipment. An Englishman in the South during the war joked, "A journey from Wilmington to Richmond was almost as dangerous as an engagement with the enemy."[42]

There had been recent Federal attacks along Quantrill's route. On December 17, dispatches reported that Federal cavalry had cut the railroad between Goldsborough and Wilmington, North Carolina, broken down the wires, and burned the bridge. During the spring of 1862, with the fall of Forts Henry and Donelson to Union gunboats, Confederate Gen. Albert Sidney Johnston realized that northern Tennessee was indefensible and retreated toward Murfreesboro. Further Confederate defeats in Tennessee forced Quantrill to take the southernmost rail from Memphis on the Jackson and Holly Springs Railroad to Jackson, Mississippi. From Jackson, Quantrill had to change to the Alabama and Tennessee Railroad until he reached Atlanta. From there, Quantrill again had to stay on a southern route that took him through Columbia, South Carolina, then on to Raleigh, North Carolina, en route to Petersburg, Virginia, the last major stop before finally reaching Richmond. Quantrill may have had time to confer with Missouri Lieutenant Governor Thomas Reynolds, who was convalescing from a severe illness in nearby Winnsborough, South Carolina. Reynolds was a close acquaintance of Jefferson Davis and a trusted adviser to Gen. Edmund Kirby Smith, commander of the Trans-Mississippi Department. Reynolds was described as "a rather handsome man [with] jet black hair and a beard [that] was always closely cut, and his dark eyes always shaded by gold-rimmed glasses."[43] Reynolds was aligned with Governor Claiborne Jackson in bringing Missouri into the Confederacy. When he learned that Jackson had died on December 6, 1862, Reynolds rode to Richmond, arriving on January 10, 1863, to confer with Missouri's delegation and other Confederate leaders in the capital. Soon afterward, Reynolds followed Quantrill back to Arkansas, first establishing a temporary Missouri capital at Camden, where he gathered the state's records before establishing more permanent headquarters in Little Rock. After Confederates were forced to evacuate Little Rock, Reynolds reestablished his headquarters in Shreveport. Finding the city too crowded to conduct business, he sent his staff to Marshall, Texas, eventually establishing Missouri's capital there.

As Quantrill's train pulled into Richmond, there was excitement on every street corner. The weather was cold, a recent heavy snowfall lay on the ground, and the rivers were frozen over. Smallpox was spreading through the city at an alarming rate, and yellow fever was raging in nearby Wilmington. Soldiers marched through the streets without shoes. Gen. Robert E. Lee had just sent a letter to the president, saying that several thousand of his men were barefoot. A portion of the people Quantrill saw looked like vagabonds. Women and children in the streets wore dingy and dilapidated clothes; some seemed gaunt and pale with hunger.[44] Richmond was only 106 miles from Washington, D.C. The 150,000-strong Federal army lay just across the Potomac River; Gen. Ambrose E. Burnside had just replaced George B. McClellan as the army's commander. Occasional firing could be heard in the distance. There were constant rumors about whether Burnside would make an attack on the capital or go into winter quarters. There was no word on the whereabouts of Lee's army, but this was not alarming since every Southerner knew that Lee would successfully defend the capital. Unlike Quantrill, Lee was politically constrained to defend large cities like Richmond. Other daily dispatches contributed to the war's bleakness: all Southern ports were blockaded; Yankees controlled New Orleans; Florida's governor was calling for immediate aid; and Gen. Albert Pike reported that Indian Territory would be lost if it was not attended to "instantly." Still, morale was high in the capital.

Like most large cities, Richmond bustled with activity. Food and goods were still available—albeit at very high prices. Salt sold at 70 cents a pound, potatoes at $5.00 per bushel, butter at $1.30 per pound, sugar at 80 cents per pound, a quart of milk at 25 cents, and cotton cloth at $1.75 per yard. "Tea is beyond the reach of all save the most opulent," reported the *Charleston Courier* in April 1862. Coffee was selling for $2.50 a pound, and many Southerners substituted such things as parched corn, parched rye, wheat, corn, sweet potatoes, chestnuts, peanuts, chicory, cottonseed, or other brewed items in its place. Speculators withheld goods needed for everyday existence, waiting to profit at extortionist levels. Maj. Frank G. Ruffin of the Commissary Department issued a statement that the army must go on half rations after January 1, 1863.

Despite the hardships, people found a way to carry on. It was Christmastime when Quantrill arrived. Because of the anticipated battle lining up around Richmond, soldiers were not allowed leave to celebrate the holidays with their families. Families that could afford to do so sent Christmas boxes to loved ones at the front. The contents gave the recipients a much-needed mental and physical boost: delicacies such as mince pie and fruitcake and maybe a bottle of brandy. If a family could procure a Christmas tree, it was decorated with holly, strung popcorn, and homemade candles. Children were told that Santa Claus was not able to run the blockade. As a result, homemade gifts were the norm. On Christmas morning children found dolls made of hickory nuts, sweets of sugarplums, cakes, and even a few coins in their stockings.

Quantrill sought an audience with Jefferson Davis. Most government business was conducted at the Customs House situated a short distance from the James River on the Kanawha Canal Basin, just down the hill from the Capitol. Here at various times was the home of the War Department, the president's office, the Treasury Department, and other high-echelon government entities. Prior to Quantrill's arrival, the president had been accessible to all; a member of Congress had no preference over the common citizen. But now Quantrill found six aides, cavalry colonels in rank and pay, and one of them, Col. William M. Browne, an arrogant Englishman, screened the president's appointments and permitted only certain ones to have access to Davis. At the time of Quantrill's visit, it was rumored that the president had left the capital for Tennessee and Mississippi, and he would not return until after January 1. In fact, Davis secretly visited Murfreesboro and Vicksburg; by December 30 he was in Mobile, Alabama, returning to Richmond and therefore was not accessible to Quantrill to personally grant the colonel's commission.

The previous month, on November 19, James A. Seddon of Virginia was appointed the secretary of war to replace G. W. Randolph, who had resigned.[45] When Quantrill was finally granted an appointment with a government official, it was with the secretary of war.

Seddon had been born in Virginia, on July 13, 1815, and admitted to the bar after being graduated from the University of Virginia in 1835. He served several terms as a member of Congress, and he was a member of the 1861 peace commission held in Washington, D.C., that had tried to avoid the war.

Also participating in the interview with Quantrill was Sen. Louis T. Wigfall. At the start of the war, Wigfall was a U.S. Senator from Texas, but he was expelled from the Senate for supporting secession. He was in Charleston during the bombardment of Fort Sumter, and he rowed out to the fort to present terms of surrender to Union Maj. Robert Anderson, in charge of the fort's defenders. After being expelled from Congress, Wigfall became a general in the regular Confederate army before resigning to take a seat in the Confederate Congress in February 1862. Wigfall could be found much of the time in the secretary of war's office, offering recommendations on military actions and troop displacement for the armies in the west.

Both Seddon and Wigfall were keenly aware of Davis's feelings toward Missourians. At the start of the war, Sterling Price had sent messages expressing his dissatisfaction with Benjamin McCulloch's constant refusal to cooperate with him. Price stated that such noncooperation endangered the loyalty of Missourians to the South since the people doubted whether the Confederate government sympathized with them and desired to aid them.[46] In one newspaper article, Price denounced the Richmond government, asserting, "With the exception of Springfield[, Missouri], not a sword has been drawn for the release of Missouri, save by her own sons."[47]

Seddon and Wigfall were acquainted with Quantrill's exploits along Missouri's western border. They badly needed a man of his caliber, but they were concerned with the accounts of Quantrill's killing of prisoners. After speaking with the two men for only a few moments, Quantrill realized that the guerrilla war in Missouri was worlds apart from the war in the eastern theater. Seddon seemed reluctant in granting a battlefield commission to Quantrill if he planned to continue his present mode of fighting. Neither Seddon nor Wigfall was shaken from the conviction that war had its amenities and that civilized men could not lower themselves to fight where they did not respect the rules of war and protect their prisoners when captured. They were appalled when Quantrill relayed some of the facts about the fighting in Missouri. He told them about the widespread house burnings and confiscations of personal property of anyone with Southern sympathies. Slaves were raped in front of their masters, and young women's clothes were ripped off them by Jayhawkers in search of money. Fierce, brutal combat caused the Federals to retaliate by killing unarmed elderly men as well as boys as young as ten years old, simply because their relatives fought in the Southern army. But even this repulsive evidence did not sway Seddon's opinion. The most Quantrill was able to obtain was an independent commission for partisan service. After failing in his purpose and excusing himself from the meeting, Quantrill made plans to rejoin his command.

He needed to return as quickly as possible. The military situation around Richmond was tenuous at best. Even though Jeb Stuart had just made a daring raid in Pennsylvania with fifteen hundred horsemen around the Federal army, other war news was not as bright. News from Kentucky signaled a Northern victory, and the Confederate army in the West had been pushed into southern Tennessee. Lee had just sent an urgent message calling for the immediate completion of the railroad from Danville to Greenville, North Carolina. Legislators were fearful of an attack on the railroad, and asked that Lee send Gen. William Mahone to Petersburg to defend it.[48] And Quantrill had to pass through Petersburg on his way back from Richmond.

What he had seen during his travel to the Southern capital and while he was in Richmond did not fill Quantrill with confidence. Taking a defensive position and waiting for the enemy to attack was not his style of fighting. The only military accomplishments he heard of were the small but daring cavalry raids being executed by Jeb Stuart, Nathan Bedford Forrest, John S. Mosby, and John Hunt Morgan; the last had just completed a raid through Kentucky that netted more than eighteen hundred prisoners.

Quantrill returned to Arkansas by the same route he had come. At least four of his men attested to the fact that he received a colonel's commission from Confederate authorities in Richmond. Harrison Trow remembered, "Quantrill, together with Captain [Andy] Blunt, returned from Richmond, Virginia, in the fall of 1861, with his commission from under the hand of Jeff Davis, to operate at will along the Kansas border."[49] (Trow's dating was not correct; Quantrill traveled to Richmond in December 1862.) John McCorkle also claimed that "Quantrill had gone to Richmond, Virginia and secured his commission as a colonel and command of a battalion of Missourians."[50] Even Quantrill's youngest recruit, Frank Smith of Blue Springs, attested to the fact that "Quantrill left men in camp in Arkansas and with Andy Blunt went to Richmond where he got a colonel's commission and promptly returned to Missouri waging warfare along the Kansas-Missouri border." In addition to these three statements, another of Quantrill's men, Lee C. Miller, asserted, "Quantrill himself had a captain's commission from General Price, and later a colonel's commission from the Confederate war department. His commission authorized him to operate on the Missouri-Kansas border as a Partisan Ranger."[51]

Somewhere on his return trip Quantrill decided to continue by rail a hundred miles farther from Jackson, Mississippi, to Vicksburg, where Sterling Price had moved his headquarters. It is a matter of record that throughout the previous summer Quantrill assisted the missions and efforts of many recruiting officers. Preceding the battle of Independence, Quantrill aided Col. Upton Hays's recruitment task, and he was also instrumental in assisting Col. John T. Hughes and seventy-five newly recruited men. Accompanying Hughes were recruitment officials Cols. Gideon Thompson, Jeremiah Vardeman Cockrell, and John T. Coffee. After the Southern victory at the battle of Lone Jack, Quantrill had remained in the area and protected Hays's recruitment mission along White Oak Creek in southern Jackson County, while the other Confederate officers returned to Arkansas with their recruits. "In those days it was easy enough to get into Missouri," wrote one Southerner, "but sometimes it was extremely difficult to get out."[52]

After the battle of Independence in August 1862, Col. Gideon Thompson personally swore Quantrill into the Confederate partisan service, commissioning him as a captain. Records after this date show that Quantrill began drawing pay as a regular Confederate officer.[53]

Reports afterward by some of Quantrill's other men claim that General Price granted Quantrill a colonel's commission as "range recruiting officer" for his efforts in assisting the recruiting officers; Price frequently commissioned men as colonels for recruiting duty. In an August 23, 1862, letter to Secretary of War George W. Randolph, Price indicated that he planned to authorize Quantrill to raise troops in Missouri. Recruiting officers had wide-ranging responsibilities. Often accompanied by their new recruits, they were temporarily attached to other military units, and as the senior officer on the field, they assumed control over military operations. As an experienced field commander, Quantrill offered his services to Price both as a recruiting officer and as a military commander. If by some accounts Quantrill did not receive his colonel's commission in Richmond, Price had the authority to award the rank of colonel to those he believed would benefit the Southern cause.[54] This fact is verified by a Federal dispatch stating that Quantrill came back to Missouri "highly elevated in his purpose" and that he was going to "conscript all of military age" and keep them in Missouri and not "take away any recruits" to go south to join the regular Confederate army.[55] It was well known that, after his meeting with Price, Quantrill was seen wearing a colonel's uniform and was photographed while wearing it. After this date, dispatches from many Southern officers refer to him with the rank of colonel. Even Gen. Henry McCulloch of Texas acknowledged that Quantrill had a commission signed by Jefferson Davis, but whether this was for promotion to the rank of colonel for recruiting or for an independent command of partisan rangers has never been determined. What is known is that Quantrill was never forced to join the regular Confederate forces and maintained his independent command for the course of the war. Others at the time conjectured that Quantrill received his colonel's commission directly from Missouri Governor Thomas C. Reynolds from his headquarters in Little Rock at the time Quantrill visited there.

Official records show that Quantrill purchased a vest in Little Rock on January 21, 1863, from Maj. W. H. Haynes, the acting quartermaster. After leaving Price's headquarters, Quantrill returned to Arkansas before heading to Texas for a few short weeks. Quantrill reportedly went to the Sherman area with about twenty-five Missouri guerrillas, and they spent a quiet winter in the city before riding north in the spring.[56]

Very little is recorded about Quantrill and his men when they came to the Sherman and Kentuckytown vicinity during the winter of 1862/63. Gen. Henry McCulloch, commander of the Subdistrict of North Texas mentions their presence during the winter of 1862 in a dispatch to Gen. John Bankhead Magruder, who had been made commander of the District of Texas. Numerous local accounts in Grayson County also mention the guerrillas' presence.

During that winter, Quantrill received his pay from Maj. John Ambler, a paymaster headquartered in Mobile, Alabama. The Treasury Department sent paymasters to chief sites throughout the South to issue payment for services rendered. Records show that pay voucher no. 1272 in the amount of $280 was paid on February 16, 1863, by Capt. A. McVey for service from December 1, 1862, to February 3, 1863, from "Headquarters, District of the Gulf, Mobile, Alabama, to W. C. Quantrill, Captain of Cavalry Scouts, Confederate States of America." Pay voucher no. 332 for $672 was paid on March 4, 1863, for the period between August 7, 1862, and January 1, 1863, from Maj. John Ambler, paymaster from Mobile, Alabama, and signed by "W. C. Quantrill, Cavalry Scouts."

Unbeknownst to Quantrill, soon after his departure for Richmond, Lt. George Todd returned to Jackson County in late November, a month after arriving in Arkansas, taking with him James Little, Fletcher Taylor, Boone Scholl, Andy Walker, and James Reed. Todd was reported back in Jackson County and operating with Cole Younger on November 29, when they ambushed a foraging party from Independence and killed five soldiers from Col. William Penick's Fifth Missouri State Militia.

Penick was equally despised by Northerners and Southerners alike. His men pillaged indiscriminately. Mrs. J. M. Thatcher of Westport recalled, "Colonel Penick, who was in command of 400 bloodthirsty men who had been taken from jails, penitentiaries and what-not, was stationed among us. Our houses were raided and ourselves subjected to indignities." A few months earlier Penick imprisoned a number of Southern women for such things as refusing to make new Federal flags and fly them over their homes. One of these, Bettie Tillery, refused to sew for the Federal soldiers or to furnish material for a flag. Penick threatened to place her in solitary confinement with only one blanket and promised that he would allow the roughest soldier in his command to sleep with her. When Tillery wrote to provisional governor Hamilton Gamble to complain, he replied that he would not and could not interfere with Penick's command.[57] Only a year after it was organized, Penick's regiment, commonly known as "Penick's Thieves," was disbanded.

The order stated that his regiment was disbanded "in view of the interests of the public service."[58]

While he was in Richmond, Quantrill's company, under the leadership of Lt. William Gregg, was attached to the brigade of Gen. Joseph O. Shelby serving under Gen. Thomas C. Hindman, commander in charge of the Trans-Mississippi Department. The Trans-Mississippi Department was an inclusive designation for the geographic area west of the Mississippi River. Shelby attached the balance of Quantrill's men to Elliott's Battalion in Col. David Shanks's regiment. The guerrillas were employed as scouts and saw considerable action during the subsequent battles of Cane Hill, Prairie Grove, and Hartville.

Quantrill's remaining men were ordered to move north to Cane Hill, Arkansas, along with two thousand cavalrymen under Gen. John Sappington Marmaduke. Federal Maj. Gen. James G. Blunt with five thousand cavalry and infantry and thirty cannon met the Confederates at dawn on November 28, 1862. The Confederates planned to flank the Federals after a diversion by cavalry under Marmaduke, using Quantrill's men to lead the assault. Blunt, realizing his exposed position, called for reinforcements from Springfield and continued his attack. The Confederates, now greatly outnumbered, withdrew slowly across the Boston Mountains, with Shelby's command fighting a fierce rear-guard action. The fighting turned into a series of running battles extending over miles of mountains and creeks, complete with saber charges and artillery assaults. A participant noted that "almost every rod of ground was fought over for a distance of ten miles." Successfully making it over one mountain range, the men of Quantrill's command were given orders to hold the Federals in check while the Confederate baggage train could get over the next mountain and safely away. While he was scouting with the rear guard, John McCorkle reported to William H. Gregg that they were in danger of being surrounded by the rapid advance of the Federals. But because they were experienced veterans, and being heavily armed, Quantrill's men successfully kept the enemy in check until the rest of the column made it to safety.

McCorkle reported an amusing incident during the battle: "During the running fight, one of our company, Dick Turpin, became separated from us, and riding up to where General Shelby was, the general asked him what command he belonged to. He replied 'Quantrill's.' Shelby replied, 'I thought those boys always stayed in their places.' To which Turpin replied, 'I can go any place you can: come on.' The general started to follow, when his horse was killed from under him. Turpin turned in his saddle and saw Shelby getting up and said, 'General, what in the hell are you stopping for? Why don't you come on?' Going up the mountain Shelby had three horses shot out from under him."[59]

Throughout the running battle, the Confederates made stands at Boonsboro and Russellville. During one phase of the engagement, Marmaduke drew the Union army into a narrow defile on the Cove Creek road. The battle raged for nine hours over fifteen miles of timber and brush roads. As night fell, Marmaduke withdrew toward Van Buren, while Blunt finally withdrew his forces back to Cane Hill. Quantrill's guerrillas were highly commended for their fighting abilities in guarding the rear of Shelby's command as it withdrew over the Boston Mountains.

During the rest of November and December, Price's troops moved out of Fort Smith to again engage the Federals. The guerrillas' next action came only a few days later, near Fayetteville on December 7. Hindman brought his entire force of ten thousand Confederates together in a maneuver to destroy Blunt's division before he could be reinforced by Union Gen. Francis Herron's division. Herron's men marched 110 miles in three and a half days to reach Blunt, but as soon as they arrived at Prairie Grove, the Confederates pushed them back after establishing a line of battle on a wooded ridge northeast of Prairie Grove Church. The Union troops assaulted the line twice and were repulsed, then the Confederates counterattacked. Just when it appeared that the Confederates would roll up Herron's infantry in the late afternoon, Blunt attacked the Confederate left flank, bringing the day's fighting to a halt.

At one point the fighting grew desperate. John Jarrette and other members of Quantrill's guerrillas helped to save Shelby's life on the Fayetteville road during the battle of Prairie Grove. As McCorkle had noted, four horses were shot out from under Shelby while he directed the rear-guard action. Hiram George and his comrades all recalled, "Shelby was a brave soldier and was always in the thickest of the fight."[60] During one engagement on December 7, 1862, the Federals pressed Shelby so closely, they captured him and several of his men. But before he could be taken away as a prisoner of war, Quantrill's men, led by Jarrette, boldly counterattacked, surprising the enemy and rescuing the general. Shelby never forgot this, and to his dying day, he defended the guerrillas whenever he had the chance.[61]

As night set in, the Confederates found themselves out of ammunition and without artillery. Hindman finally withdrew to Fort Smith then to Little Rock, relinquishing control of northwest Arkansas. The toll on both sides was severe. Confederates incurred thirteen hundred casualties, the Federals twelve hundred. "For the forces engaged, there was no more stubborn fight and no greater casualties in any battle of the war than at Prairie Grove," declared a Union officer. Despite fighting bravely, Marmaduke's withdrawal was a setback for Hindman's plans to recapture northwest Arkansas. Though Hindman was immensely popular with his men, he was replaced in August with Gen. Theophilus H. Holmes, a close friend of Jefferson Davis.

To counter the disheartening effect of this Confederate defeat, Marmaduke made a daring raid into Missouri on January 8, 1863, threatening the city of Springfield, which was an important Federal communications center and supply depot that the Confederates wanted badly to destroy before Herron's two divisions could return from his victory at Prairie Grove. In a two-pronged attack, Marmaduke sent Col. Joseph C. Porter to assault the Union posts around Hartville, Missouri. The garrison surrendered, and as the Confederates pulled back to the south, Union Col. Samuel Merrill attacked. Fearful of being cut off from his line of withdrawal, Marmaduke counterattacked, forcing the Federals back into Hartville, where they established a defensive line. Though claiming victory at Hartville, the Confederates retired to Arkansas, where they were eventually deployed south of the Arkansas River to establish winter quarters.

After this series of battles, William H. Gregg was given orders by Marmaduke to return to Jackson County for recruiting duty. Around January 1, 1863, Gregg took with him John Ross, John Koger, and Bennett Wood. The guerrillas accompanied Marmaduke into Missouri as far as Springfield before they veered north, arriving in Jackson County on January 19, having marched hundreds of miles over rough roads and in a strange country. Gregg captured and paroled nearly two hundred Federal militiamen during the trip. Owing to the extremely hard winter, Gregg's operations in Jackson County were few and far between. Others in Quantrill's command soon followed Gregg and began filtering back into Jackson County in small groups. Brothers John and Jabez McCorkle, their cousins George Wigginton and Thomas Harris and neighbor Benjamin Rice, along with Isaac Bassham, also returned home in January. Before February was half over, John Jarrette and another handful of guerrillas also returned.[62] Once these small bands of guerrillas procured winter clothing, they made their camps among the scattered hills of the Sni and the Little Blue rivers.

Several of Quantrill's men had been forced to remain in Missouri when the guerrillas headed for Arkansas. They had been hiding out at various campsites among the rugged hills. Most were suffering from previous wounds and therefore unable to make the arduous trip south. Sympathetic Southern doctors visited the camps from time to time to treat their wounds.

One guerrilla who remained in Missouri for the winter was John Kegan, who had been wounded at the battle of Lone Jack. Andy Walker had a serious wound to his hand and hid out with his cousin William Cox and Cox's brother-in-law, Al Ketchem. During the winter a company of Federals surprised them in their camp, killing Ketchem and leaving Kegan for dead. Those who managed to escape soon joined with George Todd when he returned from Arkansas. In addition to Walker, Todd now had with him James Lilly, Sam Montgomery, Sam Stone, Zachery Trochere, Lee Miller, William Hopkins, and Bill Reynolds. Cole Younger's camp was nearby, on the East Fork of the Little Blue, and Abe Cunningham and a handful of men had a camp farther south on the border of Jackson and Cass counties.

Harrison Trow reported, "[Cole] Younger was exceedingly enterprising and did not seem to be affected by the severity of the winter. At night, under a single blanket, he slept often in the snow while it was too bitter cold for Federal scouting parties to leave their comfortable cantonments or Federal garrisons to poke their noses beyond the snug surroundings of their well furnished barracks."

The guerrillas who returned to Jackson County during the winter were shocked to learn of the atrocities of Penick's men perpetrated during their brief absence. Todd issued a written warning on January 31, 1863, to Penick in Independence:

> Sir, I am now in this country and expect to remain here. You have represented us to the world as carrying on a barbarous and murderous warfare which is not so. Every word of your letter to [Brigadier] General [Benjamin] Loan, as published in the Kansas City paper, is one tissue of falsehood. Sir, we have the Orders of General Loan, Nos. 3–35. Now if said orders are carried out, we will adopt the same mode of warfare, although it is repugnant to our feelings, and should be to every human being. We have sworn that we will for every house burned, burn two, and every lady banished, we will banish one, and for every citizen killed, we will kill one Union man. All prisoners taken by our command will be treated in the same way you treat ours.[63]

With so many men available for service, Todd put them to use attacking the mails and ambushing patrols. The guerrillas waylaid roads, bridges, couriers, and routes of travel. Six mail carriers disappeared in one week between Independence and Kansas City.[64] Todd soon aroused the whole country and seemed to be giving battle everywhere at once. His wife, Catherine, was living in Kansas City, and he often sneaked into town to visit her. This is where he possibly learned that the Federal soldiers who had killed Cole Younger's father the previous summer were now assigned to garrison duty. He proposed to Younger a plan to find and kill these men.

The weather turned bitterly cold as the Christmas holidays approached. On Christmas night, while the Federals relaxed their vigilance and turned their attention to more festive occasions, Todd, Younger, and three companions went to Kansas City to find Henry Younger's assassins. The guerrillas were dressed in Federal uniforms and carried a brace of Colt Navy revolvers beneath their heavy army overcoats. Before the night was out, they found four of the men they were looking for and shot them as they played cards and drank in a saloon. The guerrillas managed to escape to Reuben Harris's farm overlooking the valley of the Little Blue. After the deaths of the card-playing Federals, Union commanders ordered constant patrols in Jackson County to run the guerrillas to ground.

In late January 1863, Quantrill returned to Arkansas to what remained of his company, now commanded by Lt. Ferdinand A. Scott. Some accounts report that Quantrill headed to North Texas. Church records dated December 11, 1862, from the moderator for the Kentuckytown Baptist Church state, "Quantrill and his men are here at this point in time and are encamped less than two miles due north of Kentuckytown along wooded Camp Branch of Mill Creek where there is plenty of spring water."[65] Additional church records note an outbreak of smallpox that winter, which reached its height during the first week of February. The illness had an immediate effect upon the comings and goings of the people. One can only imagine the problems Quantrill's men suffered if they were among those who had the disease at this time.

The guerrillas watched the leaves begin to bud and started preparing themselves for the long trip home. Quantrill left Texas sometime in late March 1863. On his way back, he purchased a new hat for fifteen dollars from the Confederate quartermaster in Little Rock on April 3. The voucher was signed "Capt. William C. Quantrill, Captain Cavalry Scouts."

In southwest Missouri, as Quantrill crossed north of Spring River in St. Clair County, he encountered Gen. John S. Marmaduke, who was patrolling north after wintering in Texas. Marmaduke apprised Quantrill of the recent actions of Jayhawker Obadiah Smith in the area. John Newman Edwards reported that Smith commanded a company of desperate thieves and cutthroats, adding, "Houses were robbed and burnt, some old men killed, much stock was driven off, and outrage and oppression dealt out with no unsparing hand."[66] Marmaduke told Quantrill that he had been trying to get rid of Smith for some time, but the Jayhawker was too cunning for him. Quantrill sought out Smith and shot him with his own gun.[67] Another account states that Quantrill sent a messenger to Smith indicating that a senior Federal officer was camped nearby and ordering that Smith report to him. When Smith showed up at Quantrill's camp, he was seized and hanged.

Smith's execution stirred the surrounding Federal militia into even more action. Some soldiers frantically raced to overtake Quantrill, a trail they easily followed since it was littered with the bodies of unwary soldiers who had crossed his path. Two hundred Federals soon gathered on Quantrill's rear column and brought on an engagement. As the Federals drew closer, Harrison Trow noted the Federal commander made a costly mistake. The Union advance was too far out in front of its main column, and Quantrill immediately grasped the opportunity and ordered a charge. Trow recalled the assault: "A revolver in each hand, the bridle reins in his teeth, the horse at a full run, the individual rider firing right and left. This is the way the guerrillas charged."[68] Of the sixty-six cavalrymen who were leading the Federal pursuit, thirty guerrillas killed twenty and suffered no casualties themselves. Wheeling back north, the guerrillas quickly forded the Osage River. Another Federal column attempted to strike a flanking blow, but Quantrill led his men into the nearby timber and escaped into the approaching darkness; three guerrillas were wounded and one horse was killed.

Preceding Quantrill's arrival in Jackson County in March, William H. Gregg took eleven guerrillas toward the Missouri River near Sibley and captured the Federal steamboat *Sam Gaty*, commanded by Capt. John G. McCloy, as it pulled along the shore to take in a load of wood. The guerrillas were well acquainted with the *Sam Gaty* from the year before; on January 12, 1862, the riverboat was involved in taking Confederate prisoners from the battle of Arkansas Post to Union prisons in the north. Hiding in the timber, the guerrillas sprung on board so quickly they surprised the soldiers and captured the boat without firing a shot. Aboard were twenty-two black soldiers and twelve white soldiers, six from Col. James McFerrin's First Missouri Cavalry and six from Col. William Penick's Fifth Missouri Cavalry. Penick previously had issued orders that any guerrilla taken captive would be immediately executed. In response to this order, the guerrillas took the six men from Penick's command off the boat and shot them. Cole Younger vouched for the black soldiers, so they were paroled. Also on board the riverboat were numerous wagons and supplies, which Gregg had thrown overboard. He destroyed an estimated half million dollars' worth of sugar, coffee, flour, and bacon.

Quantrill eventually returned to Jackson County with thirty men, all wearing Federal uniforms. Whenever the guerrillas encountered a Federal party,
they always identified themselves as "a Federal scout on special service."[69]

As soon as Quantrill returned to his base of operations, the Federal commander in Lexington notified his superiors and his troops warning of Quantrill's presence. In the meantime, Quantrill decided to temporarily disband his
men to refit. He gave them ten days to find serviceable mounts, new clothes,
and ammunition. Their journey home had been arduous. All the rivers were
swollen by recent rains, and the ubiquitous mud made the march wearisome.
Food was scarce, and the guerrillas were worn out, saddle sore, and hungry. In
short order, however, the guerrillas who had sojourned in Texas as well as
those who had remained in Jackson County for the winter joined together
under Quantrill's command.

Andy Walker remembered seeing Quantrill return to Jackson County on
a jaded horse "tired and worn out." He guessed that the Richmond errand
had somehow broken his spirit.[70] Seeing the capital firsthand, with Confederate soldiers marching barefoot, citizens suffering from lack of food, and extor-
tioners and speculators withholding necessary supplies from the army and
civilians opened Quantrill's eyes to the path the war had taken for the Southern cause. Walker stayed in camp with Quantrill for several days, and they
discussed the progression of the war. Walker recounted:

> He had been to the seat of the big war, and had seen how it was going. True,
> Gettysburg had not yet been fought, nor had Vicksburg fallen, though the
> latter eventually now seemed certain. Lee was at that very hour invading
> Pennsylvania, following up the great victories of Chancellorsville and Fred-
> ericksburg, but Stonewall Jackson had fallen at Chancellorsville. Then re-
> membering the Monitor and the Merrimac, Shiloh, the practical loss of the
> Mississippi, the loss of Southern territory, and the drain of Southern re-
> sources, the weight of evidence pointed to final defeat; so much so that Lin-
> coln felt safe in issuing his Emancipation Proclamation. The armies of the
> North, dogged and well fed, would yet, Quantrill feared, march in triumph
> through the streets of Richmond. So that a slight despondency possessed
> him in place of his gay abandon.[71]

One of the reasons that might have added to Quantrill's sadness was the
news of the death of his good friend Samuel Kimberlin. On November 8,
1862, Kimberlin had been arrested by Federals from Independence, taken to
his barn, and hanged while the barn burned down around him. Kimberlin

had taken no side in the war, and there were no specific charges against him.[72] Harrison Trow was with Quantrill at the time and described the circumstances surrounding Kimberlin's murder: "Colonel Penick's men came from Independence down to Blue Springs and burned houses, killed old men too old to be in the service. On the road from Blue Springs to Independence they killed John Saunders and a man named Kimberlin, both old men, and left them lying in the roadway. If neighbors had not offered their services the hogs would have eaten their bodies. They burned from two to twelve houses and left the families homeless."[73]

Kimberlin's four sons immediately joined Quantrill. In addition to Kimberlin, two other elderly farmers from Blue Springs had been murdered during Quantrill's absence: Jeptha Crawford and John Saunders. Both had been arrested and taken from their homes on Penick's orders. Saunders was taken to Independence and shot in front of the house of the Federal commander. Penick's men then rode to Saunders's home and burned it to the ground. Crawford was arrested away from his home then taken back on horseback. He was told to dismount then shot down in cold blood in front of his wife, Elizabeth, and their small children. The Federals then forced the widow and her children from their home and set it ablaze. As a result, Elizabeth Crawford brought her four sons to Quantrill's camp and told him to make soldiers of them to avenge their father's death. Shortly afterward, Quantrill ambushed a Federal patrol from Independence. He killed five soldiers, loaded the bodies in a wagon, and sent them back to Penick with a note warning him that such would be the fate of all his soldiers who ventured into "Quantrill Country."[74]

In February 1863, Federal Capt. Anderson Morton murdered David C. George of Oak Grove, the elderly father of Hiram and Nathan George of Quantrill's command, then the Federals burned down his house. Quantrill often camped on George's farm, two miles southwest of Oak Grove, protected by its thick woods and deep ravines.

Another close friend of Quantrill had also been killed during his absence. Fifty-five-year-old Dr. Pleasant Lea had moved to southeastern Jackson County in 1852, purchased eight hundred acres, and built a home said to be the finest house in the neighborhood. A neighbor reported that Lea had gone to the nearby home of Josiah N. Hargis to obtain a newspaper. Some of Penick's soldiers stopped him on the road; they broke both his arms trying to get information about the guerrillas, then they shot him. His home and thirteen others were burned that day.

The murders of peaceful citizens deeply troubled Quantrill. Frank Smith claimed that, after these killings, the region's elderly men feared being seen out during the day, and young boys also went into hiding. Many other young men of Jackson County probably joined the guerrillas out of feelings of desperation and self-preservation because they had few alternatives.[75]

On March 26, 1863, a citizen of Jackson County reported, "The Bushwhackers killed nine soldiers a few days since and five are missing."[76] These soldiers' deaths were apparently in retaliation for the murders of family members of men in Quantrill's company. Harrison Trow reported: "In mid-winter houses were burned by the hundreds and whole neighborhoods devastated and laid waste." Frank Smith recalled, "[The] Redlegs began to dash over the border into Jackson and Cass Counties and rob. There was a great deal of plundering by Penick's men from Independence and sometimes Jayhawkers."[77]

Trow noted that Quantrill responded to the atrocities with a directive: "In the spring of 1863, Quantrell issued a proclamation to the Federal forces of Kansas that if they did not stop burning and robbing houses, killing old men and women, he would in return come to Lawrence at some unexpected time and paint the city blacker than Hades and make its streets run with blood."[78] Federal authorities merely dismissed Quantrill's proclamation.

In addition to the killings of Kimberlin, Crawford, Saunders, and Lea, the Federals also hanged Moses Kerr, father of guerrilla Nathan Kerr. Three of Jim Cummins's family were killed, as well as the eleven-year-old son of Henry Morris. Eighty-year-old Howell Lewis was killed with David Gregg, an uncle of William H. Gregg, shot by Jennison himself. The year before, seventeen of Jennison's Jayhawkers went to the home of William H. Gregg and hanged and almost choked to death the entire family and were in the act of plundering and destroying the house when Gregg approached with three companions. Gregg was the only one armed. A fight ensued with the seventeen Jayhawkers. Gregg's two unarmed companions were captured and shot. The day after the two men were killed, Gregg saw fourteen houses in his neighborhood burned to the ground.[79]

When Quantrill resumed operations in the spring of 1863, he sent his officers into various districts to recruit. Large numbers of men joined his company, enabling him to expand his offensive operations. He first put the Federal command into a state of shock by ordering his officers to strike various targets simultaneously. Lt. Fletcher Taylor remarked, "[Quantrill] would occasionally divide his band and send small squads off in all directions, directing those in command to strike in the name of Quantrill, and thus it appeared that he was in three or four different sections at the same time."[80]

One change Quantrill implemented from the previous year was that he decentralized his command structure, delegating his authority to his individual captains so those who executed his orders would have the freedom to develop their own plans. Decentralized command allowed his orders to be executed at the lowest possible level and still reflect his intent. In this way Quantrill fostered an environment where his subordinates could act on their own initiative and still have the flexibility to execute general commands of their own while maintaining Quantrill's vision for carrying on the war in Jackson County. With this attitude of mutual support, Quantrill's guerrillas wreaked havoc with the enemy during the spring and summer of 1863.

The previous year Quantrill had kept tight control over his men. But now that Federal depredations had taken on sinister implications, Quantrill developed different tactics commensurate with his new rank. He knew that by virtue of his larger command he could reorganize his company into smaller units that would enable him to strike in several places individually or in conjunction with other units.

William H. Gregg described the change: "During the year 1862 the men were kept close together and all under the watchful eye of Quantrill. Not so in 1863, there was Todd, Poole, Blunt, Younger, Anderson and others."[81] Hiram George remembered, "In the spring of 1863 Quantrill assembled his men in the timber on the farm of David George and he outlined his work for the coming summer and fall. He said he would not command a band himself that summer but would keep all the captains subject to him, and when necessary he would command the whole force."[82]

These subordinate commanders included George Todd, Andrew Blunt, David Poole, Coleman Younger, Ferdinand Scott, William Anderson, and others with the rank of captain. This command structure allowed Quantrill to focus on higher-level concerns and to concentrate on maintaining a greater tempo of operations by devising ways to use the various units of his command more efficiently. With these smaller units, Quantrill was able to make forays into Kansas as well as Jackson and the surrounding counties. Scott was sent into Lee's Summit. Younger was sent up along Big Creek in Cass County. David Poole took with him John Ross and William Greenwood and attacked Federal outposts in Lafayette and Saline counties. Quantrill maintained overall command; William H. Gregg acted as his adjutant. Gregg remained with Quantrill while he recruited along the Sni-A-Bar Creek in Blue Springs. John Jarrette took Isaac Berry and recruited from the Kansas line all the way to Saline County. These men were assigned recruiting duties in the areas they lived in since they knew the citizens and locale intimately. But they were not limited to recruiting operations. Near Wellington, Jarrette and Poole killed ten Federal soldiers as they emerged from a brothel. Bill Anderson executed raids into Kansas and maintained a constant patrol in Cass County. George Todd's company controlled the western portion of Jackson County, while Andrew Blunt's company controlled the eastern portion.

In response to the increase in Quantrill's activities, Federal authorities greatly increased their manpower. Where there had been five thousand Union soldiers on the Kansas-Missouri border, there were now ten thousand desperately trying to combat the guerrillas. With so many Federals constantly patrolling their neighborhoods, Quantrill's decision to alter his command and control by dividing his company into ten-man squads proved extremely beneficial. Elsewhere around Jackson and the surrounding counties, these small parties ambushed columns on the march, sniped on pickets, harassed stages and searched the mails, tore down telegraph lines, attacked scouting patrols, wiped out foraging parties, and generally disrupted enemy operations whenever possible. One Independence citizen recorded in his diary: "May 6, 1863, They say there are a great many bushwhackers here. I understand Quantrill is here again. Colonel Penick I understand has sent for reinforcements and artillery."[83]

All the guerrilla units were noticeably active. Younger made his camp on the East Fork of the Little Blue River just south of Independence at the home of his cousins, George and Tom Tally. Here he maintained a constant assault on the Federals who daily abused civilian Southern sympathizers. On one occasion, Younger returned to his old Cass County neighborhood to scout an attack on the three-hundred-man garrison at Pleasant Hill. He saw that the outpost was too strong for the guerrillas to attack even with their entire force. Instead, he developed a plan to ambush a patrol outside of the town in conjunction with the guerrilla unit led by Joseph Lea.

William Hulse and Noah Webster were detailed to maintain a watch on the post and to track the number and size of the patrols that were sent out at regular intervals. Soon a patrol of thirty-two cavalrymen led by a lieutenant named Jefferson was discovered not far from town. Younger instructed Lea to take a squad and prevent Jefferson from returning to the post; in the meantime, he would follow from behind and bring on an engagement. When Jefferson encountered Lea's men to his front, he arranged a quick skirmish line. At the same time, Younger charged from behind. Instead of fighting, the Federal line broke and ran. During the running battle, Noah Webster killed four Federal soldiers. His weapons were empty, but still he dashed after the fleeing soldiers, knocking them from their saddles by clubbing them with his empty pistols. William Hulse, fifty yards behind Jefferson, shot him from the saddle.

After the news of the guerrillas' victory reached Pleasant Hill, the Federals quickly evacuated the town.[84]

Following Younger's skirmish in Cass County, a Federal company led by a German-immigrant colonel rode into Independence in search of the guerrillas. After getting drinks at a saloon on the square, they rode away, taking the Independence to Harrisonville road until they approached one of Quantrill's camps. When the Federals came into view, Quantrill ordered his men to charge. Again the Federals broke and ran. Harrison Trow and Simeon Whitsett chased down the colonel and shot him from the saddle. After the smoke cleared, only two Federals managed to escape alive.[85]

Despite the brilliant victories won in these daily encounters, Quantrill lost several of his best men. On April 15, 1863, William Haller, Quantrill's first recruit and the most respected man in the guerrilla band, was killed when Federals surrounded his camp at dawn. Harrison Trow reported that Haller fought until nightfall before being shot down.[86] A short time after the fighting between Pleasant Hill and Harrisonville in Cass County, Albert Cunningham was struck down in a minor skirmish on May 30, 1863.

After one battle, Quantrill captured three Union soldiers: a lieutenant, a sergeant, and a private. Federals under Gen. James G. Blunt had earlier captured guerrilla James Vaughn and planned to hang him at Fort Union in Kansas City. Confederate Col. Benjamin F. Parker was operating north of the Missouri River and often participated in operations with Quantrill; he was holding five Union soldiers prisoner. Parker and Quantrill sent letters to Blunt offering to exchange their prisoners for Vaughn, adding that if Vaughn were hanged, they would execute their prisoners instead. Blunt replied curtly that he intended to destroy any Rebel or Rebel sympathizer in his district. Vaughn was hanged. Parker executed his five prisoners, but Quantrill released his three prisoners. After their release, the soldiers returned to Kansas City and resigned from the service.

Blunt's actions were reason enough for the growing hatred in the guerrilla company. On May 2, 1862, with Sen. James H. Lane's backing, the War Department made Kansas a separate military department and placed Blunt at its head. This action shocked most Missourians but also stunned most Kansans. Blunt was not well known aside from having been an officer in James Montgomery's Jayhawkers earlier in the war and later becoming Lane's cavalry commander. Politically, he was a rabid abolitionist with close connections among the leading Radicals of southern Kansas. He was resolute and self-confident, but coarse and unscrupulous.[87]

In response to this appointment, Quantrill determined to strike a blow in Blunt's jurisdiction. On June 6, he led his men just across the border to

Shawneetown, Kansas, garrisoned by fifty militiamen. He surprised the town and captured the entire garrison. Quantrill was looking for certain individuals. After checking identifications and not finding the men they were looking for, the guerrillas paroled the soldiers and rode away; none were killed on either side.

The day prior to riding into Shawneetown, Quantrill sent another patrol under William H. Gregg north of the river to Clay County to strike back at the Union commander in Richfield along the Missouri River. Thirty-eight men led by a captain named Sessions and a lieutenant named Graffenstein were garrisoned at Richfield. Gregg took with him Ferdinand Scott, Frank James, James Little, Fletcher Taylor, Joe Hart, two guerrillas named Vandever and Easton, and five other men to find Sessions. Most of the guerrillas accompanying Gregg lived in Clay County and were familiar with the area. Gregg and Scott set up an ambush along an old wooden bridge, then they sent a civilian into town to report that he had seen guerrillas in the area. Without delay, Sessions led a dozen cavalrymen out of town. As soon as the horses' hooves struck the wooden bridge, the guerrillas opened fire. Sessions, Graffenstein, and seven privates were killed. Three survivors returned to town, but they were chased down by Gregg and Little and shot from their saddles. Vandever claimed to have killed Sessions.[88]

A few days later, Quantrill detailed Ferdinand Scott with a squad of twelve men to make a raid north of the river. Citizens recalled that Quantrill's men "passed through different parts of the county at times, occasionally 'getting in their work,' as they expressed it."[89] Scott's plan was to attack a Union garrison at Plattesburg in Clay County and destroy a cache of weapons. Frank James had recently joined Quantrill's company, and his home was in Clay County. He learned from family members that most of the Clay County militia was hunting for Scott. Nevertheless, the guerrillas rode four abreast into the town's main square and took fire from the forty-six militiamen still there. Scott's men captured the garrison colonel, and his soldiers surrendered. The guerrillas paroled the militiamen then destroyed more than two hundred rifles and confiscated ten thousand dollars in Missouri defense bonds.[90]

On June 16, 1863, new tactics were being developed to combat guerrilla operations when Union Gen. Thomas Ewing was named the new military commander for the District of the Border. Ewing ordered that outposts be set up at fifteen-mile intervals along the border from which constant patrols would be run; if any guerrilla movement was sighted, the outposts were to notify area commanders by telegraph. Ewing also toured the district and delivered speeches that promised to have a thousand men in the saddle every day to battle the guerrillas. While Federal units were responding to Ewing's new orders, spies apprised Quantrill that two Union companies would be moving from Westport to Kansas City on June 17. Quantrill ordered George Todd's guerrilla group to ambush the column but did not specify how the mission was to be accomplished. Quantrill instead relied on Todd's judgment as to how he might best deploy his men, allowing him the freedom to take whatever steps he deemed necessary. Todd always displayed an initiative and boldness in action; he possessed an exploitive mind-set that took advantage of every opportunity.

Todd selected an excellent spot for an ambush and placed his men on either side of the Westport to Kansas City road that was hidden behind a stone wall covered with thick brush. When the column leisurely rode past, Todd sprang the ambush. Thirty-three Federals were reported killed or wounded, but the guerrillas lost three of their best men: Ferdinand Scott, Alson Wyatt, and Boone Scholl.

Ferdinand Scott was killed by a sniper while chasing the fleeing Federals back toward Kansas City. Scott was a native of Ohio; he had been a saddler in Liberty, but for the past four or five years he had resided in Jackson County. He was one of Quantrill's ablest leaders.

Scholl was riding a new horse that was unaccustomed to combat; the animal became unmanageable and ran through the Federal lines. Scholl was shot in the back, the bullet passing through his body and breaking his belt buckle. Frank James killed the man who shot Scholl. Quantrill was heartbroken at the news of Scholl's death. He had earlier given him a Colt Navy revolver. Quantrill had the pistol engraved with his name and then presented it to Boone's brother George. The revolver has been cherished by the Scholl family ever since.[91] (The engraved .36-caliber Colt Navy revolver is now owned by Claiborne Scholl Nappier, George Scholl's great-grandson.)

3

One Man with Courage

Quantrill sighted—Expect hell in Texas soon.
—UNION DISPATCH, OCTOBER 1863

NION ATROCITIES IN JACKSON COUNTY during 1863 were simply heinous. The war was in its third year, and the heavy-handed actions of the Federal authorities against the civilian population in their efforts to combat the guerrillas in Missouri only made the situation worse. Loyalty oaths were required and bonds were levied as guarantees for good behavior. Unconstitutional assessments exacted by local commanders on citizens for repairs to damaged rails and telegraph lines led many to view the government as despotic. Provost marshals were empowered to banish people, and they often exercised that authority even though no act of disloyalty could be proven against those who were banished.[1] In addition to banishment, even harsher penalties were levied against those suspected of disloyalty: Southern sympathizers were denied their right to vote or hold civil office, their homes were torched, their possessions were seized, and many were executed without trial. On their patrols, local commanders employed civilians as human shields. As a consequence of the suspension of habeas corpus, thousands were imprisoned without trial or even made aware of the charges against them. Kansas Jayhawkers murdered anyone who stood in their way of plundering the Missouri border. Even the pro-Union newspaper in St. Louis extolled the horrible facts to its readers: "The people of Missouri,

95

on the Kansas border, are being slaughtered without mercy under the authority of the Yankee commander of that department, [John M.] Schofield."[2]

During the summer of 1863, frustrations reached their peak. After failing
to capture or kill Quantrill, and feeling themselves powerless against his attacks, Jayhawkers of the Ninth and Eleventh Kansas Regiments stationed in
Kansas City under Gen. Thomas Ewing concocted a plan to torment the
relatives of the guerrillas. Scores of women related to the guerrillas were subsequently arrested.

Fourteen of these women were related to men of Quantrill's command.
They were separated from the rest and confined in a brick house at 1425
Grand in Kansas City that belonged to Gen. George Caleb Bingham; he had
been paroled earlier by Price at the battle of Lexington and now served as the
provisional state treasurer in Jefferson City. Since his home was vacant,
Ewing seized it to house the women prisoners. Guards were quartered next
door. Over the course of a week, the soldiers undermined the structural integrity of the building, and the house collapsed on August 13, resulting in the
deaths of five of the women. Two of the victims were Riley Crawford's sisters;
Federal soldiers had cruelly murdered their father six months prior to the sisters' apprehension. William Anderson's sister also died in the house collapse;
Union troops had killed their father and uncle at the beginning of the war.
Another victim was the sister of John McCorkle; her home had been plundered and destroyed by Federal soldiers a few months earlier. A fifth woman
later died as a result of injuries sustains in the collapse of the house.

This atrocity against these women raised the level of guerrilla warfare to a
fever pitch. The guerrillas added this incident to the barbarities perpetrated
by the Jayhawkers since the beginning of the war. In 1861, Kansans under
James H. Lane had burned the small town of Osceola to the ground. Out of
three hundred buildings in town, only three were not torched. Quantrill's veterans were eyewitnesses to the heightened atrocities committed by the Federals in Jackson County. Old men who had not taken part in any of the
hostilities had been hanged or shot. Boys as young as ten years old were ripped
from their mother's arms and executed for having relatives in either the regular Confederate army or among the guerrillas. Visions of their homes destroyed, their relatives slain, their sisters abused, and their slaves raped were
too much for them to bear.

The center of Jayhawk activity and the headquarters of the abolition
movement in the area was at Lawrence, Kansas. The city's newspapers fomented inflammatory unrest by supporting the armed incursions into Missouri
motivated by revenge and the possibilities of plunder. On August 21, 1863,

after having gathered the guerrillas along the border, Quantrill marched on Lawrence and destroyed the homes and businesses of those most responsible for the destruction in Missouri. Quantrill's men carried death lists bearing the names of Jayhawkers, abolitionists, members of the New England Immigrant Aid Society and the Underground Railroad, free-state politicians, soldiers, and newspapermen who encouraged the assaults on Missourians. The guerrillas also had lists of buildings to be destroyed. In all, eighty-six buildings were put to the torch and 150 men were killed.

An account of Quantrill's success reached Richmond: "Major Quantrill, a Missouri guerrilla chief has dashed into Lawrence, Kansas, and burnt the city, killing and wounding 180. He had Gen. Jim Lane, but he escaped."[3] Guerrilla J. G. Cisco explained the motivation for the raid: "Quantrill's raid on Lawrence was consummated in retaliation for the inhuman treatment of Southerners in Missouri by Kansas Jayhawkers. No Confederate, whether of Quantrill's command or not, ever fell in the hands of Kansans in any of the border counties of Missouri and came out alive, and there was also the murdering of four Southern women in Kansas City by the undermining of a house in which they were held as prisoners."[4]

Missourians understood all too well why the guerrillas attacked Lawrence. Local histories reported: "Hordes of men, many of them claiming to be soldiers from Kansas overrun this territory . . . killing men, robbing and burning houses, driving off horses, mules, and cattle, loading wagons with household and kitchen furniture, leaving in their wake absolute desolation. In retaliation for these acts the sons and relatives of those who had been murdered or plundered, whose houses had been burned or property stolen, went to Lawrence, Kansas, and there committed what is known as the 'Lawrence Massacre,' committing murders and other atrocious crimes."[5]

Missouri partisan A. B. Barnes also justified the Lawrence raid: "In the Lawrence (Kans.) raid one hundred and sixty-three men were killed by Quantrill's band. Of these, all were identified except three. It was not a massacre, as Northern people maintain, but an execution. Every man (except the three) was identified and pointed out as a murderer, a robber, or thief. In many instances they were pointed out as: 'You murdered my father, you killed my brother, you burned my mother's home.'" Barnes added: "The best evidence I have ever heard that many people in Kansas did not sympathize with the Lawrence gang was a statement made to me by the editor of a Republican paper, a friend of mine in Kansas. We were discussing the so-called Lawrence massacre, and I remarked that if there were any innocent men killed at Lawrence I had failed to discover the evidence. He replied: 'If you had fired a gatlin gun into that crowd for an hour, you could not have hit an innocent man.'"[6]

A Lawrence resident who survived the raid was given the responsibility of identifying the dead and wounded. Robert S. Stevens was one of the most respected men in the city, a Democratic attorney with a variety of financial interests in Kansas. At the time, he was working on acquiring grants to build a railroad through Kansas; he had just arrived in Lawrence the previous evening and was staying at the Eldridge Hotel. When the occupants of the hotel surrendered to Quantrill's men, Stevens wisely called upon Quantrill for protection for himself and the other residents. Before the war, Stevens had successfully defended Quantrill in Douglas County, Kansas, against spurious charges brought against him by Jayhawkers. Quantrill readily agreed to protect the prisoners in the hotel, and he directed that they be taken to another building since the hotel was to be burned. Quantrill assigned George Todd, one of his captains, to head the prisoners' escort and to guard them from the havoc around the city. Another officer, Fletcher Taylor remarked, "Quantrill was humane and kind, as some can testify at Lawrence, where he saved a great many."[7]

After a hot pursuit by Federal troops, Quantrill returned to Jackson County and maintained his tight grip on the border counties. Though thousands of Union soldiers scoured the Blue and Sni hills for the guerrillas, Quantrill continued to strike at will. Federal officers confronting Quantrill were baffled by his maneuvers. Ewing wrote to Schofield, commander of the Department of Missouri, about Quantrill's tactics: "Being familiar with the fastness of a country wonderfully adapted by nature to guerrilla warfare, they [guerrillas] have been generally able to elude the most energetic pursuit. When assembled in a body of several hundred, they scatter before an inferior force; and when our troops scatter in pursuit, they reassemble to fall on an exposed squad, or a weakened post, or a defenseless strip of the border."[8] Guerrilla Lee C. Miller claimed that the guerrillas "could whip four or five times [their] number, because we fought at short range with six-shooting pistols and short six-shooting rifles. We could fire twenty-four to thirty-six times without reloading. The enemy would discharge their arms at long range and we would then rush in upon them. No body of men could stand such a charge. They would run and we would pursue. Many more were killed from behind than in front."[9]

IN EXASPERATION, Ewing directed his energy and resources against those who supported the guerrillas and those of questionable loyalty. On August 25, Ewing published General Orders No. 11, a banishment decree. In effect, this order depopulated entire counties bordering Kansas. George Caleb Bingham, whose home had been destroyed in the Jayhawker plot that murdered six women related to Quantrill's men, was violently opposed to Ewing's order. He wrote:

> Of its purpose as revealed by its actual results, in the ruin of thousands of our citizens and the speedy transfer of their movable wealth to their dishonest neighbors in Kansas. It is well known that men were shot down in the very act of obeying the order, and their wagons and effects seized by their murderers. Large trains of wagons, extending over the prairies for miles in length, and moving Kansasward, were freighted with every description of household furniture and wearing apparel belonging to the exiled inhabitants. Dense clouds of smoke arising in every direction marked the conflagrations of dwellings.[10]

Ewing's order granted residents fifteen days either to vacate the area or to move within one mile of a Federal outpost. Eight days after the order was published, Federal troops and Kansas Jayhawkers swarmed through Jackson County, plundering the countryside and murdering Southern sympathizers before they had a chance to leave. Jayhawkers led by Lt. Col. Charles S. Clark, in addition to enforcing the evacuation order, sought to engage and capture Quantrill. But Quantrill predictably avoided the Federals. Frustrated, Clark chose to execute Missourians whom had been identified as having aided Quantrill in any way.

Zion Flanery, whose relatives had already suffered significantly at the hands of Jayhawkers, moved his family to another county, but he was murdered by Federal troops when he returned to harvest his crops. When questioned as to why they had killed Flanery, the soldiers replied, "Because we knew he was a Southern man."[11]

On September 6, a Sunday morning and three days prior to Ewing's evacuation deadline, a small group of Missourians was halted near the town of Lone Jack by a detachment from Lieutenant Colonel Clark's Ninth Kansas Jayhawker Regiment. The ten men and their families were en route to Johnson County, near Basin Knob. Martin Rice was a farmer, a dairyman, and a Unionist, traveling with his son and his son-in-law, William C. Tate. Rice was the only one in the party with a certificate of loyalty. Fellow travelers included Andrew Ousley, John S. Cave, brothers David and William Hunter and one of their young sons, and seventy-five-year-old Benjamin Potter's family. It was common knowledge that Quantrill had stopped at the Potter farm on his way to Lawrence and that Potter and his neighbors had fed the guerrillas and provided forage for their horses. Laura Flanery was also in the group.

Clark ordered Capt. Charles F. Coleman to detain the Missourians until their identities could be verified. Coleman separated the men—except for Rice and his son and son-in-law—from the women and then sent the women farther down the road. Soon shots rang out. The women were immediately alarmed for their men. Rice tried to assure them that the soldiers were only shooting some game for breakfast, but the women were not convinced. Jane Cave asked Amanda Potter to join her and search for her father. The two women ran back to where they had been stopped by the soldiers. The troops were gone, but the seven men, ranging in age from seventeen to seventy-five, lay dead on the ground, some bearing multiple bullet wounds.[12] Clark reported to his superiors that the men were bushwhackers.

Information eventually leaked out as to what had transpired. The soldiers were supposedly reluctant to kill Potter, but a young trooper volunteered and executed the man. David Hunter, a large man, attempted to flee and knocked down two soldiers in the process. He was felled on the edge of the timber and then shot repeatedly in the face. Ousley, a nephew of the Hunters, also attempted to flee, but someone shouted, "Five dollars to the man who drops the boy," and he was quickly cut down. The beardless boy looked like a child as he lay on the ground.

Clark was allegedly aghast at Coleman's actions, saying, "Those were innocent men. I could have saved them and I didn't." He told Coleman that the blood would be on Coleman's hands alone.[13]

Southern newspapers carried the story throughout the South. One St. Louis newspaper reported: "On Sunday last the desire for blood manifested itself in the southeastern part of Jackson County, not far from the village of Lone Jack. Although it was Sunday, the people of that region, alarmed and terror-stricken by threats from Kansas, and cruel edicts from headquarters of the district, were hard at work straining every nerve to get ready to leave their homes before this memorable 9th day of September, 1863." The account added: "There lay six lifeless forms, mangled corpses, so shockingly mangled that it was difficult, my informant stated, to identify some of them. They were buried where they were murdered, without coffins, by a few friends who had expected to join them on that day with their families, and journey in search of a home."[14]

David and William Hunter's father had to bury his sons without shrouds or coffins, merely covering them with quilts and placing them in the ground. When the war was over, several Confederates, relatives of the slain men, returned home and learned of the tragedy. They found out where Coleman was and were planning to kill him when they learned that he had died. Gaius Cave, one of the murdered men's relatives, often told the story of the Federal atrocity and always concluded the story by saying, "And he *died* before we got to *kill* him."[15]

Benjamin Potter's son Marion joined Quantrill after hearing of his father's murder. He was motivated not only to fight but also for his safety, as matters had become so hazardous for any men to remain at home. In the spring of 1865, Marion was seriously wounded and staying with friends in Waverly, Missouri, when he was captured by Federal soldiers. They took him to Marshall, Missouri, still unconscious, to a cemetery, placed him on a casket, and shot him.[16]

Months after the Lawrence raid, Missourians were still being assaulted by Jayhawkers. Jacob Hall recorded in his diary on December 10, 1863: "But we might say that we still 'dwell in the midst of alarms.' The whole three counties of Jackson, Bates and Cass are depopulated and a mass of smoldering ruins."[17]

Upset with Ewing's policies, George Caleb Bingham published a statement in the Jefferson City newspaper: "General Ewing has doubtless discovered that this, his crowning military achievement of 1863, was not of a nature as well calculated to secure the favor of the Democracy with whom he is now associated, as it was to win to his support the 'Jayhawkers' and corrupt rabble of Kansas, through whose aid, there is reason to believe, he then looked for political preferment."[18] Returning to his hometown of Independence, Bingham purchased a house at 313 West Pacific Street. In his studio here he painted his most famous work, *Martial Law*, popularly known as *Order Number Eleven*, in retaliation for the injustice of Ewing's order.

Col. William Weer of the Tenth Kansas Jayhawker Regiment desperately scoured the hills of Jackson County for any signs of Quantrill's company. On September 15, he reported:

> I am in pursuit of Quantrill and his gang, but that, being scattered into small parties, hiding in the brush, they are difficult to find. . . . After a week spent in search of Quantrill's guerrillas, I became convinced that his band continued to secrete themselves upon the waters of the Sni-Bar and Blue Creek in Jackson County, Missouri. . . . The country is very rugged, and filled with almost impenetrable thickets. . . . The enemy fired but one volley, and at once disappeared in the thick underwood, where pursuit was impossible. . . . The expedition demonstrates the fact that Quantrill's band is still secreting itself in Jackson County, though evidently preparing for another raid.[19]

(Weer commanded the Fourth Kansas Jayhawker Regiment that was later consolidated on April 3, 1862, into the Tenth Kansas Jayhawker Regiment along with the Third Kansas Jayhawker Regiment and a small portion of the Fifth Kansas Jayhawker Regiment in Paola, Kansas. On August 20, 1864, Weer was dismissed from the service for drunkenness.)

Rather than being demoralized or unable to fight back, Quantrill proved that he still commanded a powerful force that was able to strike at will. Harrison Trow reported, "Six thousand Federals were in the saddle, but Quantrill held his grip upon these counties despite everything." A Yankee officer patrolling through Quantrill country discovered that *he* was being hunted by Quantrill. He reported, "When we returned to Pleasant Hill we found that he [Quantrill] had been following us and burning and killing in retaliation for the punishment he had received and for Order No. 11."[20] Trow added, "Not a single Federal scouting or exploring party escaped paying toll. Sometimes the aggregate of the day's dead was simply enormous. Frequently the assailants were never seen. Of a sudden, and rising, as it were, out of the ground, they delivered a deadly blow and rode away in the darkness—invisible."[21]

On November 18, 1863, Kansas Governor Thomas Carney of Kansas, foolishly thinking that he could ignore Quantrill's military status, tried to label Quantrill and his men as criminals by issuing a warrant for the guerrillas' arrest. Carney erroneously accused Quantrill of killing George Burt in Lawrence, but witnesses identified one of Quantrill's men as the assailant. The warrant also listed the names of thirty-four other guerrillas.

Twenty-four-year old William Maddox was listed on the Douglas County grand-jury indictment. After the war, Maddox was captured at Olathe, Kansas. He was not taken to Lawrence, because he would have been lynched immediately. Instead, Maddox was taken to Ottawa for trial. There was a strong movement in favor of lynching him at Ottawa, but the argument prevailed that he would be found guilty and hanged anyway, and the legal hanging would be public. Maddox produced witnesses who proved he did not participate in the Lawrence raid. The jury acquitted him.[22]

WHEN THE leaves began to change color n 1863, Quantrill passed the word to his men to assemble at their old rendezvous in Johnson County with their horses freshly shod and a good supply of ammunition. Accompanying Quantrill were many men who had come north after the defeat at Pea Ridge on March 6, 1862. When the guerrillas gathered on September 10, 1863, all wore Federal uniforms.

Frank Smith recalled: "Late in September we began marching south for the winter. All the guerrillas assembled at Captain Perdee's. Anderson's men and Holt's company joined them. They had some new recruits but many of the old faces were missing."[23]

As the men began gathering into companies, several joined Capt. Andy Blunt's new company instead of George Todd's, as Todd had expected. This angered Todd. Shortly afterward, Blunt's company captured a Federal wagon train near Pleasant Hill, including a wagonload of badly needed flour. The flour was taken to the woods and guarded by John Hicks George until it could be distributed. Todd heard of the capture and sent a few men to get some flour. George said that he needed an order from Blunt before he could dispense any. This too angered Todd. Blunt later said he would have given Todd all the flour he wanted if he had asked for it.

Blunt's and Todd's companies were camped about three-fourths of a mile apart. Al Ketchem of Blunt's company rode to Todd's camp to visit some friends. Upon Ketchem's arrival, Todd attacked him without a word of explanation and almost beat him to death.

Blunt decided not to winter in Texas, but to stay in Johnson County. Amanda George, Hiram and John Hicks George's sister, was Blunt's sweetheart, and many believed this may have been an incentive for him to stay in Missouri that winter. But Hiram George knew otherwise. When the guerrillas were about to march south, he noted, "Todd's insolence and arrogance kept increasing and the relations between [Todd and Blunt] became more strained because of Todd's unreasonable course, he [Blunt] would have to kill Todd or be killed by him. He preferred to send his company under command of another, and avoid trouble."[24]

In addition to the George brothers and Ketchem, many guerrillas were apprehensive regarding Todd's leadership. On the second day of the march, Cole Younger warned Hiram George that Todd was threatening to kill the George brothers. Several days later, Todd rode up to Blunt's old company, but Hiram and Hicks George drew their pistols, and Todd rode away.

William Gregg and Sylvester Akers declared, "When Quantrill and his men started south in the fall 1863, owing to a disagreement between Blunt and Geo. Todd, Blunt remained in Missouri." Blunt had asked Hiram and Hicks George and others from the original band to enlist in his company. But Todd had wanted the veterans to enlist under him. Gregg and Akers said that from that day on, Todd was the uncompromising enemy of Blunt and most of his men. Another guerrilla added, "Todd was jealous and intolerant and he would have been killed of necessity by the guerrillas themselves had not he met death at the hands of the Federals."[25]

Blunt was not the first officer to leave because of Todd's overbearing character. Todd was also jealous of William Haller because Quantrill had chosen him as first lieutenant over Todd. Because of Todd's animosity, Haller soon left the company to join Sterling Price.

Andy Blunt's stay in Missouri was a fatal choice. During January 1864 he conspired to free guerrilla Otho Hinton, who had been captured and was being held in a Lexington jail. During the escape attempt, Hinton was killed and Blunt barely made it out of town alive. About March 10, 1864, as Blunt and John Watson stopped at a house three miles south of Oak Grove, they were surrounded by thirteen Federals under the command of Capt. John T. Burris of Col. James McFerrin's regiment. Blunt tried to escape through an orchard but was knocked from his horse by low-hanging limbs. As he turned back to fire on the pursuing Federals, he was killed.

While the guerrillas were gathering to head south, another guerrilla company under Capt. Bill Anderson arrived. Together the collected guerrilla bands amounted to 150 men. When the column began the march to Texas, the guerrillas kept twenty men in an advance squad, ten men on either flank, and ten to twenty men as a rear guard. The remainder rode two abreast in the main column, which also included wives and other women, either on horseback or in wagons.

The advance squad carried a Union flag. Shortly after the march began, an unsuspecting squad of six Federals, led by a lieutenant with military dispatches from Springfield to Kansas City, joined the column and, in the usual fashion, was shot from their saddles.[26]

Leaving Jackson and Cass Counties, the guerrillas crossed the Grand River and entered Bates County. It was heavily wooded around the river, and the ground was level, with a few open areas. The countryside was sparsely populated, and only Federal patrols were encountered. Before leaving Bates County, the guerrillas attacked a foraging party from companies A and F, Third Wisconsin Cavalry, near the Marais des Cygnes River. One soldier was killed, and four others were wounded.[27] The skirmish proved to be the pattern for the guerrillas throughout their southward trek, fighting every day. Thus their 1863 march to Texas became one long skirmish.

Still, Quantrill kept the column moving at a rapid pace so the guerrillas would be long gone by the time anyone reported their presence and picked up their trail. Fearing Quantrill was heading south as part of another raid on Kansas, Lt. Col. Charles S. Clark reported that Quantrill was near Rose Hill on October 2 with between five hundred and six hundred men.[28]

As the guerrillas approached the Osage River on the southern border of Bates County, they came across a detail of thirty cavalrymen guarding a flatboat across the river. Quantrill ordered a charge. When the firing stopped, all but three Federals had been killed. Twenty-five miles farther south, Quantrill's column encountered sixteen cavalrymen herding stolen cattle across the border to Fort Scott. After a brief fight, no Union soldiers survived. Another skirmish with the Ninth Kansas Jayhawkers cropped up at Hog Island as they were headed toward Lamar.

Quantrill next halted his column near Carthage, south of Lamar, a generally flat but heavily wooded area. Shortly afterward, two men rode into the camp claiming to be Southern men. Since the guerrillas were traveling by night, they let the men ride with them, hoping they might guide them south across the Spring River. A little before midnight, John McCorkle, who was somewhat familiar with the country, told Todd that the guides were leading them toward the Union garrison at Fort Scott, Kansas. Quantrill shot the guides for their treachery and turned over the scouting duties to McCorkle, who soon had the column headed safely south on the correct road.

There had always been men who attempted to pass themselves off as Southern sympathizers or guerrillas. The most noteworthy was J. W. Terman, better known as Harry Truman. At the outset of the war, Terman lived in Jackson County. He offered his services as a scout and a spy to the Federal authorities. In early 1863, Terman was working for Gen. James G. Blunt, and he infiltrated the guerrilla band led by George Todd. On March 9, 1863, Terman was arrested in Lawrence by Federal authorities as a "bold secessionist" who was using his cover as a spy to terrorize the people of the Missouri border counties. Under Federal auspices, Terman sacked Union homes as well as Southern properties, passing himself off as one of Quantrill's guerrillas. He moved into the Keytesville area in 1864, posing as a guerrilla, then returned to plunder and kill those who had openly expressed Southern sympathies. On June 7, 1864, Terman hanged sixteen-year-old James Starks from a tree a quarter mile from his house and threatened the local citizens not to cut Starks down. By the time Terman left, the people of Chariton County were flooding Union authorities with complaints about Terman and the men who were riding with him. William A. Hall declared: "These soldiers have done more mischief in one week . . . than the rebels have done in that county since the war broke out." Hall wrote Union Gen. Clinton Fisk that if something were not done to stop Terman, he would "drive the whole population to the brush."[29]

Meanwhile, on October 6, 1863, Quantrill's column arrived in McDonald County, the furthermost corner of southeast Kansas, and prepared to cross into Indian Territory, in what was popularly known as the Cherokee neutral lands. After taking breakfast at Redding's Mill, the guerrillas resumed their march. They had been in the saddle for six days.

Just after sunup, scouts from David Poole's company, with Capt. John Brinker leading the advance column in charge of twenty men, came across several Federal soldiers in the timber tearing down a shanty and loading the stolen lumber into a wagon. Other nearby Union troops were shooting squirrels.[30] All of the Federals were part of Company D, Third Wisconsin Cavalry, commanded by Lt. John Crites. They shared a newly built fort with a company from the Second Kansas Colored Infantry commanded by Lt. R. E. Cook. The fort was under the military jurisdiction of Fort Scott. Days before, on October 4, Lt. James B. Pond arrived from Fort Scott with brothers George and Homer Pond and part of Company C, Third Wisconsin. James B. Pond took command of the post, known as Fort Baxter but officially designated as Fort Blair, in honor of Lt. Col. Charles W. Blair of the Fourteenth Kansas Jayhawker Regiment. Pond was an ardent abolitionist who had fought alongside John Brown in Kansas in the mid-1850s. Pond also held the confidence of Brown associate James Redpath, a foreign anarchist and revolutionary. After gaining experience in a newspaper office, Pond moved to Lawrence and joined the staff of the abolitionist newspaper *Herald of Freedom*. He also became involved with the Underground Railroad, ushering untold numbers of slaves into Canada.

Fort Baxter began as a military camp in the spring of 1862 consisting of some log cabins facing east toward the Baxter Springs River, a half mile away. Behind the buildings was a large space enclosed by earthen embankments and designated a *fort*. The enclosure was about four feet high and open on one end, where Pond intended to increase its size. A two-story log blockhouse was erected in the center and served as a barracks for the black soldiers. The site was a poor location for a fort: a quarter mile below the crest of the road. Thus, the command could not easily detect an advancing enemy. Only a hundred yards to the east was a stand of heavy timber. The water source and the fort's cooking camp were more than a hundred yards to the southwest, forcing the soldiers to leave their defensive perimeter three times a day to get food and water.

Pond's tent was two hundred yards west of the fort. He allowed some of the married men to have their families bivouac with them in the tents outside the walls, just east of the enclosure. Early on October 7, a foraging party of sixty men with eight wagons was sent out, leaving about twenty-five white soldiers and seventy black troops to man the fort. After the foraging party departed, Pond had the remaining men begin dismantling the western wall in order to expand the perimeter. About 11:00 a.m. he ordered the men to break for noon chow. Some of the soldiers walked into the woods for some casual pistol practice, including R. E. Cook and Johnny Fry, who had gained notoriety as the first Pony Express rider. Fry had only recently appeared at the fort after being chased across the Neosho River by local guerrillas. Now, as Quantrill's advance scouts came across the two men, Cook and Fry were run down and shot. Guerrilla Bud Story stripped Cook of his coat and pistols.

Poole captured some of the returning lumber-laden wagons. After interrogating the drivers, he learned about the newly established fort and quickly relayed this intelligence to Quantrill. As soon as he received the information, Quantrill told chief scout John McCorkle to find William H. Gregg, who was commanding Blunt's company of the rear guard, and tell him to come to the front as quickly as possible. Meanwhile, Quantrill brought the main column up alongside Poole's right. Gregg was to support them both if necessary.

At noon, the guerrillas came charging out of the timber between the fort and the river. The soldiers were at lunch at their makeshift kitchen a hundred yards from the fort. Poole's sudden charge cut them off from the fort. All the Federals had foolishly left their guns inside their tents or stacked inside the earthen barricade. Thirteen of the black soldiers were wounded in the first charge.

After seeing his men frantically run from the guerrillas, James B. Pond shouted at those closest to him to rally at the earthen enclosure, realizing that it was the only area that could offer some sort of defense. Many of the soldiers ran past the charging guerrillas and made it to the relative safety of the earthwork. Several guerrillas, including Fletcher Taylor, Ike Berry, George Shepherd, and Peyton Long, followed the soldiers into the open end of the fort, firing at them and stampeding the horses that had been corralled inside.

Gregg's company attacked the fort from the east, through the soldier's tents and the tents of their dependents. Realizing that there were women and children in the tents, Gregg immediately ordered his men to cease firing and withdraw. When Poole saw Gregg withdraw, he also fell back and regrouped for another attack. Suddenly Quantrill arrived with the guerrilla column's main body. The guerrillas combined forces and prepared for a second assault from the north.

Pond had a small howitzer and screamed at his men to help him load and fire it, but the soldiers were too frightened to respond. Pond single-handedly manned the gun. One successful shot decapitated guerrilla Dave Woods. The guerrillas fell back and turned to pursue the soldiers who had fled for the tall grass around the fort.[31]

While Poole continued firing, Quantrill received word that a Federal column was approaching from the north, down the old Fort Scott to Fort Gibson road. It was Gen. James G. Blunt, commander of the District of the Frontier, with an escort of forty men from Company I, Third Wisconsin Cavalry, and forty-five men from Company A, Fourteenth Kansas Jayhawker Regiment. Company A was Blunt's personal bodyguard recruited during the spring and summer of 1863. Blunt was en route from Fort Scott to Fort Smith in Arkansas. He had been informed that a Confederate force was threatening the Fort Smith garrison, and he was hurrying to aid their relief.[32] Including the teamsters, musicians, and soldiers in his column, he had about one hundred men.

Blunt had an elevated opinion of himself, still basking in the glory of having driven Price's forces from Missouri and over the Boston Mountains in Arkansas during the battles of Cane Hill and Prairie Grove the year before. In a recent battle on July 17, 1863, he had defeated Gen. Douglas H. Cooper's Indian Brigade at the battle of Honey Springs. During this campaign, in addition to the use of Federal Indians, Blunt was reinforced with troops from Colorado, Kansas, and Wisconsin. With these forces, Blunt's command occupied Fort Gibson in northern Indian Territory. In response, Cooper determined to drive them out. Blunt decided on a preemptive strike before the Confederates could be reinforced from Fort Smith. In the engagement, Blunt managed to turn Cooper's flank twenty miles southwest of Fort Gibson, causing a widespread route of the Confederate Indian forces.

In the following few weeks, Blunt had marched from Fort Gibson to find and destroy the remaining Confederate army in the Indian Territory. Blunt's scouts discovered Confederate Gen. William Steele's rear guard as he was withdrawing south across the Canadian River. Cooper was still pulling his forces back to Perryville to refit and resupply. Instead of pursuing Steele toward the more important Confederate garrison at Fort Smith, Blunt moved south to attack Cooper's forces. Perryville was a major supply depot for the Confederates, situated halfway between Boggy Depot and Scullyville on the Texas Road. Blunt attacked the Confederates at night. The Confederates, sensing that their forces were being encircled, retreated and abandoned their supplies. Blunt ordered the depot and town burned, crippling the Confederate forces in the area. After the battle, Union forces consisting mostly of Kansas troops maintained control of Indian Territory north of the Arkansas River.

On September 2, the Federals gained control of Fort Smith, including Little Rock. With the Confederates' defeat at these battles, and Missouri firmly under Federal control, Southern strategy was altered in northwest Arkansas. The Confederate Trans-Mississippi Department shifted to a plan that included disruption of enemy communications, raids on supply trains, and general small-unit actions that many hoped would shake Federal control of Missouri, northwest Arkansas, and Indian Territory. This strategy switched from large-scale encounters that were designed to draw much-needed Federal personnel west, away from Vicksburg and the eastern campaigns. In this strategy, Quantrill's tactics greatly aided the Confederates in Missouri.

Blunt prepared to move his headquarters from Fort Scott to Fort Smith. On October 6, 1863, as Blunt neared Fort Baxter, he saw blue-uniformed soldiers to his front. He halted his headquarters column and waited for his men to close ranks. He had with him a fourteen-piece brass band adorned in new uniforms with new revolvers in a specially outfitted wagon. Riding with them was James O'Neil, a reporter for *Frank Leslie's Illustrated Newspaper*. Also in the wagon was driver Henry Pellage, a soldier with the Third Wisconsin, and a twelve-year-old boy, the bandleader's servant. Behind the bandwagon were eight baggage wagons, two ambulances, and two buggies. The wagons were loaded with official documents and supplies. Flying at the head of the column was a flag trimmed with yellow fringe and the words, "Presented to Gen. J. G. Blunt by his friends, the ladies of Leavenworth." At the bottom of the flag was an American eagle trimmed in black, meaning "no quarter."[33] Blunt had up to this time been riding in a buggy with chief of staff Maj. Henry Zarah Curtis, son of Gen. Samuel Ryan Curtis, commander of the Department of Missouri. Blunt's horse was tied behind, saddled and bridled. In the second buggy were driver Pvt. Charles H. Davis and an attractive young woman. Blunt had a reputation for traveling in the field with numerous women, known as field servants. Most were Indian or black or white; there was no secret as to their real purpose.

Riding alongside Blunt was the notorious Redleg Capt. William S. Tough, described as a ruthless killer. Charles Chase, a reporter for the Sycamore, Illinois, *True Republican and Sentinel*, wrote that Tough's name "carries with it a degree of terror in Kansas of which people in peaceable society can have no conception." Besides being a terror to Missourians, Tough had no compunction about killing Federal soldiers. On July 28, before leaving for Fort Baxter, Tough murdered one of the privates of the Third Wisconsin Cavalry in a confrontation at Fort Scott.[34]

It took approximately fifteen minutes for Blunt's column to close up. The forty-five men from Company I dismounted and rested, waiting for the rest of the column to arrive. As the soldiers fell into line, the band held their instruments at the ready and began playing "Yankee Doodle," serenading the general as he made his way into the fort. Blunt remained about three hundred yards behind, intending to be the last to ride through the military parade accepting all the military honors.

Meanwhile, Quantrill formed his men east of the road north of the fort. The guerrillas fell into line so quickly they did not have time to tighten their saddle girths or to check their weapons. Blunt saw approximately 150 mounted Federal soldiers to his left, coming out of the timber. He thought they were soldiers from the fort sent out to salute him. Not absolutely certain that they were Pond's men, he had his men fall into line and face the approaching soldiers, keeping the wagons and ambulances in the rear. Blunt's men all carried carbines. The Wisconsin troopers were also armed with either Remington or Colt Army pistols.

Blunt ordered Tough to ride out and ascertain who the approaching Federals were. Within minutes, though, Tough returned at a dead run, telling Blunt that the soldiers to his front were Quantrill's men and that he personally recognized the guerrilla leader. Terror spread through the Federal ranks.

In the meantime, Quantrill prepared his men for a charge. His officers quickly rode among the men, issuing final orders and making sure the guerrillas were properly in line. They were instructed to advance at the double quick and charge after the first volley as fast as their horses could carry them.

Despite Tough's report, Blunt still could not believe the enemy was in his front. Some attributed his condition to the whiskey he had been consuming all morning.

The Federals nervously formed a line of battle, with the Third Wisconsin Cavalry to the left of the Kansas soldiers. Everything was happening so quickly. The cry, "It's Quantrill!" spread rapidly through the ranks. Sensing Tough's desperation in trying to get away, several soldiers of the Fourteenth Kansas started to turn and run. At the same time, the guerrillas started their horses on a steady walk toward Blunt's line. The Kansas troopers knew the fighting reputation of the guerrillas and realized that being caught out on the open prairie was certain death. Where a few seconds before a couple of Kansas soldiers tried to run and were goaded back into line, now the tide gave way, and the company broke and could not be rallied.

Quantrill had been riding behind his men as they dressed in line. Once he arrived at the center of the formation, he rode to the front, tucked his hat into his coat, and shouted orders to his men. The guerrillas spurred their horses into a run, and the wild charge commenced.

At a hundred yards, the Wisconsin troopers fired a volley at the guerrillas then braced for the onslaught. In their excitement they fired inaccurately;

Quantrill later wrote that the volley was too high to hurt anyone. As the guerrillas raced toward the Union line, pistol shots mingled with the wild Rebel Yell. The remaining Federal line soon fell apart, each man defending himself as best he could. With the guerrillas now on top of them, it was primarily pistol work. Plunging and screaming horses mixed with the smoke of revolver fire. This was familiar work for Quantrill's men; dismounted men had no chance of surviving. The only hope for the Union troopers was escape, and this illusion lasted only momentarily.

In describing the scene, Andy Walker claimed, "Many of them fell at the first volley, and every half mile of the stampede saw new victims reel to the earth. It was a mad, sickening race." Walker was joining in the pursuit when his horse was shot out from under him. Those that came riding back said that, as best as they could make out, fifteen of the Federals, those best mounted, escaped.[35] Accounts of the battle stated, "The ground on which the fight took place is rolling prairie, extending west a long distance, covered with grass, and intersected with deep ravines and gullies, on the banks of which grow willow bushes, sufficient to conceal any difficulty in crossing, but not sufficient to protect from observation: and in retreating, many of the [Federals] were overtaken at these ravines, and killed while endeavoring to cross."[36]

Blunt and several of his officers were among the first to flee, leaving the Wisconsin troopers to their fate. Frank Smith recalled: "Blunt was sitting in a buggy with a woman when the charge began. When he got out and mounted his horse and fled he was followed by [Frank] Smith, John Jarrette and Dick Yeager."

Lt. Col. Cyrus Leland Sr. rode a gray horse his son had obtained from Gen. Thomas Ewing and followed Blunt in the panic-stricken rout. Several guerrillas took notice of Curtis, whose uniform was hard to miss as he attempted to escape in another direction. One account reports that Peyton Long was the first to ride down Curtis. Long yelled at him to stop and surrender, but Curtis fired and emptied his pistols until Long came within range. About a half mile from the fort, Curtis's horse tried to jump a ravine, and the animal's flank was struck by a bullet, causing him to stumble and toss Curtis to the ground. When the guerrillas approached, Curtis held up his gauntlets, showing his rank and expecting to be spared. Long was the first to ride up. He disarmed the Federal and then searched him.

Found in one of his pockets was an order he had written on behalf of his father, Gen. Samuel Curtis, commanding the soldiers of his division to raise the "black flag" and not to take prisoners of any of Quantrill's men. Curtis emphasized that Quantrill's men were outlaws, and as such, they were not to be considered prisoners of war. Curtis's issuance of the order was to correct the assumption that Quantrill was a legitimate Confederate officer with the power to parole or exchange prisoners. In fact, Quantrill had recently captured and paroled thirty to forty soldiers of Company H, Twelfth Kansas Jayhawker Regiment, during an attack on Olathe, Kansas, in September, thus denying them further service as soldiers in the army. They were compelled to take an oath not to take up arms against the Confederacy and discharged upon their parole. After returning to their homes, they were arrested by provost marshals. Only an exchange of prisoners would legally permit these men to take up arms again. General Curtis wrote that these men were not prisoners of war because Quantrill was an outlaw. He ordered the soldiers back to duty but warned them not to surrender if they were again confronted by Quantrill's men, since their capture without being exchanged would result in their execution.[37]

Long asked Major Curtis if he had written the order, and the Federal admitted that he had. When Long asked him if he would have obeyed it, Curtis said that he would. Without any hesitation, Long shot him where he stood.

Blunt and nine of those around him were able to escape to safety. Federal reports stated, "The general, turning in his saddle to order his bodyguard to advance and fire, saw, with shame and humiliation, the whole of it in disgraceful flight over the prairie."[38] Pvt. Charles Davis, driving the buggy with the woman, whipped the horses into a frenzy and got away. They later joined Blunt after the guerrillas gave up the chase. Many of the Federals who managed to escape did not stop running until they reached Fort Scott, thirty-eight miles away. Besides the initial volley fired by the Wisconsin troops, the remaining soldiers of the Fourteenth Kansas made only a feeble attempt at defense. Unmounted soldiers were run down and shot at close quarters.

The guerrillas' usual practice proved most efficient by dispatching the enemy with a single shot to the head, which proved fatal and didn't spoil the victim's desperately needed clothing. Only a few wounded soldiers shot this way survived to tell the bloody tale.

Soldiers in the horse-drawn vehicles fared as badly as the soldiers afoot. Their fates came only moments after the infantry soldiers were shot down. The drivers in the baggage wagons and ambulances tried to escape by scattering in different directions across the prairie, but they were soon caught and dispatched. The large and cumbersome bandwagon with its large number of passengers drew considerable attention. Guerrilla William Bledsoe, followed by George Todd and William H. Gregg, gave chase. Bledsoe was the first to reach it, riding alongside the wagon and demanding its surrender. A band member shot Bledsoe from his saddle. A half mile farther, the left-front wheel flew off, pitching the band members into the dirt. Instruments and scattered sheet music flew across the prairie, as did the sketches by the newspaper artist riding in the wagon. The drawings showed Federal soldiers bayoneting frightened guerrillas and caused considerable anger. Some band members waved white handkerchiefs at the approaching guerrillas. Todd angrily asked why they had not waved their white handkerchiefs at Bledsoe instead of killing him. In fearful silence, each one was shot down. They were then dragged and piled beneath the wagon, which was set on fire.

Mopping up after the battle, some of Quantrill's men rifled through the supply wagons, while others talked about their victory. Quantrill rode up to Todd and Anderson and proudly stated, "By God, Shelby could not whip Blunt. Neither could Marmaduke. But I whipped him."[39]

In the fading late-afternoon light the guerrillas looked over the battlefield and saw scores of bodies covering the earth like a blue blanket. Afterward several of the Federals were discovered to be wounded and unconscious. The guerrillas had no way to care for prisoners, especially wounded prisoners. So the wounded were dispatched with a bullet to the head.

One unfortunate soldier, Jack Splane, lay bleeding and semiconscious with wounds in his side, arms, and legs. A guerrilla walked up and said, "When you get to hell, tell the devil the last man you saw on earth was Quantrill." The next thing he heard was a shot. Splane was fortunate that the bullet did not kill him; he recovered and later wrote of his ordeal.

Fifteen-year-old Riley Crawford was with a group of guerrillas who jokingly shouted at the dead Federals around them to stand up and fight. A nearby Union soldier was feigning death but thought he had been discovered. To everyone's surprise he stood up. Crawford immediately shot him.

John Koger was searching one of the supply wagons when a soldier ran from the fort and fired his rifle, hitting Koger in the back. In one wagon were found military documents and Blunt's personal papers and commission as brigadier and major general, plus his saber and a magnificent saddle. Scout John McCorkle discovered an officer's coat, six white shirts, a pair of fine cavalry boots, and two fancy revolvers in a trunk. Also found was Blunt's sash, made of fine, heavy silk adorned with beautiful tassels. One of the guerrillas reported that the sash was appropriated by Quantrill and worn as a war trophy; "he prized it highly and wore it for the rest of the war."[40]

Keeping with military necessity, most of the dead were stripped of their uniforms and worn afterward by the guerrillas. Bud Story posed for a photograph while wearing the uniform he had taken from R. E. Cook. All but one of the ambulances was later burned.

When the guerrillas searched the bodies, many canteens were found to be full of whiskey.[41] Captured weapons were distributed among the guerrillas. Federal casualties amounted to eighty killed and eighteen wounded. In the initial attack on the fort, the guerrillas killed nine and wounded ten. Official Federal reports claimed that eleven guerrillas were killed and twice that number wounded, but Quantrill's company only had two casualties: John Koger, who was too wounded to ride, and William Bledsoe, who had been killed by a band member. The other reported deaths—Robert Ward, Dave Woods, and William Lotspeach—apparently belonged to other commands being escorted south by Quantrill.

After the fighting had ended, the Confederates took muster and discovered two men were missing. Wanting to ascertain if Pond had taken any prisoners, Quantrill sent Todd under a flag of truce to inquire. Todd approached Pond's camp at 2:00 p.m. and demanded the surrender of the fort in the name of Colonel Quantrill of the First Regiment, First Brigade, Army of the South, along with an exchange of prisoners. Pond responded that he had no Southern prisoners.[42] William H. Gregg recorded that Pond informed Todd that the two men he was looking for were dead.

Protected now behind the earthen walls of the fort, with loaded weapons and a good supply of ammunition, the remaining Federals refused to surrender and awaited another guerrilla attack that never came. Todd and Anderson argued for another assault on the fort, but Quantrill overruled them, saying that additional assaults would be foolhardy and he didn't want any more casualties to slow his progress. He had wounded men, and they still had a long way to travel.

Quantrill's decision greatly endeared him to his men. Hiram George recalled that Quantrill "usually restrained the ardor of his followers and never sacrificed a man needlessly."[43] He realized this victory was just a means to a larger end, and his object had already been accomplished: he had achieved an outstanding battlefield victory by reducing the fighting to the slenderest possible proportions.

After rifling through the captured wagons and tending to their wounded, the guerrillas re-formed into a column and around 4:00 p.m. continued their march. Quantrill wanted to put some distance between himself and Fort Baxter while it was still light. He only had an hour and a half before darkness to get his men as far away as possible and set up a defensive perimeter for the night.

Blunt waited until sundown before riding back toward the fort. He had suffered the worst defeat of his career. Pond's men noted that Blunt appeared "much crestfallen and mortified."[44] The general's mind was already becoming unhinged partly due to his defeat at Quantrill's hand and partly from the excesses he took in his personal lifestyle. For years afterward, Blunt was heard to utter every time he recalled the battle, "I cannot throw it from my mind. It haunts me night and day."[45] Quantrill's victory was so astounding that one Federal dispatch reported the strength of his command to be 600 men strong even though Quantrill only had around 350 men with him at the time. In his official report, Pond asserted that Quantrill had attacked with about 650 men. Other Federal reports put the guerrillas' strength at up to 1,000.[46] These inflated figures were the norm in Federal reports; such numbers made their defeats seem less embarrassing.

About a month after Blunt's defeat at Fort Baxter, an article appeared in the November 8, 1863, issue of the *New York Times:* "General Blunt has made a demand on the rebel General [D. H.] Cooper for the surrender of Quantrill and his men as murderers and assassins. Otherwise, when captured all the soldiers in Quantrill's command will be ordered shot." No doubt Blunt and many others were responding to the inaccurate reports given by the Federal survivors at Baxter Springs. One such description by Pvt. Jesse Smith contradicts all battlefield reports and eyewitness accounts by Quantrill's men; Smith asserted that Quantrill took seventy-five prisoners and then executed them: "On the sixth of October 1863 he [Quantrill] surprised General Blunt's bodyguard and captured seventy-five of which I was one. After we were captured we were shot in obedience to his [Quantrill] orders. . . . Five of us lived and seventy were killed."[47]

Ten black Union troops were captured. One was a barber named Zack who had worked in Kansas City before the war and was well known to George Todd. Another black prisoner was Jack Mann. He had committed several crimes in Jackson County and was forced to flee the area when things became too hot for him. Mann was forced to dig a grave for William Bledsoe, Quantrill's one casualty. Bledsoe was buried in his saddle blanket near an abandoned farmhouse at the junction of the Fort Gibson and Fort Scott roads. After burying Bledsoe, Mann was forced to dig his own grave then was killed and dumped into it.[48] Quantrill placed a detachment of twenty-five men in Federal uniforms and carrying Blunt's captured flag a quarter of a mile in advance of the main column. He hoped that any Federals who had been apprised of Blunt's expected arrival would assume that the guerrilla column was his command.

The land south of Fort Baxter becomes very hilly with many woods and very little open spaces. The column pushed through Indian Territory, following the western branch of the Texas Road, and crossing the Arkansas River eighteen miles north of Fort Gibson. Quantrill moved rapidly, keeping any opposing forces from having time to confront him or to mass their forces in his rear. Before reaching the area around Fort Gibson, Quantrill came upon a wagon train with an escort of twelve Federal Pin Indians belonging to the First Indian Home Guards. They were captured then shot. Andy Walker recalled, "Each day, ten to twenty Pin Indians [Federal] would join us, and each night we would shoot the recruits of the day." Some were reported to be part of a larger group of Pin Indians that had accompanied Kansas Jayhawkers in killing and scalping a number of women and children.[49]

The Pins were Unionist Cherokees who had organized a secret society known as "the Pins" because the insignia they wore was formed by two common pins in the form of a cross on a shirt or coat lapel. The Pin Indians who fought for the North caused considerable trouble after joining the army. One black man writing from Indian Territory recalled, "The Pins came to the farm one day and broke down the doors, cut feather beds open and sent feathers flying in the wind, stole the horses, killed the sheep and done lots of mean things."[50] Another settler remarked: "We hear today that the Pins are committing outrages on Hungry Mountain and in Flint, robbing, destroying property and killing. It is so dreadful . . . Alas, alas, for this miserable people, destroying each other as fast as they can."[51] In his book *After the Trail of Tears*, William McLoughlin states, "Whenever the Pins 'stole' slaves, they claimed to be liberating them, but they may have sold some to slave traders from Southern states."

South of Fort Gibson was the Canadian River. Night was approaching, and the guerrillas made camp on the north side of the river. They found a campsite close to a farm with a cornfield, hogs, and abundant water. This may have been the home of Tom Starr, a Cherokee who had joined the Confederacy against the leadership of tribal leader John Ross. Quantrill had been a guest at Starr's ranch earlier and occasionally fought beside him.[52] Six miles south of the river was the camp of Gen. Douglas H. Cooper at Boggy Depot. Quantrill planned to send scouts in the morning to signal his approach. He had Blunt's ambulance, with the wounded guerrilla Koger inside, placed on the edge of the river, and he and Todd slept beside it as guards. Todd had ridden in the ambulance with Koger for two or three days after being hurt when his horse fell on him. The remainder of Quantrill's men slept in the timber across a ravine and fanned out around the ambulance in a half circle that faced north in a defensive perimeter. Always keeping part of his command vigilant as a security element, Quantrill ordered all the soldiers but Gregg's company to remove the saddles from their horses, relax in the tall grass, and get some sleep. Gregg's men slept with their horses bridled, saddled, and tethered next to them.

Before daylight the stillness was shattered by the blare of a bugle. Quantrill jumped up and ordered the command to mount and form a line. He and Todd ran to their horses and mounted without saddles. Armed troopers approached the ambulance, where Koger kneeled behind the seat with a pistol in each hand. The commander approached and asked Koger who they were. Koger responded, "Don't fire. It's Quantrill's men. If you fire, you'll be cut to pieces!" One of the soldiers tied a white cloth on a ramrod and rode toward the guerrillas, shouting, "Don't fire, boys; we are friends."[53]

The troops were Confederates commanded by Col. Daniel McIntosh. They observed the blue uniforms of Quantrill's advance guard the evening before and had been directed to wipe out the approaching company. McIntosh was an Indian political and military leader in charge of an Indian cavalry brigade known as the First Creek Mounted Volunteers belonging to Gen. Stand Watie's command. His brigade consisted of fifteen hundred men, two companies of Indians and one Texas company, comprising Col. Peter Hardeman's Texas Battalion.[54]

After breakfast, McIntosh escorted Quantrill to his camp at Cooper's headquarters in the foothills surrounding Boggy Depot. There the men were issued rations for themselves and their horses. Andy Walker recounted, "The general treated Quantrill well, providing him with everything we were in need of."[55] The guerrillas were now in the Chickasaw Nation. The area around Boggy Depot was inundated with small timber-covered hills as far as the eye could see. From here the guerrillas could snake their way south through the countryside unobserved. Here they rested for five or six days. On October 13, Quantrill took the opportunity to compose a report to Sterling Price explaining his recent experiences along the border.

I have the honor to make the following report of my march from the Missouri River to the Canadian, a distance of 450 miles.

I started on the morning of October 2, at daybreak, and had an uninterrupted march until night, and encamped on Grand River for three hours; then marched to the Osage. We continued the march from day to day, taking a due southwest course, leaving Carthage 12 miles east, crossing Shoal Creek at the falls, then going due west into the Seneca Nation.

On October 6, about 2 p.m., the advance reported a train ahead. I ordered the advance to press on and ascertain the nature of it. Captain [John] Brinker being in command of the advance, he soon discovered an encampment, which he supposed to be the camp of the train; in this we were mistaken. It proved to be the camp belonging to Fort Baxter, recently built and garrisoned with Negroes, 45 miles south of Fort Scott, Kans. When the advance came near the camp they saw that they were not discovered, and they fell back a short distance to wait for the command to come up. I now ordered the column to close in and to form by fours and charge, and leading the head of the column myself with Captains Brinker and [David] Poole, took about one-half of the column to the encampment which they had discovered, being ignorant of the fort. This they charged, driving everything before them, and in two minutes were in possession of the fort. The Negroes took shelter behind their quarters. Having no support, my men were compelled to fall back. Not knowing myself where the fort was, I moved with three companies, Captains [George] Todd, [Noah] Estes and Garrett, in all 150 men, out on the prairie north of the camp, and discovered a train with 125 men as an escort, which proved to be Major-General (J. G.) Blunt and staff with bodyguard and headquarters train moving headquarters from Fort Scott, Kans., to Fort Smith, Ark. I immediately drew up in line of battle, and at this time I heard heavy firing on my left, and on riding out discovered, for the first time, the fort, with at least half of my men engaged there. I ordered them to join me immediately, which they did, on the double-quick. General Blunt formed his escort, still in doubt as to who we were. I now formed 250 men of all the companies and ordered a charge. Up to this time not a shot had been fired, not until we were within 60 yards of them, when they gave us a volley too high to hurt any one, and then fled in the wildest confusion on the prairie. We soon closed up on them, making fearful havoc on every side. We continued the chase about 4 miles, when I called the men off, only leaving about 40 of them alive.

On returning, we found they had left us 9 six-mule wagons, well loaded; 1 buggy (General Blunt's); 1 fine ambulance; 1 fine brass band and wagon, fully rigged.

Among the killed were General Blunt, Majors Curtis, Sinclair, and (B.S.) Henning, Captain Tufft (Tough), and 3 lieutenants of the staff, and about 80 privates of the escort. My loss here was 1 man killed (William Bledsoe) and 1 severely wounded (John Koger). In the charge on the fort, my loss was 2 men killed (Robert Ward and William Lotspeach) wounded, Lieutenant Toothman and Private Thomas Hill. Federal loss at the fort, 1 lieutenant and 15 privates killed; number wounded, not known.

We have as trophies two stand of colors, General Blunt's sword, his commission (brigadier-general and major-general), all his official papers, etc, belonging to headquarters. After taking what we wanted from the train; we destroyed it, fearing we could not carry it away in the face of so large a force. We then sent a flag of truce to the fort to see if we had any wounded there. There was none.

I did not think it prudent to attack the fort again, and as we had wounded men already to carry, and it was so far to bring them, (I concluded) that I would leave the fort. So at 5 p.m. I took up the line of march due south on the old Texas road. We marched 15 miles, and encamped for the night. From this place to the Canadian River we caught about 150 Federal Indians and Negroes in the Nation gathering ponies. We brought none of them through.

We arrived at General (D. H.) Cooper's camp on the 12th in good health and condition.

At some future date I will send you a complete report of my summer's campaign on the Missouri River.

P.S.—In this report I neglected to say that Colonels Holt and Roberson and Captain Tucker, who have been in Missouri on business for the army, were with me, and took an active part in leading the men on the enemy.[56]

On October 13, Quantrill gave his report to Capt. John Brinker and forwarded it along with General Blunt's sword and general's commissions. Spies in the Indian Territory discovered Quantrill's arrival and forwarded the news. Before Quantrill rode away from Boggy Depot, a Federal dispatch was hurriedly sent to Union headquarters: "Quantrill sighted—Expect hell in Texas soon." Brinker delivered Quantrill's report to General Price's headquarters at Camp Bragg, Arkansas, along with a requisition of what the guerrillas would need during their stay in Texas. They declined funds but did make Price aware of their need for clothing, arms, ammunition, and horses. They also asked to serve him solely as independent cavalry.

News of Quantrill's victory over Blunt quickly spread. On October 15, 1863, Confederate Gen. William Steele wrote to Gen. Henry E. McCulloch at his headquarters in the Northern Sub-district of Texas at Bonham: "Quantrill is reported to have brought with him some 300 well-equipped men. I am anxious to see him, as I am confident that he is better posted as regards the enemy in Southwestern Missouri and Western Arkansas than any one else."[57] McCulloch added his congratulations in General Orders No. 187, which reads in part:

With much pleasure the major-general commanding makes known to the troops of this district the following cheering intelligence from Northern

Texas, congratulating them on the brightening of our prospects in that quarter: Very good news from our front. Brigadier-General Blunt, of the United States army, killed by Colonel (W.C.) Quantrill 30 miles from Fort Scott. The Federals fallen back. North Fork Town burned. Blunt had gone to Kansas, it is supposed, to organize and start his jayhawkers and Indians to the Texas frontier. On his return with his body-guard of 130 men, Quantrill attacked him, killing him, his adjutant-general, and many, if not all, of his men, capturing everything he had, including his sword, carriage, etc. . . . Our prospects are brightening in the north, thank God, and for the present, at least, Northern Texas is safe.

McCulloch considered Quantrill's recent battlefield successes so effective that he wrote Gen. John B. Magruder that he felt no fear of a Federal attack along his northern frontier.[58]

On November 2, Price replied to Quantrill's report. Addressing him as a colonel, Price congratulated Quantrill on the Baxter Springs victory and thanked him and his men for their "gallant struggle" against Northern oppression in Missouri. He added that he was anxious to have a report on the Lawrence raid, so that "your acts should appear in their true light before the world." Also, he desired information on the treatment accorded captured guerrillas, in order that "the Confederacy and the world may learn of the murderous and uncivilized warfare" being conducted by the Federals and "thus be able to appreciate their cowardly shrieks and howls when with a just retaliation the same measure is meted out to them." Price concluded, "The expedition to Lawrence was a gallant and perfectly fair blow at the enemy," one that served the "malignant and scoundrely people of Kansas right."

Even as far away as Richmond, Quantrill's daring exploits made headlines: "Quantrell and other bold raiders in Missouri have collected some thousands of desperate men, and *killed* several regiments of the enemy."[59] Department of Texas commander Magruder published a general order congratulating "Colonel Quantrill" for his victory over Blunt.[60]

On November 2, 1863, the same day that Price responded to Quantrill concerning his victory, Price wrote a letter to Missouri Governor Thomas C. Reynolds at Marshall, Texas, where the Missouri government in exile had relocated.

I have the honor to enclose to you an official copy of Colonel Quantrill's report of his march from Missouri River to Canadian, detailing in a terse but graphic style his attack upon Fort Baxter and upon Major-General Blunt and escort. This report was handed to me by Captain Brinker, who you see bore a conspicuous part in the attack. Colonel Quantrill has with him some 350 men of that daring and dashing character which has made the name of Quantrill so feared by our enemies, and have aided so much to keep Missouri, though overrun by Federals, identified with the Confederacy.[61]

Some Confederate officers were suggesting that partisan units be joined to the regular army while they were away from Missouri. Price pointed out that many of the guerrillas feared to be attached to the army since many of them had belonged to the commands of Gens. Thomas Hindman and T. H. Holmes the previous winter, where they grew bored with garrison duty and wanted to serve a more active role in the war and so joined Quantrill's command. Holmes had previously admitted to the secretary of war on November 15, 1862, regarding his army: "There are in this army about 6,000 Missouri recruits. They are in the service in all sorts of ways, having been raised, some under the Missouri authorities, some under the Confederate authorities, and some under no authority at all."[62] Price told Governor Reynolds that, as an additional incentive for the guerrillas to remain in partisan service, they feared being captured if the army had to surrender, because their lives would be forfeited since the Federals had classified them as outlaws rather than soldiers. The guerrillas were more than willing to serve as scouts and rangers for the regular army and in this capacity could protect themselves.[63]

After submitting his report to Price, Quantrill and his guerrillas resumed their march down the Texas Road toward the Red River. South of Boggy Depot, the hills leveled out and there was very little timber. The only trees were those surrounding the rivers and creeks.

During their march to Texas, orders arrived from Gen. Edmund Kirby Smith, commander of the Trans-Mississippi Department, to General Cooper, directing Quantrill to arrest Gen. Albert Pike, the commander of Choctaw troops at nearby Fort Washita for treason, cowardice, and incompetence during the battle of Pea Ridge. Records stated: "In November Pike was arrested by a captain and forty-eight men of Shelby's brigade of Missouri troops. He was seized near Tishomingo, less than fifty miles above Colbert's Ferry just in the Chickasaw country on November 14, when returning to Fort Washita from Fort Arbuckle."[64] Quantrill was purported to be involved in the arrest. From the start of the war, Pike had been at odds with his military superiors, charging them with an entire disregard of the treaties with the Indians. During the battle of Pea Ridge, Pike caused a great deal of anxiety in the Confederate ranks by spreading the rumor that both Generals Price and Van Dorn had been captured and instructing regular Confederate troops to throw down their arms and go home.[65]

Pike's difficulties were made worse when he and Thomas Hindman exchanged charges related to mismanaging funds and materials. Under provisions of an act by the Confederate Congress, Pike was given $681,869 in treasury notes, $265,927 in gold, and $65,000 in silver to be delivered to the superintendent of Indian affairs in Indian Territory. Some of the money was handed over and some was held by Pike on questionable grounds. Finally, Pike resigned his military command and delivered an address to the Indians of such violent and unmilitary nature that Gen. D. H. Cooper was instructed to arrest him. To protect himself, Pike resigned his position, but the resignation was held up so he might be tried "for falsehood, cowardice and treason." The court martial was never held, and Pike's resignation was afterward accepted. With Pike out of the way, Cooper was in a position to command all of the Indian Territory. After Pike's arrest, Quantrill continued to move south until he arrived at the Red River.

4

Proud to Be a Soldier

It was a stirring example to free people throughout the nation of what a
few brave men could accomplish once they refused to submit to tyranny.
—SOUTHERN WRITER

HE ROAD FORKED AT the Red River, one road going west to Preston and the other going to Colbert's Ferry, where a ferryboat
ran on a cable across the river. The ferries were large flat-
bottomed boats capable of holding a four-horse team and wagon, drivers, and
passengers. The boats were too large to be poled across the river, especially
against the current. Round trips took twenty-five to forty minutes under ideal
conditions. Quantrill first crossed here in 1861 with the Gill family. Now, in
1863, after getting all of his men across the river, Quantrill spurred his horse
for Sherman, the county seat of Grayson County.

Shortly after the courthouse was built in 1846, a water well was dug in
the shadow of an old pecan tree on the southeast corner of the square. Water
was brought up by a hand pump to fill a large four-legged vat. Families drew
their water from the vat, and animals drank from a nearby trough. Post Oak
Creek supplied the well; the creek ran across West Cherry, Jones, Lamar, and
Houston streets, winding its way through the city before emptying into
Choctaw Creek. Roads were the next order of business for the community.

Sherman was a very small town, but it was the only town of any size in
the countryside. A three-hundred-foot-square lot bounded by Travis, Lamar,
Crockett, and Houston Streets became the town square. Travis Street was
the dividing line for all streets running east and west, and Houston Street was

the initial point for all streets running north and south. A post office opened in 1847, and letters were no longer deposited in the pockets of an old coat hung from the pecan tree on the square. The pecan tree became a central landmark. On Sundays, church services were held under its shade, with guns stacked nearby in case of Indian attack. On weekdays, court was in session under its branches, even after a log courthouse was built. In time, two sa- loons, a district clerk's office, a doctor's office, and a church were also built. Austin College opened on North Grand Avenue in 1849. It is now the oldest college in Texas operating under its original charter; it was the first to open a law school in the state and the first to award graduate degrees in 1856.

In 1857, two fires destroyed virtually all of Sherman south and east of the city square, but the townspeople rebuilt. By January 25, 1858, eight post of- fices served Grayson County. Sam Houston visited the area in 1859 during his gubernatorial campaign, touting his independent bid for the governorship and voicing opposition to secession. Because of his anti-secession sentiments, he was not allowed to speak at the Sherman Opera House but was offered a plat- form in a cow lot from which to give his speech. Houston accepted and drew an overwhelming crowd. Sophia Butts stood at his side and held a parasol over him while he spoke under a broiling sun. When election returns were tabu- lated, he not only carried Sherman and Grayson County, he won the election.

By 1860 the county was considered a thickly settled community. Sher- man served as a supply post for a wide region of North Texas; it was far more important both in trade and population than Dallas. But because of a lack of transportation facilities, farming did not develop as quickly as it could.

E. F. Jones, one of the oldest pioneers of Grayson County, settled in the area in 1856 and reported what he saw:

> When I first came to this district there were not hardly any of the land in cultivation. There were plenty of deer and wild chickens to be found on the prairies. The principle crop was wheat, corn, and oats and a very little cot- ton. There was just enough raised to make clothes for the people who raised it. The houses that we lived in these days were very poor, boxed or log houses, with stick and dirt chimneys, which smoked very badly on windy days. The houses sometimes had cracks in the walls large enough for the cats and dogs to come in. We had very little furniture and what we had was some that we had brought with us. For beds, we would drive poles up in the floor and run poles through these to holes in the walls and lay boards across these and put our bedding on this. We used a substitute for coffee, parched wheat or barley. I know some people that used parched okra seed for coffee.

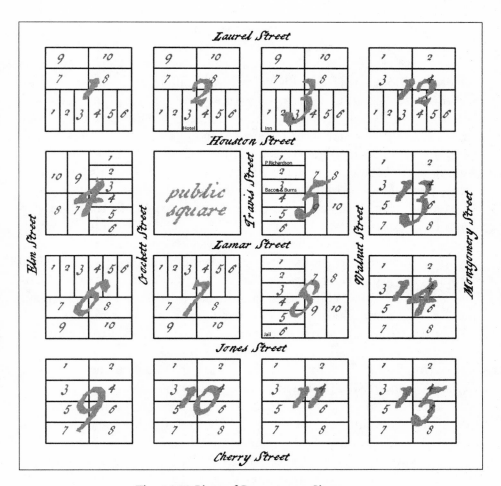

The 1860 Platt of Downtown Sherman

There were plenty of cattle on the prairies and you could buy the best cow for twenty dollars. There were mustang ponies running all over the prairies, more ponies than cows. All of the work was done with oxen in the fields.[1]

Despite the hardships imposed during the Civil War, Sherman continued to grow and develop during the early 1860s. In 1861, the community's first flourmill began operation, becoming the foundation for the area's industrial development.

In addition to Sherman, another important town was growing in North Texas. Marshall was about 160 miles from Sherman and had a population of two thousand. On January 1, 1863, the city became the unofficial capital of the duly elected government of Missouri that had been expelled from Jefferson City by Federal bayonets. Shortly after the death of Claiborne F. Jackson, Missouri's governor in exile, in Little Rock in December 1862, Lieutenant Governor Thomas C. Reynolds visited Marshall to find facilities for his government's operations and to select an executive mansion. Reynolds's government still controlled a remnant of the State Guard, issued bonds and currency, and performed other state government functions. The establishment of Missouri's capital here was inspiring to Quantrill and his soldiers because it lent substance to the politics of the struggle. Soon Marshall, barely twenty years old itself, was abuzz with all the noise of a state capital.

Marshall's location was a logical decision for Reynolds. In 1854, the Marshall newspaper linked the town to New Orleans and the national news. By 1860, Marshall was one of the largest and wealthiest towns in East Texas. Reynolds noted that in addition to overcrowding and the city's exorbitant wartime rents, it was reasonably close for easy communication with both Gens. Edmund Kirby Smith,* commander of the Trans-Mississippi Department, and Sterling Price, commander of the Confederate armies in southern Arkansas.

The importance of Marshall was emphasized by the fact that many bureaus of the Trans-Mississippi Department either operated here or moved here during Reynolds's stay. These included the ordnance, quartermaster, subsistence, and medical bureaus, the post office, the treasury, and a tax collections bureau. Marshall also attracted a number of local war agencies, including a powder mill, a Confederate hat factory, and a home for transient soldiers. The community also had outstanding lawyers and political leaders, which included the first and last governors of Confederate Texas.[2] To further highlight Marshall's significance, after Vicksburg fell into Federal hands on July 4, 1863, Smith moved the headquarters of the Trans-Mississippi Department to the city.

Before the Missouri capital moved to Marshall in 1863, the area witnessed a peculiar brand of Unionist revolt in reaction to the conscription law. Pockets of Union sympathizers began to run a fifth column in Texas. A secret organization, seventeen hundred strong, formed in Collin, Cooke,

---

* Smith had been born in St. Augustine, Florida, on May 16, 1824. He graduated twenty-fifth in the West Point class of 1845 and gained notoriety during the Mexican War, where he was cited for bravery. After contributing to the Confederate victory at the battle of First Manassas, Smith was named commander of the Trans-Mississippi Department. In 1863 he was thirty-eight years old and described as an active man of very agreeable manners. He wore large spectacles and a thick black beard. In addition to his renowned military reputation, Smith was also a devout Christian and contemplated entering the ministry in 1863.

Denton, Grayson, and Wise counties to oppose the Confederacy and secession and foment unrest among slaves and Indians. Plans were made to seize ammunition and guns at Sherman and Gainesville and to kill all who were not members of the secret organization. But the conspirators' plan was discovered, the militia was called out, and around 150 men were arrested and brought to Gainesville, thirty-three miles west of Sherman, for trial. Col. James G. Bourland, provost marshal of the district, oversaw the matter. Because some of the suspects wore Confederate uniforms, they appeared before Bourland in a separate military tribunal and were promptly declared guilty and sentenced to death. Of the 150 men arrested, 40 were found guilty and hanged. Two of the condemned men broke away from their guards and were shot and killed.[3]

In addition to large organizations of Union sympathizers in North Texas, individual leaders were identified and hunted down. Dr. Robert Lively of Sherman was linked to the Unionist movement by an article in the *Dallas Herald;* he was later killed in an ambush. Sherman's Methodist minister, the Reverend John H. McLean, a boarder at the Binkley home, was saved from a violent mob by his landlord when he learned a mob was intent on harming McLean because of his antislavery sentiments.

By October 1863, when Quantrill's company returned, the area had settled down somewhat.[4] One citizen reported: "In the midst of these most turbulent times came the Missouri guerrillas establishing their camps along the numerous streams that inundated the county. The county seat in Sherman was said to have presented a very martial appearance when any men were in town, as they were all in military dress. The town showed the effects of the war, business dwindled to little or nothing and producers whose work lies in the earth are the only persons busy and comparatively unaffected by the stopping of the ordinary current of business."[5]

Quantrill's experience in North Texas the year before satisfied him that it was an ideal site for winter quarters. Reports at the time stated, "The climate is all that could be desired. A cool breeze blows from the south during the summer, and the winters often pass without forming ice. For good health Northern Texas cannot be surpassed. There are few swamps and consequently the country is comparatively free from malarial diseases. Few prairie counties are better supplied with springs and running streams. In nearly any portion of the county good well water can be found at a depth of between twenty and fifty feet."[6]

Quantrill stayed in Sherman two days, establishing a camp near the intersection of College and Broughton streets before going into camp about two miles outside of town. During this time he became reacquainted with the people. One resident recollected:

> When I first saw Quantrell's men after their arrival to Texas I must confess that I looked upon them with feelings of profound respect. . . . I saw them soon after their arrival, and was struck with their manly forms and chivalrous bearing. They were generally dressed in rich Federal uniforms, rode good horses and wore an air of jaunty nonchalance, peculiar to the life they lead, all of which with a knowledge of their prowess, their unsatiated hate of

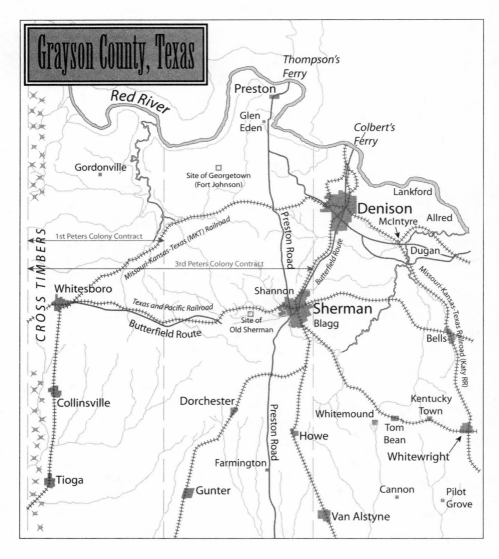

Marcus Gill was a wealthy Missouri settler who hired William C. Quantrill to escort his family to safety behind Southern lines and into Texas at the beginning of the war to escape the Jayhawker attacks in Jackson County.

Capt. Joel Bryan Mayes commanded the First Cherokee Regiment, composed of both whites and Indians. Quantrill joined Mayes's regiment at the start of the war, after returning from Texas.

Gen. Benjamin McCulloch commanded Confederate forces from Texas and Arkansas at the battle of Wilson's Creek near Springfield, Missouri. He was killed in action at the battle of Pea Ridge, Arkansas.

Gen. Henry Eustace McCulloch was Ben McCulloch's brother and the commander of the Northern Subdistrict of Texas while the Missouri guerrillas were in winter quarters in the area.

Colbert's Ferry, north of Sherman and Denison, was the site of Quantrill's crossing of the Red River into Texas. After the war, in 1872, former guerrillas John and William Maupin rented the ferry from "Chickasaw Ben" Colbert and added a second boat.

During the winter season, Quantrill and his men often came to Sherman, Texas, to relax and celebrate their victories. On the first Monday of every month, farmers would come to town to barter for goods at informal auctions. Note the O.K. Saloon and Gabe's Picture Gallery in the background, where many of the guerrillas had their pictures taken.

During a visit to Richmond in his quest for a partisan ranger commission, William C. Quantrill met with Secretary of War James Seddon in the Confederate Customs House (above), where most military affairs were conducted. The Confederate Capitol can be seen in the background, on the right, between the two buildings.

Col. Daniel N. "Dode" McIntosh commanded the First Creek Mounted Volunteers, consisting of fifteen hundred men (two companies of Indians and one company of Texans).

Col. Douglas H. Cooper, commander of the First Choctaw and Chickasaw Regiment, was a Baptist minister and physician and a close friend of Jefferson Davis, whom he served with in the Mexican War.

Glen Eden, the home of George and Sophia Butts, was the most prominent plantation in North Texas. Many of the state's leaders, both political and economic, and some of the most notable figures of the nineteenth century attended dinners and parties at this social center. During the winters of the Civil War, Quantrill and his men also enjoyed the hospitality of the Buttses.

George and Sophia Butts had met and married in 1853 in New Orleans. They were the most prominent couple in North Texas and were devoted to the Southern cause.

George Butts was bushwhacked in 1864. Sophia left North Texas and did not return until after the war. She remarried and rebuilt her cattle and cotton empire.

Lawyer Robert S. Stevens defended Quantrill against spurious Jayhawker allegations prior to the war. During Quantrill's August 21, 1863, raid on Lawrence, Kansas, Stevens and other occupants of the Eldridge Hotel were protected by Quantrill.

Lt. James B. Pond commanded the Union garrison at Baxter Springs, Kansas, that was overrun by Quantrill's company on October 6, 1863. Pond was awarded the Medal of Honor for his actions in this battle with the guerrillas.

Johnny Fry was the first Pony Express rider and a Federal scout during the war. He was one of the first soldiers killed by the guerrillas led by Dave Poole at the October 6, 1863, battle of Baxter Springs, Kansas.

Frank Leslie's depiction of a Richmond food riot illustrates a similar incident in Sherman, Texas, in 1864 that was quelled by Quantrill.

Neal Henderson lives near the site of Quantrill's camp at Mineral Springs, Texas, and displays a trough carved by Frank James to collect water from a hillside spring.

The waterfall of Brogdon Springs still flows at the Mineral Springs campsite. As many as fifteen men could bathe here at a time.

JACKSON COUNTY HISTORICAL SOCIETY, PATRICK MARQUIS HISTORICAL ARCHIVES

William Clarke Quantrill and Kate King were married by a country preacher not far from his Blue Springs camp in Missouri. Although a marriage certificate has not yet surfaced, many of Quantrill's men attested to the marriage, probably officiated by Pastor Hiram Bowman from Oak Grove, who performed other marriages for members of Quantrill's company.

This gravestone marks the last resting place of J. B. Blundell of Company C, Fourteenth Kansas Cavalry, one of the many Federals interred near Quantrill's Mineral Springs camp. Hundreds of Union soldiers are believed to have been killed during Gen. James G. Blunt's failed December 1863 invasion of North Texas. Yet any records of Federal fatalities in this action are mysteriously missing from the files of the adjutant general's report of the state of Kansas.

COURTESY OF TONY SWINDELL ARCHIVES COLLECTION

George Caleb Bingham's 1870 painting depicts Union atrocities perpetrated in Missouri's border counties after Quantrill's raid on Lawrence, Kansas.

Union Col. Charles Jennison led the hated Seventh Kansas Jayhawker Regiment that devastated the border counties of Missouri during the war. Jennison personally executed elderly Missourians merely for their Southern sympathies. One of his victims was the father of guerrilla John House. In some instances, Jennison disfigured individuals (for example, cutting off a person's ears) as a warning rather than kill them.

Capt. Dave Poole was one of Quantrill's officers and commanded a company of guerrillas. He led the initial attack on the Federal garrison at Baxter Springs, Kansas. After the war, he assisted Federal authorities in convincing numbers of guerrillas to give up the fight and surrender. He then relocated to Sherman, Texas, and became a rancher.

The Valley of the Little Blue River in Jackson County, Missouri, is eight miles south of Independence. Most of the Missouri-Kansas border skirmishes and battles occurred here.

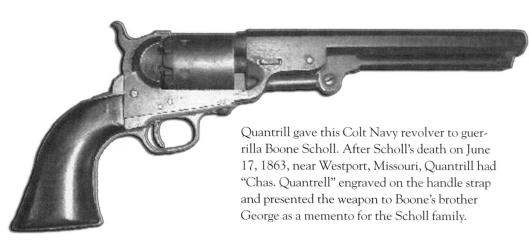

Quantrill gave this Colt Navy revolver to guerrilla Boone Scholl. After Scholl's death on June 17, 1863, near Westport, Missouri, Quantrill had "Chas. Quantrell" engraved on the handle strap and presented the weapon to Boone's brother George as a memento for the Scholl family.

Guerrilla Riley Crawford (below) was only fourteen years old when his mother brought him to Quantrill after her husband had been murdered and their home burned down. His two sisters were murdered by Union soldiers in Kansas City. Riley was sixteen when he was killed in 1864 in Cooper County, Missouri.

Below is a postwar photograph of guerrilla George Scholl, who participated in all of Quantrill's major battles, including the Lawrence raid and the battles of Baxter Springs, Centralia, and Fayette.

The Hill brothers—Francis Marion "Tuck" (upper right), James W. "Woot" (lower left), and Tom (lower right)—settled in McKinney, Texas, after the war and raised livestock and traded mules. All were well respected, and Tuck served on the city council. Tuck and Woot married sisters whose father, Albert Graves, was a refugee from Cass County, Missouri.

Tuck had been a captain under Quantrill, and his brothers had been lieutenants. They attended many Quantrill reunions after the war.

Tuck had been captured several times during the war, but he escaped in every instance. He also was wounded twelve times and had seven horses shot from under him.

Payne Jones was one of Quantrill's best fighters. He accompanied his commander to Kentucky at the end of the war and later surrendered to Federal authorities at Samuel's Depot in the Bluegrass State.

This image of William "Bloody Bill" Anderson was made in 1864 in Sherman, probably for his wedding. It may be the last known photograph of Anderson taken while he was alive.

James Anderson was William's brother and served by his side until Bloody Bill's death. In 1864, James married his brother's widow, and the couple had one child. James was killed in 1869, and this photograph was worn as a mourning pin by his sister Molly. The back of the pin contained a lock of his hair.

Nate Teague served in Bill Anderson's company and fought at the September 27, 1864, battle of Centralia as well as other battles with Quantrill's command.

Sylvester Akers and John Barnhill were captured and photographed near Harrodsburg, Kentucky. They were held in Lexington before they were transferred to the Federal prison at Louisville.

Guerrilla Bob Thompson was photographed in a Federal uniform, but the time and the place are unknown. Thompson was killed in a skirmish with local militia near Boonville, Missouri in the summer of 1863.

The George brothers—Hiram "Hi" James and John Hicks "Hix"—were from Oak Grove, Missouri. They joined Quantrill after Union troops killed their father, hanged their brother, and plundered and burned down their home.

Oll Shepherd was from Independence, Missouri. He rode with Quantrill for most of the war, including the Lawrence raid. On April 4, 1868, Shepherd was killed by vigilantes at his home in Lee's Summit, Missouri.

Three Missouri guerrillas show off their battle trophies, including captured Federal officers' sashes probably seized after the October 1863 battle of Baxter Springs. The photograph was found in Higginsville, Missouri, but the image purportedly was made in Texas. Revenue stamps on the back of the photograph indicate it was taken after June 30, 1864.

This is the earliest known image (above) of Frank James as a Quantrill guerrilla. Because Frank rode with Quantrill, Federal troops severely beat Frank's brother Jesse, hanged his stepfather, abused his mother (causing a miscarriage), and imprisoned his mother and sister.

Frank James (above left) was photographed with John Jarrette. Both men fought as guerrillas in some of the most savage fighting of the war. When James tried to return to farming after the war, vigilantes stole his livestock and tried to kill him and his brother Jesse. In southern Missouri, Jarrette was ambushed by vigilantes, and his wife was gunned down and their home was torched with their children inside.

Guerrilla Jesse Hamlet (left) served under Bill Anderson. After the war, Hamlet became a U.S. marshal at Lexington, Missouri.

B. Nauschuetz.

San Antonio, Texas.

Carpetbaggers like the one pictured above swarmed into the South after the war with the goal of making themselves rich at the cost of the ruin of former Confederates.

In the postwar photograph above, Lee McMurtry is flanked by his brother and Dick Poole (on the right). McMurtry was the sheriff of Wichita County, Texas, at the time, and his badge is apparent.

Jim Cummins's mother was abused by Federal troops because she was a Southern sympathizer. After Jim joined Quantrill, his uncle was hanged. Cummins survived the war, but he relocated to Texas with George Shepherd.

the male Yankee race and their high respectability as gentlemen, inclined me to huzzah! for Quantrell's men.[7]

A member of the Sherman Methodist Church recalled: "After they settled in, the outrages credited to them in Kansas and Missouri seemed to have abated and their presence created a sense of protection. Intercessory prayer had prevailed at least temporarily and Quantrill conducted himself in a gentlemanly manner. By 1863 men who chose not to go to war had drifted into Indian Territory. Cattle rustling in North Texas and Southern Indian Territory was rampant, with Quantrill's intervention it stopped."[8]

Sherman resident Juanita Beach told neighbor John P. Proctor that both Quantrill and Bill Anderson had visited her home and that she was distantly related. She remembered Quantrill as "A man of quiet demeanor and genteel manners."[9]

The people of Sherman opened their homes and hospitality to the weary refugees. Quantrill divided his command, keeping part of them in camp outside Sherman. Most of the married men, like H. T. Ritter and Jim Chiles, whose wives and families were with them, were housed more comfortably in town. Only the married men were allowed to live in town; single men were required to be billeted outside of town, per orders from Gen. Henry E. McCulloch. Eventually the remainder of Quantrill's command camped about fifteen miles north of Sherman, in an area called Georgetown, just south of the Red River.

A report describing the citizens of Sherman who welcomed the guerrillas stated, "They were also to have compassion toward the incoming families who had been expulsed from their homes in Missouri and who were beginning to arrive here."[10] The citizens were overjoyed at having the guerrillas among them. Local reports described Quantrill's leadership: "He has kept at bay the legions of the Yankees on the plains of the Missouri, kept thousands of the murderous enemy hunting him down, and thus diverting them for two years from an extensive invasion of Arkansas and the Indian Territory, between the Canadian and Red Rivers, and consequently thereby, from the soil of Texas. It is a notorious fact that the operations of the guerrillas in Missouri for the last two years have ensured vastly to the benefit of the Southern cause in Arkansas and Texas."[11]

Many of the guerrillas sought out old friends, relatives searched for cousins or brothers, and all inquired about news from home. William H. Gregg found some Missouri friends and stayed with them for two weeks before returning to the camp northwest of Sherman.

Frank and Jesse James brought their sister, Susan Lavinia James, with them, and she began teaching school. She also became better acquainted with Allen Parmer of Quantrill's company. Parmer was only fourteen years old when he joined Quantrill's command. Allen and Susan were later married on November 24, 1870, in Missouri, settled in Arkansas, then returned to Grayson County.[12]

The James brothers were not charged with any crimes in North Texas, according to available information. Several settlers remember Jesse as a youngish-looking man with blue eyes and a mild manner. E. J. Parker of Sherman knew Jesse and Frank after the war and remembered Jesse's descriptions of the beginnings of his and Frank's outlawry: "An outrage visited upon the James home turned the James boys against constituted authority and gave them a thirst for revenge."[13]

The guerrillas built cabins and made themselves modern conveniences. According to one source:

The Missourian's cabin was from fourteen to sixteen feet square, built without glass, nails, hinges, or locks. Large logs were placed in position as sills. Upon these were laid strong "sleepers," and upon them rough-hewed puncheons served as floors. Logs for cabin walls were raised until the desired height for the eaves were reached. Long logs projected some eighteen inches over the sides, and butting poles were placed on these projections. Heart pieces of timber were made into billets for chinking the cracks between the logs, and a bed of mortar was made for daubing the cracks and sealing the jambs of the rough stone chimney.[14]

Quantrill picked the area known as Cross Timbers for his camp because of its abundant grazing lands. Here the terrain was similar to what they had known in Missouri. Protective woods surrounded a prairie of lush grasses, which supplied bountiful forage for horses. The camp was just southeast of the confluence of Big Mineral Creek and the Red River, near Brogdon Springs and east of the Bounds Ferry Road, one mile due south of the ferry and fifteen miles from Sherman. Fifty yards north of the campsite, an eight-foot waterfall at the confluence of Brogdon, Stout, and Dripping springs cascaded into a deep pool on the east side of the Bounds Ferry Road. The huge pool could accommodate as many as fifteen people, and the bathers were able to stand beneath the waterfall. Here Frank James carved a cedar water trough to funnel water from a hidden hillside spring, and this proved to be very useful during dry spells. The camp area was lined with daffodils and lilies, probably collected from the greenhouse of nearby Glen Eden plantation. Abundant oak, sycamore, cedar, elm, walnut, and pecan trees provided lumber for buildings and corrals.

Quantrill named the place Camp Lookout because it was situated at the highest point in Grayson County and had a clear view of the countryside for half a mile in all directions. The site offered a strong defensible position with rocky bluffs and thick timber that skirted the surrounding prairies.

Other military units were also stationed in the area. The Eleventh Texas Cavalry had been organized at nearby Preston, which was three miles north of Quantrill's camp. Many men of the Eleventh Texas were members of the nearby Kentuckytown Baptist Church and became acquainted with Quantrill and his men during the winter of 1862/63.[15] The Fifth Texas Cavalry was also quartered nearby. Several horsemen of the Fifth Texas had joined Quantrill after the battle of Pea Ridge, and they may have discussed the strength of this area as a camp site. Also in the area was the Ninth Texas Cavalry, which consisted of a thousand volunteers from Cass, Grayson, Hunt, Hopkins, Lamar, Red River, Tarrant, and Titus counties. Their headquarters was at Brogdon Springs, where they had been mustered into the army before seeing action at Pea Ridge.

The guerrillas were well supplied during their winter stay. Game was abundant around the Mineral Springs camp. While deer were plentiful, wild long-horned cattle were the most sought after, because they furnished meat, milk, leather and tallow, and could be tamed for easier handling. During the fall and spring, innumerable files of ducks and geese could also be found. Because the area was so bountiful in game and crops, the men did not have to rely on government rations. They actually ate better here than they did in Missouri. The guerrillas took turns supplying sides of beef for group gatherings; their menus included roast pig, wild turkey, prairie chicken, doves, quail, deer, bear, wild cattle, buffalo, and antelope, as well as nuts, berries, and fruits.[16] John McCorkle recalled, "During the winter Quantrill's men spent their time hunting, fishing and going to dances."[17]

One of the first things Quantrill did after settling in the Mineral Springs camp was to sell some of James G. Blunt's captured equipment in order to buy supplies for his men. Frank Smith recollected: "Quantrill sold a 6 mule team ambulance captured at Baxter Springs then used the money to buy a hundred pound sack of green coffee for the outfit. Quantrill got enough money from the wagon and mules to buy enough coffee that he made it a present to other families that supported him while he stayed in Texas. The gift of coffee Quantrill gave his men soon ran out largely because the men often traded with the farmers in the countryside." Frank Smith, Jim Little, John Barker, and Andy

McGuire went into Sherman to purchase more coffee for the outfit, but when a storeowner refused to sell to them, they wound up "confiscating it."[18]

Col. John Potts owned a prosperous plantation near the Mineral Springs camp. Potts had emigrated to Texas from Mississippi with one hundred slaves, and his home was known as a social center in North Texas. He and Quantrill became friends, and the guerrilla leader frequently stayed at the Potts home. One of the most cherished possessions of the Potts family is a December 11, 1863, letter from Quantrill to Mrs. Potts:

> After my compliments, you will allow me to present you with some coffee. And, in consideration of your kindness to my men who have been at your house. We are all under many obligations to you and your daughters, and when we are far off in danger, we will often think of the hospitality received at your hands. And, should it happen that the enemy should invade your home, you will remember that we will strike a blow for you all. My respects to all your family, Respectfully yours, W. C. Quantrill[19]

The area around Camp Lookout was mostly prairie covered with native grasses that came up to a horse's saddle. Innumerable cattle grazed on the green grass all summer and fed on the dry hay during the winter. The countryside was open range, and the grass was free to all.

Six miles west of Colbert's Ferry, connected by old Indian trails, was another well-known Red River crossing, called Thompson's Ferry. James George Thompson, the first chief justice of Grayson County, had operated this ferry. The Thompson home also became the first post office in the county and its first courthouse. Thompson was a wealthy cattleman and the first person to trail cattle from Grayson County to St. Louis and Abilene.

One mile southwest of Camp Lookout was Cedar Mills, one of the earliest settlements in Grayson County and a trading post. Situated on the banks of the Red River, it was surrounded by forts, actually log cabins with portholes built in to defend against Indian attack. Gristmills sprang up along the river with its many springs and deep waterfalls. In 1863, thriving Cedar Mills had several general stores, a post office, a sawmill, and a carpenter shop. The surrounding land grew corn, cotton, and alfalfa. In fact, most of the grain that supplied the Confederate army came from Grayson County.[20] Bumper crops were harvested beginning in 1860 and continued for several years after.

IN 1857, the town of Sherman was made up of only two or three little stores. The west side of the square was residential; clapboard business houses lined the east side of the public square. On the northwest corner stood a frame building called the Red Store, which had been moved from Preston and served as a warehouse and was occupied by A. M. Alexander as a place of business. Next to it was a three-story brick store, the first brick building in Sherman. The bricks had been hauled from Preston, where they had been used in another building. Next to the Red Store was the residence of Hugh F. Young. Another building on the square belonged to John Dorchester, the local tinsmith. Shaw and Allen operated a gunsmith shop next to Dr. John Brooke's drugstore. T. J. Patty owned the other general store in town. A bakery was also located along the square.

N. Byrd Anderson ran a hotel on the north side of the square. The one-and-a-half-story "hotel" was a double log house with a walkway in the middle, offering six rooms—two bedrooms above and four rooms below. Two additional shed rooms were available in the back. The reception area was also used as a ballroom, and to the right of the entrance was the dining room, which was very popular with many locals.

Twice a week, the Butterfield stage stopped in front of the hotel, drawing huge crowds and adding a little excitement to the drabness of routine frontier life. Before the war halted the service, a passenger recorded his impressions of the arriving stage: "He knows that it brings tidings from the hearts and homes he left behind him; it binds stronger and firmer to his beloved country. So regular is its arrival that the inhabitants know almost the hour and the minute when the welcome sound of the post horn will reach them."[21] Because of the celebrations initiated with the stage arrivals, the Anderson Hotel became the town social center.

In 1858, forty-nine-year-old Benjamin F. Christian from Tennessee took over the management of the hotel; he also owned a freighting business in town. Christian was familiarly called "Uncle Ben," and he was a member of the Cumberland Presbyterian Church. Near his hotel, lawyers C. C. Brinkley, G. A. Edwards, W. N. Mayrant, W. M. Kirk, and the firm of Woods & Diamond practiced their profession. Beside Christian's hotel, on the east side of the square was a building occupied by M. Schneider, general merchant under whom Walter and Ernest Jones started their careers in dry goods and general merchandise. Next to it was the general merchandise business of Henry & Andrews. Also on the east side was a long row of cabins, one of which was used as a courthouse. There were no sidewalks.

Chief justice James G. Thompson supervised the building of a log courthouse in January 1847. It was said to have had a rough floor, no ceiling, no chimney, and the cracks between the logs were not sealed well. In 1859, a new courthouse was built in the center of the square. The courthouse was used for everything from dancing to preaching to hanging. It could be rented for shows when it wasn't being used as a dance hall. In 1860, the courthouse ordered sawdust placed on the floor three inches thick.

Ben Bradley occupied a small log house on the south side of the square as the district clerk's office and the post office. On the east side of the square was I. Heilbroner's general merchandise store, with a photographer's shop run by his son Gabe on the second floor. In the middle of the block was the Iron Post Grocery and saloon. Other businesses on the square included John Fitch's grocery store on the southeast corner, John Shaw's barbershop, and a newspaper, the *Grayson County Monitor*.

The town jail was one block south of the square, on the corner of Jones and Travis streets. Its manner of safekeeping prisoners was unique: the heavy-log building had no doors or windows. An outside ladder gave access to the roof, where a trapdoor was cut. Prisoners were lowered into the one-cell structure. Even then, with the aid of friends, some managed to break out.[22]

Benjamin Moore's blacksmith shop was down on Jones Street. Frank Richards occupied a log house on the south side of Houston Street; on the opposite side of the street stood P. T. Wells's home. Close to town, on the corner of North Broughton and College Street, was W. H. Lucas's store.

Another noteworthy building in Sherman was a temporary home for Confederate soldiers established by Mary Ellen Falconer. She came to Sherman after fleeing from Fort Smith. Quantrill and some of his men stayed here for a brief time.[23]

Other businesses in town off the square included a livery stable owned by Ed Sacra. On Houston Street, F. W. Sumner owned a cobbler and a watch-maker's store; he also owned a business on the corner of Houston and Travis streets that sold Mexican goods. Joel Hagee was the only tailor in town after his partner enlisted in the army. J. P. Hopson was an architect and builder. Three doctors practiced in Sherman at this time. Next to the small post office near the square was Tom E. Bomar & Son's blacksmith and wagon shop. Bomar also advertised a sign-painting firm, and he was later the editor of the Sherman newspaper. William S. Bomar was later attached to the gun works in Bonham. H. A. Anderson who engaged in "stock hunting," charging ten dollars a head to round up lost or stolen cattle.[24]

SHERMAN HAD two churches and one school, which was established and supported by the Odd Fellows. The more prominent church was the First Methodist Episcopal Church South. It had been established in 1858 on

South Travis Street. The church's first permanent building was a one-story frame structure on the east side of the 300 block of South Travis Street, between Jones and Cherry streets. Crowning its steeply pitched roof was a tall, slender spire on which a heavy wooden globe was mounted. The name of the church was chiseled in stone and built into the corner of its structure. Inside the one-room sanctuary were handmade pews, a balcony, and an altar with a kneeling rail, where the sacraments were served from a common cup. The west portion of the lot provided hitching posts and space for horse-drawn vehicles and saddle horses. Many Methodists chose baptism by immersion, which was administered in a pond owned by a man named McMahon at the corner of Washington and Crockett streets.

Pastor John Howell McLean arrived in Sherman in 1861, when the term of the Reverend Jacob Monroe Binkley expired. Binkley was a man of distinction, always wearing a Prince Albert coat and high silk hat. He was a large man with a warm personality, a generous heart, and a rare Irish wit. Binkley was an outstanding leader, a fluent and dynamic speaker who drew great crowds. He believed that churches could significantly influence the moral character of a community through their ministries and by sponsoring and supporting schools. Accordingly, he aggressively encouraged the organization of churches in all denominations, resulting in Sherman's being called "the Holy City," a label that Binkley and his brothers used to promote the city.

In 1861, Binkley applied for a leave of absence to join the Twenty-sixth Confederate Volunteers as chaplain. His decision was personal. All ministers were exempt from military duty, unless they chose to serve.[25]

As Binkley's replacement, McLean held church services and prayer and class meetings regularly. On Sunday afternoons, special services were held for the blacks, who were loyal to their masters and gave no trouble in the community. The Methodist church in Sherman was divided on the war issue, but McLean managed to enjoy the goodwill of both sides, and none left the church on account of the differences in opinions. McLean remembered, "During church worship reckless ones would sometimes obtrude and act in a defiant manner, and I realized a few times that I incurred risk in insisting upon the maintenance of order in the house of God, but no hurt came to me." Recounting the soldiers who attended worship services, one worshiper remarked, "Although the boys 'fairly sizzle' on other days in the week, the most attentive respect was manifested by all the volunteers to the delivery of the sermon, and all joined most sincerely and devoutly in singing the concluding hymn."[26]

The new pastor recalled his first encounter with Quantrill in Sherman:

The day I was leaving Sherman to attend a conference in Jefferson, Quantrell and his men arrived in Sherman and stopped on Travis Street, in front of a little brick office I had been occupying. They were very quiet and civil in appearance. Quantrell was pointed out to me. He had a refined and civil look and was dubbed "parson" by some of his men. He was said to have been at one time a school teacher but because of certain outrages committed by Kansas Jayhawkers on the Quantrell family in Missouri, he became desperate and showed no quarter to such foes. This was told me by one who was a near neighbor of the Quantrells in Missouri at the time the offenses were committed.[27]

Other Sherman acquaintances also commented about Quantrill: "Dynamic he must have been, for he frequently maintained his gang at above two hundred men, and the loyalty of his friends in Missouri was absolute."[28]

SHERMAN OFFERED many amusements to the guerrillas to occupy their time. In addition to church services, dancing in the homes was very popular, and fiddlers played the strains of many favorite tunes where both young and old square-danced. A Masonic lodge had been organized in nearby Preston in 1852, and it furnished many social opportunities for the members. County fairs were held a mile northwest of Sherman, on Post Oak Creek, beginning in October 1858 and usually lasting several days.[29] On the first Monday of every month, hundreds of people came to town to buy and sell. Mostly there was trading or "swapping," but sometimes informal auctions were organized after the farmers arrived. No one thought of spending money for anything except necessities.[30]

Quantrill and Jim Chiles decided to establish a horse track for the amusement of their men. Chiles had a great love for animals, especially horses. Frank Smith remembered that some guerrillas rode daily to the track just outside of town to race their mounts. The only other track in the area was in a glade in the lower bend of the Red River, near the Coffee plantation, called the Race Track Prairie. With a track closer to town, the guerrillas held horse races among themselves and engaged in horse trading with the locals.

Quantrill usually won whenever he raced. He had one of the best horses in the command, and it was useless to try to buy him. Frank Smith remarked: "Ol' Charley, Quantrill's horse, would permit itself to be ridden or touched only by Quantrill. If anyone else tried to, it would kick, paw and bite but it was very gentle with Quantrill."

When the guerrillas congregated in Sherman at the racetrack, many of them entertained the Sherman residents as well as each other. Frank Smith commented: "Dick Maddox was the best rider among the guerrillas and also an expert rope thrower. Maddox would get drunk every time he got the chance, then he would give an exhibition of bronco busting and rope throwing."[31]

Guerrilla Jim Chiles lived in town with his wife, Sarah. They had married in 1861 in Jackson County. Chiles was described as dashingly handsome, and he was nicknamed "Jim Crow" Chiles. With all the dances being given in Sherman for the guerrillas, Chiles was known as a very agile, graceful dancer and earned the nickname from his skillful maneuvers to the then-popular dance called the "Jim Crow Set." There were numerous Chiles families in Jackson County during the Civil War, probably more than any other family. Joanne Chiles Eakin, a relative of Chiles's, noted that the main trait of the Chiles men in Jackson County was "they were always ready to take a gamble. Whether it was with money, horses, chickens, cards, mules, wagon trains, politics, war, new lands or just adventure, they could always be found in the forefront. There are many entries in the Jackson County court books of the 1850's that include Jim and his brothers, Henry and Elijah, paying fines for gambling and racing on Sunday."[32]

Jim was probably with his father, Col. James C. Chiles, during the border-war fight at Osawatomie, Kansas, in 1856, against the abolitionists under John Brown. In April 1857, the *Independence Dispatch* reported that a quarrel between Jim "Crow" Chiles and a T. E. Moore of LeCompton, Kansas, resulted in Moore's death. The newspaper noted: "The quarrel commenced at the supper table, and was ended in the hall in a fight, in which Chiles was cut about the face with a knife, and Moore was shot twice through the body, killing him almost instantly, one shot passing through his heart."

Chiles's father-in-law, Solomon Young, was one of the wealthiest men in Jackson County, owning more than five thousand acres. Even though Young was a freighter whose wealth in 1860 was listed as fifty thousand dollars with a contract to sell goods to the government, he was branded a Southerner because he owned slaves. Only a few days after the surrender of Fort Sumter, James H. Lane from Lawrence led his Jayhawkers on a raid of Young's farm. They stole 15 mules and 13 horses, then shot 400 hogs, cutting off the hams and leaving the rest to rot. They killed the hens and set the hay and stock barns ablaze. Next they threatened to kill the black servants unless they revealed the hiding places for valuables such as silverware. The following September, Federals stole 150 head of cattle, and a year later Jayhawkers attacked again, stealing sixty-five tons of hay, five hundred bushels of corn, 44 hogs, 2 horses, a bridle and saddle, and the family featherbeds. A month later, Jayhawkers returned and stole thirty thousand nails, seven wagons, twelve hundred pounds of bacon, and seized the house. They hanged Solomon's fifteen-year-old son Harrison to make him reveal where his father was. The Federals rode off and left him hanging, but his mother and a servant cut him down in time to save his life. In the summer of 1863, Col. Andrew G. Nugent—whose men murdered Henry Washington Younger, the father of Cole Younger, the year before—stole twenty thousand dollars in gold from Solomon that he was bringing home from a California and Salt Lake City freighting expedition.[33]

Already known as a frontiersman, Jim Chiles was well respected when he arrived in Sherman with Quantrill. In town, Chiles established a residence large enough to take in guests with a saloon and gambling hall attached. He was never one to see his comrades in need of a drink and entertainment, and it was here that he was responsible for killing two men in gambling disputes. With an established business and a place of residence in town, Chiles became known for his hospitality. The front door of his home was always open to anyone from Jackson County.[34] Many of the refugees from Missouri called the Chiles home "their home" while in Texas.

Besides the men befriended by Chiles, many Southern women had stories to tell. Laura Harris Flanery, whose brothers rode with Quantrill, left Jackson County in a wagon train of other women and children for safety in Texas after being banished during Ewing's Order No. 11 in the fall of 1863. In later years she would never forget the kindness of Jim "Crow" Chiles during this traumatic period. Laura recalled the frightening times she had before leaving Jackson County: "On October 27, 1861, our house, the church, and twenty-seven other houses were burned by the Federal troops, who had been defeated only two days before at the battle of White Oak Creek [August 18, 1862]. After the battle eleven of us girls gave first aid to the wounded and dying soldiers. Southern people after the battle of White Oak, drove the Federal troops into Kansas City, killing all but twenty-three." The Federals pulled Laura's baby boy from her arms and held him upside down, threatening to kill him if she did not reveal Quantrill's whereabouts. Also burned was the house of her brother, John Flanery. Laura's husband, Martin, joined Quantrill's company after his life was constantly threatened by Jayhawkers.

In accordance with Ewing's Order No. 11, Laura walked all the way from Clinton, Missouri, to Sherman, Texas. She remembered:

> There was nothing of value left in our formerly well furnished and spacious homes. We had one crippled horse and a blind mare. There were twenty-three families whose fathers, husbands, and sons were in the rebel army, that

set out eight days after the order was issued for a mutual meeting place. Into my wagon was loaded one hoarded feather bed, and two pair of pillows, and one small trunk, a prized object brought from Virginia, by my parents. It contained a few bare necessities in the way of cooking utensils, etc., for myself and small son. Our pilots were two feeble men, Buckner Muir, 84 years old, and his blind son, Sam, who was 56, the rest of the party consisted of sixty-one women and children.

Other women whose husbands rode with Quantrill were Mattie Yeager, Ida Irvin, Mary Ann Irvin, Laura Jane Flanery, and Elizabeth Johnson (a widow whose only son was with Quantrill). Several other women's husbands were with Gen. Sterling Price.

As the women approached Clinton, three hundred Jayhawkers surrounded the small party and stole most of their horses. Laura described the scene: "They took all but one team of horses and what part of our provisions they did not steal, they scattered on the ground. Since the lead oxen were hitched to my wagon, I was forced to lead them every step of the way from Clinton, Missouri to Sherman, Texas. That was a long walk. We were only able to walk four or five miles a day."

They trudged on, subsisting on sweet potatoes and cornbread. The caravan of women and children advanced through Indian Territory and came to Boggy Depot, where they were met by a Confederate detachment of fifteen hundred men. A Southern officer wrote,

> They expressed a decidedly favorable opinion of the rebels they met there, stating that the generous conduct of the soldiers was greatly in contrast with that of the insolent wretches who are bowing at the feet of Father Abraham; and they felt once more like they were with their brothers, and that they could breathe free again. Both citizens and soldiers at this place vied with each other in giving them every assistance in their power, to alleviate as much as possible their distress, and to show them every courtesy due them from a gallant and brave people, battling for freedom's cause.

Two of Quantrill's men—Martin V. B. Flanery, Laura's husband, and Dick Yeager, whose wife, Mattie, was in the group—had been given a leave of absence to find the women since they had been gone so long and the men were uneasy about their journey. When they were reunited, Laura commented that the women were so overjoyed that they were unable to sleep the first night. "We felt we were now under the protection of our own natural protectors," she said. "My husband procured a mule which he and I rode into Sherman, Texas. I stayed there at the home of Jim 'Crow' Chiles for a week and then went on to the home of Alec [Alexander] Chiles, ninety miles farther, on the route half way between Fort Worth and Dallas."[35] Three months after leaving Blue Springs, they finally arrived in Clarksville, Texas.

A SHORT distance from Camp Lookout was the most renowned Southern plantation in North Texas: Glen Eden. It received its name *Glen* from its location in the horseshoe-shaped curve of the Red River, and the name *Eden* as an expression of the first couple's happiness. Col. Holland Coffee opened a trading post at a twist in the Red River known as Preston Bend. It was at the extreme western edge of Cross Timbers and about two miles east of his home at Glen Eden. The town of Preston developed around the enterprise in 1845. Nearby was a ford called Rock Bluff, popular because it cut through the steep bluff and offered a natural chute for herding animals into the river. In 1851, Coffee helped build a fort that served as a defense against Indians and as a supply depot. Some of the buildings at Fort Preston were constructed of brick made in the area. Preston Road ran one hundred miles, from Preston to the ford on the Trinity River at Dallas.

Coffee came to the territory in 1836, gaining a reputation by trading whiskey and guns with the Indians and becoming one of the most prominent men in Texas. He spoke seven Indian dialects fluently, and thus he was instrumental in negotiating treaties with the Indians. Coffee's trading post became the principal trading and social center for Indians and early settlers. White captives were brought to his fort from Indian raids around Austin to be ransomed for blankets or bolts of red calico. To his landing came boats with both passengers and freight from Shreveport. Two years later, he was elected to the congress of the Republic of Texas. Coffee was granted a huge tract of land for his military service against Mexico.

In 1837, as a Texas representative, Holland Coffee traveled to Houston and met a woman who would become the most famous pioneer woman in Texas. Having been abandoned by her husband, Sophia Suttenfield Aughinbaugh was staying with Coffee's sister near Waco. Her husband was Jesse Augustine Aughinbaugh, a German officer whom Sophia met and married at age eighteen in 1833. Records show that her first Texas home was in Waxahachie, but her husband's desertion during the Texas revolution left her a refugee protected by the army of Sam Houston. Sophia was born in Fort Wayne, Indiana, on December 3, 1815. She was the eldest child of Col. William and Laura Suttenfield, and her father was in command of the fort.

Holland Coffee urged Sophia to seek a divorce from Aughinbaugh through the Republic of Texas; it was granted on January 19, 1839. He married the dark-haired twenty-four-year-old a month later, on February 19. A grand ball was held in their honor, and Sam Houston was there to dance with the bride. Sophia had served as a nurse during the revolution, and she had tended Houston's wounds at the battle of San Jacinto.

Accounts of the wedding report that Sophia was married in "high style" and then rode six hundred miles on horseback to Preston Bend. To avoid Indians, the trip back was by the Old San Antonio Road to Nacogdoches, then north along the Trammel Trace to Clarksville, and then west on the Chihuahua Trail to Warren's Trading Post on Red River, where the newlyweds were feted with another grand ball. After celebrating at Warren's, Coffee brought his wife back to his trading post at Preston Bend.

A one-hundred-foot square log stockade enclosed several small huts and cabins at Preston Bend, one of which was the trading post. The fort was about eighty yards west of the eastern bend of the river, on a bluff about forty or fifty feet overlooking the Red River. Sophia described her new home: "We lived in a clapboard house with puncheon floors, and our table consisted of a goods box with legs on it. The first quilt I had, I picked the cotton with my fingers and Colonel Coffee laid the quilt off with a square, and I quilted it. I then made me a rag carpet and put in on the puncheon floor, and a goods box nailed up on the side of the wall was my wardrobe. And on viewing my carpet, quilt and wardrobe, I was the happiest women in Texas."

Sophia loved flowers, and the odd corners of the stockade soon bloomed with flaming blossoms during the spring and summer months.[36]

Coffee's house had to be constantly guarded against Indian attack. Sophia recalled: "Often in the night the Indians would come around and imitate wolves, and the men would stand at the portholes in the fort on guard all during the night. I would make coffee for them during the night to keep them awake."[37] In 1843, Coffee began building a new home for his wife. The house was built in stages, in the classic two-story Southern fashion with massive rock chimneys and broad galleries. It was built of white oak log slabs with outside planking, and upper and lower porches; a kitchen was added in the mid-1860s. The first phases consisted of a double log cabin with a walkway between the two cabins. The house had six fireplaces, two large white chimneys at each end of a long parlor, one in the kitchen, one in the dining room, and two in the upstairs bedrooms. The kitchen and dining area were made of brick. A porch on both the front and back ran the full length of the double cabins, separating the brick portion from the main house. A second story was later added. Included in the construction were a hand-dug cellar and a brick flower pit in the middle of the yard. Milk and wine were stored in the cellar.

Sophia had a stockade pen built across the road from her house, and there she kept fifty or more peacocks. Baked peafowl was the crowning dish on her table. Meat was provided from stock raised on the plantation and kept in the smokehouse, which used a hollowed-out cottonwood log as a trough for preserving meat.[38]

Glen Eden was the largest two-story log house in Texas. The Coffee home became quite a social center, and Sophia was noted for her fondness for parties and her imagination.[39] The new house opened with a housewarming party that lasted several days and became the talk of the countryside. That pattern was repeated often whenever the Coffees entertained. People came from across the state and often remained for a week at a time. Young people would, on their own initiative, get together and descend upon the place for two or three days, dancing all night long. The rooms were large enough for two or three sets of square dancers to share the space. For many years, Glen Eden was known as the center of hospitality throughout the surrounding counties. In return, the Coffees often attended parties at military posts in Arkansas and Indian Territory. Among their friends were Jefferson Davis, Robert E. Lee, and Ulysses S. Grant—lieutenants who served at the nearby forts. Sophia noted that Lee was very dignified in bearing, neat and prim in his dress, while Grant was free and easy in his deportment, not unlike most gentleman of the frontier. Sam Houston, likewise, was a frequent visitor at Glen Eden.

The mistress of Glen Eden became as infamous as she was famous. Some afforded her the title of heroine, while others claimed she was notorious. Rumors that Sophia was once Houston's sweetheart circulated, and local busybodies speculated that she "played fast and loose with the U.S. officers at Fort Washita."[40] Accounts at the end of the war noted, "Sophia was a remarkably well-preserved woman at the age of 50, and her charms compelled the admiration of the brave and the chivalric. In later life she frequently boasted of friendships with more than one military figure in the Texas army. Her absence from the memoirs and histories of these figures is amply explained by her reputation at the time." Another account added, "Though past 50 she was spirited and attractive and was still socially popular."[41]

Neighbors remembered Sophia as a perfect hostess, remarking, "Sophia's ability as a hostess became known throughout all North Texas and the Indian Nation. [She] was much in demand and a great favorite as a dancing partner. Colonel Coffee had the means to provide plenty of food and drink and

Sophia had the talent to provide the entertainment. She was gay, she was kind, she was smart and quick. She got on with everybody."[42]

Sophia added much to the beauty of Glen Eden, and she and her husband prospered on the three-thousand-acre plantation. Most of their money came from cotton and cattle. Due to the Northern blockade, Texas was the only state from which England could import cotton during the war, and the venture became very profitable. Before the war, Sophia shipped Glen Eden cotton to New Orleans. With the income from her cotton sales, she purchased furniture and knickknacks for the house: carved walnut pieces, fine glass and china, silver and wines, silks for her wardrobe and linens for her dresses, which she transported by ox wagon from Jefferson, Texas.

Sophia loved flowers and had two greenhouses built for her hobby. She raised beautiful blossoms in her gardens until the day she died. The south side of the house was mostly windows, which created one of her greenhouses, and shelves on either side of a walkway were covered in flowers. The Coffees had no children, but they raised two of Holland Coffee's nieces. One of those nieces recalled, "Two Negroes were employed the year round in the two greenhouses that were Aunt Sophia's pet hobby."[43] In the yard was a large magnolia tree that Sam Houston brought to her as a gift when he attended one of the Coffees' lavish parties. It grew to more than sixty feet in height. Other guests brought seeds of new flowers to add to her collection. Catalpa trees were planted up and down the banks of the nearby creek, grown from seeds that Albert Sidney Johnston was said to have carried in his saddlebags from California. Sophia also had a large rock garden filled with rocks and plants given to the Coffees by friends when they returned from travels to foreign countries during their army service.[44]

As the daughter of an army officer, Sophia felt a particular kindness toward soldiers on duty on the frontier. So the Coffees frequently entertained officers from the nearby forts. Area residents remembered:

> The latchstring of the old mansion was always out, and as the home stood near the government crossing, numerous officers from the frontier forts, Fort Gibson, Fort Smith, Fort Arbuckle and Fort Washita were attracted to the elaborate repasts, to the music and laughter of the early Grayson residence. Often the parties here lasted for days with the merrymakers dancing all night. When such social events were in prospect, invitations were sent broadcast over the countryside by the many Negro slaves on the plantation, and in response, guests came eagerly in all directions carrying their party clothes in their saddle bags.

In addition to Davis, Lee, and Grant, Fitzhugh Lee, George B. McClellan, and William Clarke Quantrill were among the many guests at Glen
Eden. Someone observed, "Aunt Sophia, as she was later called, became a
great favorite of Quantrill's men, whom she feted and dined."[45]

A niece recalled that Sophia "was very proud and was immaculate in
her appearance, and she carried herself as straight as an Indian."[46] Others
said that she was "a lady of more than ordinary intelligence and possessed
of extraordinary business qualifications, controlling and owning thousands
of acres of land."[47] Her neighbors always remembered her kindnesses toward
others: "Sophia was often known to ride horseback to take food to the sick
in the community." Many recalled, "Sophia was highly regarded among
area residents. Whenever anybody was sick, you always knew Sophia would
come by on a horse with a big basket of fine food and things. She'd have a
little black boy with her to open gates for her to go through. If they were
poor she would give them cash too. She was the richest woman around
these parts."[48]

But then tragedy struck Glen Eden in 1846. Several accounts are given of
Holland Coffee's death, but the gist of them all is that Coffee was killed in a
duel with a man who insulted Sophia. When Coffee tried to dismiss the com-
ment, Sophia reportedly said, "I'd rather be married to a dead hero than a live
coward." The offending person was twenty-eight-year-old Charles Ashton
Galloway, an Indian agent at Fort Washita; he accused Sophia of having an
affair with Justice of the Peace Thomas Murphy.

Interestingly, Galloway had only recently married Coffee's fourteen-year-
old niece, Eugenia. Galloway's brother owned a grocery-saloon in Preston. In
a heated exchange of words with Galloway, Coffee replied to Galloway's insult
that he would "horsewhip him on sight." Early on the morning of October 1,
1846, Coffee learned that Galloway was at his brother's store. He grabbed a
double-barrel shotgun loaded with buckshot, a revolver, a single-barrel pistol,
a Bowie knife, and a club, and headed for the store. When he approached the
door and called Galloway's name, Galloway answered, "Yes sir?" and came to
the door. Coffee knocked him down and fell on him. In the struggle that followed, Galloway managed to get out his knife, striking upward three times,
each thrust being mortal. Holland Coffee was carried home on a shutter. In
the local newspaper, his death was remembered kindly: "Coffee was a warm
friend and a true hearted gentleman, and fell in a difficulty respecting a matter
of honor."[49]

Charges were filed against Galloway, but the grand jury returned a no-bill
finding, meaning there was insufficient evidence to warrant a formal charge.

Galloway was acquitted by public sentiment because several witnesses said it had been a clear case of self-defense.[50] The jury afterward praised Galloway: "Having showed a laudable, but scarcely an exampled forbearance, [he] act[ed] at all time the part of a gentleman." Presiding Judge Thomas Murphy was later indicted and acquitted for misconduct because he knew Holland Coffee was going to assault Galloway but did nothing to stop the fight. Murphy later married Sophia's sister, Mary Francis Suttenfield.

Coffee left everything to Sophia. He was buried at Glen Eden in a tomb made of bricks from his own kiln. After his death, Sophia closed the trading post and devoted all her time to the management of the estate. The plantation's operations included the Red River ferry, livestock, corn and cotton fields, orchards, and freighting operations. In 1853, on a trip to New Orleans to dispose of her cotton, thirty-eight-year-old Sophia met and married Maj. George N. Butts, a planter from Norfolk, Virginia. He was in New Orleans to sell horses and slaves after disposing of his plantation. Butts was described as a large man, handsome, and aristocratic in manner. Sophia related that her husband insisted on high etiquette at mealtime, adding that he was so fastidious concerning the table settings, even when only the two of them were present, that she never trusted the servants with the arrangements.

Butts took over the management of the estate. The 1860 census lists him as being forty-seven years old with real estate worth $17,000 and $311,500 in his personal estate. With her new husband overseeing the plantation, Sophia devoted more of her time to her flowers and landscaping. Double rows of flowering trees lined the front walk. Her gardens and orchards produced fruit in abundance, and as before, her hospitality was always courteous and open. A relative recalled, "We were seldom alone at Glen Eden. Aunt Sophia loved to entertain and surrounded herself with the notable persons of the day from whom she could learn of the state of politics and social life of Texas." She was said to also entertain Union officers and gathered much important military information that she passed along to Confederate officers. Local citizens remembered that Quantrill was a frequent visitor whenever he camped nearby. They recalled, "Quantrill, who was more acceptable in the society circles of Sherman, had been welcomed into the homes of the plantation owner John Potts, and the party giver Sophia Butts."[51]

AFTER FIRST arriving in Sherman, Quantrill took some time to become acquainted with his neighbors in the surrounding plantations prior to reporting to the district military commander. Gen. Henry McCulloch's headquarters was in Bonham, the county seat of Fannin County, just twenty-five miles east of Sherman. But Quantrill's presence was well known to McCulloch since the guerrillas' advance party had entered Sherman proudly displaying James G. Blunt's captured headquarters flag.[52]

Bonham was an agricultural center with a small population. The town was named for James Butler Bonham of South Carolina, who had died a hero at the Alamo three months after his arrival in Texas. Although no major battles were fought around Bonham during the war, the town was an important center for the Confederate war effort. It housed a military hospital and a commissary that supplied clothing, blankets, harnesses, saddles, and rations for at least seven brigades. H. L. Peters operated a gun shop in town, and a tannery made leather goods for the army.

One person currently serving on McCulloch's staff, Capt. Samuel Bonham, had a close connection to the border strife in Missouri. Prior to his position on McCulloch's staff, Bonham had been an adjutant for Braxton Bragg in Tennessee. Bonham was born in Virginia in February 1832 and completed his college education at Berryville with a civil engineering degree. For three years he was a county surveyor in Nebraska, and before the war he was a surveyor in Lafayette County, Missouri. Bonham had been acquainted with John Brown in Kansas, but he disliked the man. He found out that Brown had frequently visited the home of Bonham's sister, Lucy Sowers, and demanded food. She complied because she was afraid not to. When Brown was hanged at Harpers Ferry, near Bonham's old home in Virginia, the surveyor said that he was "one of the delighted spectators."[53]

McCulloch's pride was insulted when Quantrill did not immediately report to his headquarters. He became upset after hearing rumors of Quantrill's tactics at Lawrence. On October 22, 1863, McCulloch expressed his concerns about the guerrillas camped in his district to Capt. Edmund P. Turner, assistant adjutant general, in Houston.

> A good many of Quantrill's command have come into this sub-district, and it is said that he is now within it. He has not reported here, and I do not know what his military status is. I do not know nearly as much about his mode of warfare as others seem to know; but from all I can learn, it is but little, if at all, removed from that of the wildest savage; so much so that I do not for a moment believe that our government can sanction it in one of her officers. Hence, it seems to me if he be an officer of our army, his acts should be disavowed by our government; and, as far as practicable, he be made to understand that we would greatly prefer his remaining away from our army or its vicinity.

I appreciate his services, and am anxious to have them; but certainly we cannot, as a Christian people, sanction a savage, inhuman warfare in which men are to be shot down like dogs after throwing down their arms and holding up their hands supplicating for mercy.

This is a matter to which I wish to call the serious attention of our commanding general, and with regard to which I desire their advice and instructions as early as practicable.[54]

There had been bad blood between the Missourians and the McCullochs for a long time. Most Missourians blamed Henry's brother Ben for not helping Sterling Price enough to protect Missouri from Federal invasion, and the McCullochs reciprocated these ill feelings. The Missourians also faulted Benjamin McCulloch for his ineptitude at the battle of Pea Ridge, Arkansas, in March 1862, which added to the Confederate defeat. If McCulloch's division had done well at Pea Ridge, the outcome would have been different. Instead McCulloch attacked in a piecemeal fashion, led his men into action as if he were a captain rather than a general, and thus set the stage for the disastrous defeat. In contrast, the Missourians fought gallantly at Pea Ridge, and when Price was given the order to withdraw, the Missourians couldn't believe they were losing. Many claimed that they had "retreated from victory." One Texas soldier wrote to his parents after the battle: "Major General Sterling Price has immortalized himself at the Battle of Elkhorn [Pea Ridge] for his bravery, never was a man more beloved by Southern soldiers than by his."[55]

On October 26, Quantrill reported to McCulloch's headquarters. One of the general's officers described the guerrilla as being approximately five feet ten inches tall, weighing about 150 pounds, with fair hair, blue eyes, and a florid complexion. Gen. Edmund Kirby Smith ordered McCulloch to furnish the guerrillas with anything they needed from the military stores. Sylvester Akers acknowledged that animosities soon developed: "Quantrill sent a requisition to McCulloch for a four-mule wagon-load of flour, and bacon enough to load a similar vehicle. McCulloch refused it. Quantrill then renewed the requisition and said that if the rations were not sent he would come and take them. McCulloch sent them."[56]

General Smith recognized Quantrill's command as a military asset and ordered McCulloch to use the guerrillas to help round up deserters and conscription dodgers in North Texas. As the war went on and the Confederate cause looked more hopeless, evasion of conscription and desertion from the army became commonplace.

When the new governor, Francis R. Lubbock, had taken office on November 7, 1861, he issued a call for more men to meet the state's quota of men needed for the army. Texas was required to supply as many men as the other Confederate states. Lubbock suggested that no exceptions to the draft laws should be permitted, and Texas militia laws allowed men serving in the home defense to be ordered into the field when necessary. Such marching orders persuaded many Texans to "take to the bush." In addition to the conscription laws, confiscation laws were enacted, allowing the state to seize what it needed for the war effort. And early in the war, Texas was placed under martial law. Overzealous provost marshals enforced these legal requirements, sometimes prohibiting traveling without passports and interrupting business transactions. Many Texans felt humiliated and believed the government's actions were an intolerable infringement of the rights of freemen.

John S. Ford served as the superintendent of conscription in Texas during 1862/63, and he regarded the conscription laws as an "unfortunate enactment" that did great harm. Ford maintained that it was an error to force Unionists into the Confederate army. Such men, he believed, would be of no value to the Confederacy and would desert at the first opportunity. Ford also believed the conscription act that exempted individuals with twenty or more slaves was a mistake, leading many to believe the conflict to be a "rich man's war and a poor man's fight." During the war, forty-five hundred Texans were listed as deserters; more than three thousand of them were hiding out in the thickets of North Texas in the fall of 1863.[57]

McCulloch estimated that the deserters were organized into companies of two hundred men and regularly patrolled the roads leading into their camps. They ventured out only to prey on defenseless farmers, resulting in pillage and murder. When he first arrived in Sherman, Quantrill heard about the deserter problem in North Texas and soon after sent some men into the area to find out what was going on. At this time all of North Texas was swarming with draft dodgers, deserters, and fugitives with around fifteen hundred to two thousand in General McCulloch's district alone. Morale problems among Texas regiments serving in Arkansas and Louisiana forced General Smith to consider sending Texas units back into their home state to curtail threats of mutiny and desertion. McCulloch admitted to Gen. John Bankhead Magruder, commander of the District of Texas, that he had deserters in nearly every county. These men had taken to the brush to keep from fighting along with new conscripts who had failed to report for military duty. Smith told his departmental commanders that "conscripts who came in voluntarily would be allowed to select any regiment from their State serving in the department. If they bring a good serviceable horse and equipments, they can join a cavalry regiment; otherwise they must serve in the infantry. When they do not come willingly, they are to be sent to a camp of instruction, and then assigned to such regiments, as most need them."[58] Previously Lt. B. G. Duval, the Confederate adjutant-general, wrote to Gen. Richard M. Gano, commanding a cavalry brigade in Texas, alerting him that many citizens trying to avoid the conscription laws were arming themselves and trying to cross the Red River into Indian Territory. Following this announcement General Magruder issued orders to his military commanders to stop them. In August 1862, Fritz Tegener, a citizen of North Texas, led sixty-five Unionists, mostly Germans from the Hill Country, in an unsuccessful attempt to cross the Rio Grande and flee from Texas. They were overtaken near the Nueces River by state troops commanded by Lt. C. D. McRae. Thirty-five of the Unionists were killed, and several others were wounded in what was called the battle of the Nueces.

In the canebrakes north of the Red River, a group of bandits with no allegiance to either the Union or the Confederate governments preyed on everyone, without distinction, killing and looting indiscriminately. On October 16, 1862, a North Texas gang killed Col. William Cocke Young, who had organized the Eleventh Texas Cavalry of men mainly from the Sherman area and operated mostly against the Indians north of the Red River. Young was murdered while searching for a friend who had been killed by this same gang.[59]

With Quantrill's men now in Texas, both Gens. Edmund Kirby Smith and John B. Magruder urged McCulloch to employ harsher methods to round up the deserters and draft dodgers. Both generals saw Quantrill as the most able commander to solve McCulloch's problems. Smith and Magruder urged stronger methods in dealing with the problem, but native Texans like McCulloch and Governor Pendleton Murrah were reluctant to employ harsher treatment of their fellow Texans regardless of the crimes they committed. McCulloch received a dispatch from Smith:

> If you resort to force in bringing in the absentees and collecting the conscripts in your district, no better force could be employed than that of Quantrill's Missourians. Their not being from the state, will make them more effective. They are bold, fearless men, and moreover, from all representations, are under very fair discipline. They are composed, I understand, in a measure of the very best class of Missourians. They have suffered every outrage in their person and families at the hands of the Federals, and being outlawed and their lives forfeited, have waged a war of 'no quarter' whenever they have come in contact with the enemy.[60]

In his reply, McCulloch repeated his low opinion of Quantrill and his men: "It may be said that Quantrill will help you, but I have little confidence in men who fight for booty and whose mode of warfare is like that of the savages."

McCulloch refused to recognize that his perception of the guerrillas was a more appropriate description of the draft dodgers and deserters themselves. Some were simply criminals; others were Unionists whose sympathies were not determined by their roots in either the North or the South. Many also withdrew from their communities, instead hiding out in remote and inaccessible areas. For some of these dissenters, safety meant disappearing into the tangled brush thickets of North Texas known by various names: Mustang Thicket, Black Jack Thicket, and Wildcat Thicket. But these thickets also served as the rendezvous points for army deserters, slackers, and fugitives. These men were called "brush men" because they hid in the wild and remote undergrowth.

North Texas was filled with rolling hills and deep creeks with banks ten to twenty feet high. The soil was black loam and impassable when wet. The thickets were home to countless critters that bit or stung; they were infested with rattlesnakes. The mesquite and chaparral were so thick in these areas that it was impossible for a man to ride a horse into it, much less walk. The most notable hiding place was known as Jernigan's Thicket, a dense thicket of ten to fifteen square miles. It was made up of hardwoods, particularly bois d'arc, pecan, oak, juniper, pine, and rattan vines. Mesquite grew on its outer fringes. The North Sulphur River flowed through the upper section, and the West Fork of Jernigan Creek traversed its southwestern edge.

McCulloch preferred to coax the deserters and draft dodgers back into the ranks. He counseled that wayward Texans should be brought in "by kind and gentle means" to report for duty.[61] Deserters were promised a pardon if they returned voluntarily to the army. During the fall of 1863, McCulloch formed several hundred former deserters into a "Brush Battalion," promising them that they would only be used to search for fellow deserters and Indians. They soon deserted again, and the battalion was disbanded in March 1864.

McCulloch's agony over the deserters in his district turned to despair. He expressed his frustrations in a January 23, 1864, letter to Turner, the assistant adjutant general:

> There is not one bit of reliability in the deserters that have returned to service up here as a mass; here and there a good man, generally bad, and steps must be taken to put the last one of them into his former command, the grave, or prison. To do this I must have more force, and the sooner 'tis done the better.

The brush command are deserting constantly and going back to the brush or to the Federals. I have never been in a country where the people were so perfectly worthless and so cowardly as here. I am now trying as a last resort to get them to organize a company in each county for police duty. If I can effect this in time to root out the men in the brush before spring I may save the country; otherwise it will go up certain if the Federals make any demonstrations. I would like to get out of this country, I assure you, but am unwilling to ask to be allowed to leave a sinking ship.[62]

McCulloch's weak measures proved highly unsuccessful. Smith continued to urge him to use force in rounding up these men. In a dispatch dated November 2, 1863, Smith instructed McCulloch: "I fear your conciliatory measures will not bring the results you desire. My experience in Louisiana proves that the most determined and stringent measures are now necessary. Colonel Quantrill, I understand will perform that duty, provided rations and forage are issued to his men and horses; this you are authorized to do."

Smith wanted to meet Quantrill and told McCulloch: "In the event you have no immediate service for him and his command, direct him to report in person at these headquarters. His command should go into camp at some convenient point, where they could receive rations and forage until Colonel Quantrill's return. You can issue the rations and forage required for Quantrill's command, provided they remain under your command. The best disposition you can make of them will be in breaking up and bringing in the bands of deserters in your district."[63] Instead, McCulloch chose not to use the guerrillas and directed them to remain in their Mineral Springs camp while Quantrill was ordered to report to Smith's headquarters at Shreveport.

To explain his actions, McCulloch wrote on November 9, 1863, that a few days previous three hundred deserters and absentees emerged from the brush in a body. He had promised them that they would only be used on the western frontier and not sent out of the state to fight Federals. Because they were so poorly equipped, they were immediately given fifteen-day furloughs to get warm clothing. In fact, McCulloch was fearful of what these deserters would do if he tried to bring them in by force. He stated: "These men occupied positions from which it would have been difficult to have routed them by force without leaving enough of them behind to have divested a good deal of this country in part, and I have no doubt that the use of force would have driven them to acts of outrage upon our friends, and involved us in a domestic war."[64]

In Shreveport, Smith and Quantrill conferred on the military situation in North Texas. Quantrill reported that his men had infiltrated the deserters' camps and learned that the deserters planned to turn themselves in only so they could obtain arms and ammunition before deserting again and heading north. Quantrill returned to his command on November 19.[65] Smith agreed with Quantrill's summation of the deserter problem in North Texas and was disappointed to learn that McCulloch had failed to follow the general's November 2 directive to abandon his lenient approach. On November 19, he dispatched a formal order to McCulloch through his aide, E. Cunningham:

> The lieutenant-general commanding directs me to say that Captain Quantrill leaves Shreveport today to join his command, and passes your headquarters in route. He is informed by this officer that several of his men, whom he regards as entirely reliable, went to the rendezvous of the deserters in your district, pretending that they also had deserted from their commands. They mixed among these outlaws freely, and they, thinking that Captain Quantrill himself was not loyal to our Government, fully disclosed their condition and plans. Captain Quantrill thinks that in giving themselves up to you it has been simply their purpose to get arms and ammunition, of which they were in need, so that in the spring they can go north. This they are resolved to do. It is the opinion of the commanding general that these men are unreliable and should be trusted in nothing. He disapproves of your agreement with them, and thereby relieves you from all responsibility as to its fulfillment. The concession to them of the privilege of serving where they are, would increase the number of deserters and greatly demoralize the troops in the commands from which they have deserted. He therefore directs that all those who have already given themselves up be sent to their commands immediately. . . . The lieutenant-general commanding thinks that the only thing to be done now is to go vigorously to work and kill or capture all those who refuse to come in. The commanding general thinks the ringleaders should have no quarter.[66]

McCulloch had already disappointed Smith by having furloughed half the state's troops when they were direly needed to guard against imminent invasion. His conciliatory measures toward deserters did nothing to endear him to either his commander or his fellow Texans. A resident of McKinney noted: "These renegades were called 'Bushwhackers' and made life miserable for the surrounding area. At night they would slip out and steal food and anything else they could find. With nearly all the able bodied men of the country away at war, they had things just to their liking."[67]

Eventually McCulloch issued orders to Quantrill's men to flush out the deserters and draft dodgers hiding out in Jernigan's Thicket in order to bring the men into the regular army. But he insisted they should be rounded up and brought in without force. The guerrillas, however, rather than capture the draft dodgers and deserters, shot many of them on sight.[68]

Guerrilla Sylvester Akers recalled: "McCulloch told Quantrill to go to Jernigan's Thicket near McKinney, Texas and arrest Federal guerrillas hiding there and robbing and murdering people in Texas. McCulloch insisted that these guerrillas should not be killed, but arrested and brought before him for trial. Quantrill said he would kill them if they fired on his men. Much correspondence passed back and forth on the matter and bad feelings were aroused. Quantrill finally went to arrest the deserters, but in doing so killed one or more of them. He captured but few."[69]

IT WAS a godsend that Quantrill chose to ride south with his company for the winter of 1863/64. The week before Christmas 1863 brought fear and panic into North Texas. On December 21, from an upstairs window of the Glen Eden plantation, Sophia Butts saw Yankee soldiers ride up the Preston road. According to one account, she greeted the Union cavalry graciously and entertained them lavishly. They were an advance scouting party of Kansas Jayhawkers who had forded the Red River above Preston Bend. Sophia supplied them with enough wine until they were drunk. Then she sent them to the cellar to get more wine and locked them in the cellar. They had already told her that a larger force of Federals—commanded by Gen. James G. Blunt and composed of the Fourteenth and Fifteenth Kansas Jayhawker regiments and a mob of Jayhawkers—had crossed at Bounds Ferry and had advanced as far as Gainesville. The Jayhawkers were intent on attacking Quantrill and annihilating his command as payback for their past defeats at the guerrillas' hands.

Sophia saddled a horse and headed for the ferry crossing, where she found the ferryman asleep. Rather than cause alarm, she rode across the swollen river. But the cold wind and her wet clothing forced her to seek refuge at a house she knew was loyal. From there, she sent messengers to Quantrill's camp, which was a little over a mile away, and to McCulloch at Bonham and to the Texas militia at McKinney. That night Sophia herself rode north to Fort Washita to inform sixty-two-year-old Col. James G. Bourland that Union troops were at her estate. For her efforts, Sophia gained the sobriquet "the Confederate Lady Paul Revere." As a result of her midnight ride, Sophia suffered ill health for many years. When Bourland received the news, he ordered Pvt. James W. Dougherty and a detachment of soldiers to ride to Glen Eden and bring back the captive Yankee scouts locked in Sophia's cellar.[70]

THE ONLY advantage the Yankees had was their strength in numbers, so they combined two regiments under Blunt's leadership. Their march through Indian Territory was expected to be uneventful, but no one knew what awaited them in Texas. Union spies relayed the exact location of Quantrill's camp and reported that he had four hundred men with him. Blunt had been constantly criticized about his leadership failures, and his defeat at the hands of Quantrill's irregulars (which Union authorities wouldn't admit were soldiers) was his worst nightmare. Now Blunt was intent on avenging Quantrill's raid on Lawrence and his success at Baxter Springs. The Federal commander planned to sneak into Texas, catch Quantrill unaware, and annihilate the guerrillas. After crossing the Red River, Blunt's advance scouting party hoped to initiate the surprise attack on Quantrill's Mineral Springs camp.

When warned of the Jayhawkers' approach, Quantrill had no place to run, no time to be afraid, and no time to be nervous. His officers barked quick commands, and the guerrillas checked their weapons and swung themselves into their saddles.

At his headquarters in Bonham, McCulloch saw his worst fears realized: Kansas troops had penetrated Indian Territory and crossed the Red River without his knowledge. He immediately sent couriers to his outlying camps to bring his command together to confront the invaders. On December 22, McCulloch immediately relayed the information to Houston:

News of a reliable character reached me this morning at daybreak that the Indians or jayhawkers in considerable force (number not known) had penetrated as far as Gainesville at 9 o'clock last night, and news of a less reliable character has just come in that they occupy that place this morning, Indians and Federals, 400 strong.

I sent all the cavalry force I had this morning at 8 o'clock, numbering only some 200 men, from this place, directing Quantrill, from Sherman, to meet them at once, and have sent orders to all of Colonel Martin's companies that are within reach to concentrate at McKinney and Pilot Grove, to move forward as rapidly as possible.

If the last report be true, it is the advance of a Federal and jayhawking force, or a heavy raid of some character.

I have not more than 150 infantry here, and all the cavalry I can concentrate in three days will not amount to over 500, and not a single piece of artillery, from which you will see but too plainly that I have no force to defend the granary of Texas with if I should be called upon to do so. A general without troops is worth but little in defending a country.[71]

McCulloch summoned all available units in North Texas, Quantrill's company being one of them. Without waiting for Col. Leonidas M. Martin's Fifth Texas Cavalry or for Col. James Bourland's force from Fort Washita, the guerrillas found and attacked Blunt's two regiments.

Quantrill tried to swing north and get behind the Jayhawkers, forcing them between him and Martin's cavalry. But the Jayhawkers were on him before he had time to maneuver. So he dressed his line smartly and charged. The Rebel Yell exploded in the air over the din of rifle fire. As the guerrillas bore down on the enemy, they bent low over their horses' necks, spurs digging into the animals' flanks, manes stinging the faces of their riders. There could only be one outcome. Official accounts report that the blue coats, trying to avoid Martin's regular cavalry from McKinney, approached from the south and blundered into the guerrillas, who cut them to pieces.

With the killer instinct that came from years of guerrilla warfare, Quantrill's men chased down the surviving Jayhawkers. Some Federals made it as far as eight miles west of the guerrillas' Mineral Springs camp. The Jayhawkers were caught in a deep defile of Walnut Creek called Devil's Backbone, a high limestone ridge about two hundred yards long. When the firing ended, blue-coated bodies lay like bloody rag dolls along the base of the ridge. Confederate Choctaws reported that only a handful of Federals escaped. Local farmers buried the slain Jayhawkers. Among the hundreds of Union gravesites lying near Quantrill's Mineral Springs camp are memorials listing the fallen members of the Fourteenth Kansas Cavalry. Because of the rocky soil and iron ore, most were buried in shallow graves.[72]

The guerrillas' action saved North Texas from invasion. After the annihilation of Blunt's force, a great celebration ensued. John McCorkle reported, "During Christmas week, quite a number of us attended a big ball in Sherman. We also received an invitation to visit General McCulloch at Bonham, Texas."[73] McCulloch was indeed thankful at this particular time, not just for the religious significance of the holiday season, but for Quantrill's stunning victory over the Federals intent on destroying his meager forces in the area. But with Quantrill receiving all the praise for this recent accomplishment, McCulloch may have turned resentful. Whatever conciliations were extended to the guerrilla chieftain were not realized in McCulloch's subsequent military dispatches.

Meanwhile, as evening approached in Sherman, and the citizens prepared to celebrate, 250 guerrillas thundered into the downtown square, reveling in their recent triumph. Everyone was expected to be in town for the occasion, including many women and young girls. The townspeople considered the guerrillas to be Southern patriots, so Quantrill's entire company was invited, plus any Confederate soldiers that had taken part in the victory. The guerrillas wore their best clothes and arrived excited and boisterous. The ball commenced at 7:00 p.m. with strains of music from fiddles and banjos, and the partygoers were prepared to dance all night. The hostess at Christian's Hotel offered pies and cookies, and the host opened a jug that never ran dry.[74]

What began as a harmless celebration, however, turned into a boisterous display of one-upmanship. The guerrillas began their celebration a little early. Some became drunk on eggnog then began an exhibition of marksmanship and horsemanship, which led to the victorious guerrillas shooting up the town.[75] First, they shot doorknobs off doors, shot out streetlights, and then rode their horses on the sidewalks and into the stores.

While their men attended the festivities, Quantrill and George Todd stayed behind to watch over the camp. Quantrill himself was not known to be a reveler. A Sherman citizen commented, "Quantrill did not drink and was a man of few words."[76]

The guerrillas' victory celebration was monumental. Frank Smith recalled that they traveled from Jim "Crow" Chile's place to the Iron Skillet to the O.K. Saloon and then fanned out and shot the town to pieces, riding their horses up to the storefronts and even inside Ben Christian's hotel ballroom, where they used the festive decorations on ladies' bonnets for target practice—while the ladies were still wearing them. A few guerrillas rode their horses through windows. Some staggered up the steps to Gabe's Picture Gallery to have tintypes made in their best uniforms and highly decorated "guerrilla shirts" and proudly brandished their pistols.[77]

The celebration lasted all week, and the center of activity was the Christian Hotel on the north side of the square. Sophia Butts was the belle of the ball, and she was feted for her daring adventure in warning of the enemy attack. Most interesting is the report that "someone was dancing a waltz with her, when suddenly two shots reverberated through the hall simultaneously with the falling of two of the tassels that adorned Sophia's hat. She never missed a step, and the dance went on." Dick Hopkins noted that one of guerrillas had bet another that he could not shoot the tassels off Sophia's hat while she was dancing.[78]

W. L. Potter recounted the activities in a letter:

> I was not at Sherman at the time. I was about ten miles northeast in Grayson County and was there a few days after it occurred. The only hotel in town at that time was owned and managed by Ben Christian, a friend of W. C.

Quantrill and all of his men, and every other Confederate soldier. He was as good a citizen as there was in Texas. He told me that the men first got started at a house of their friends on eggnog. They then got hold of some whiskey and were like all other men on a Christmas spree and soon became wild and full of reckless fun. That the actors had all been at his hotel before and naturally they came there in the frolic. Some two or more rode on the porch in the hall and the main reception room, discharged their revolvers in front of the hotel, their horses feet broke some few of the flooring in the hall of the hotel and they also done some damage to the furniture. Mr. Christian said the men were his friends and would settle for whatever damage they done to him and others, which was done in a few days afterward. They also went to a photographer in town to get their photographs and destroyed his instruments, all of which was paid for a few days after as soon as they sobered up.[79]

Frank Smith also recalled the celebration:

On Christmas day, a number of guerrillas rode into Sherman for a spree. [Dick] Maddox found a barrel of whiskey in a cellar and the guerrillas got wildly drunk. They rode their horses in the town hotel, shot out the lights and doorknobs off the doors. They went to the town photographer gallery and had pictures taken then destroyed the studio and its equipment. Quantrill and Todd who were remaining in camp went to Sherman and rounded up the inebriants and took them back to camp. The next day, Quantrill and Todd told them to go back and pay for the damage done which they did.[80]

Most of the misbehaving was by William Anderson's men, and it probably annoyed Quantrill to have to ride fifteen miles in order to discipline Anderson's men because Anderson didn't have the leadership skills to handle it himself. Quantrill proved his mettle in rounding up the perpetrators and forcing them to make reparations.

With most of the men in town now in the army, many of the jobs formerly performed by men were now done by women. Sixteen-year-old Bush Smith worked as a clerk in Benjamin Christian's freighting business. She was known as "one of the fine young ladies of Sherman" and was a member of the Methodist church.[81] Many of the guerrillas naturally became attracted to the local girls. And a Sherman resident recalled, "At a Christmas ball given by the young people of Sherman, Bill Anderson of the Quantrill gang met Miss Bush Smith of a prominent Sherman family. His attachment for the young woman soon became serious, and he determined to marry her." Anderson and Smith were married on March 2, 1864, just before Anderson returned to Missouri for the spring campaign. Guerrilla John McCorkle recorded, "During Christmas week, Captain Bill Anderson married a Southern lady in Sherman, all of us attending the wedding."[82]

Another townsperson recalled, "One of Quantrill's captains married a popular young lady of Sherman, and was afterward killed in guerrilla warfare." Anderson was apparently intending to return to his wife after the spring campaign was over. When he held her in his arms for the last time, he assured her that he would return. They lived in a house he had built for her at 1213 East Cherry Street by a local carpenter friend, F. M. Richardson.

Bush Smith's real name was Mary Erwin, and she was also known as Molly. She had been born in 1848 in Tennessee. After being orphaned, along with her brother Price Erwin, they were adopted by the Smith family of Sherman in the late 1850s, making her name Mary Erwin Bush Smith. Her adopted mother's family name was Bush; the Smith and Bush families had been prominent families in Sherman since the early 1850s. Five individuals named Bush Smith can be found in Grayson County's records, with at least one noted in three successive generations.

5

Troubled Waters

The greater the odds—the greater the glory.

—USMC SAYING

FTER THE CHRISTMAS CELEBRATIONS in Sherman, the guerrillas returned to the Mineral Springs camp. The talk of the camp was the story of the guerrilla who shot the tassels off Sophia Butts's bonnet while she was dancing. Shortly after this, around New Year's Day, about twenty guerrillas went to Sherman to attend a dance at the house of Jim "Crow" Chiles. The rest of the outfit had not been invited, but a number of them went to town to break up the dance. Fistfights broke out, but there was no shooting.

Quantrill and George Todd again remained in camp. When they learned of the disturbance in town, they set out to round up their men. But the Missourians were no longer at the Chiles place and could not be found. The next morning, however, all of the guerrillas were back in the Mineral Springs camp.[1]

Many people were inspired to help the indigent families of soldiers in the field and the women who had lost husbands and sons by sickness or in battle. There was so much destitution and privation, however, that relief soon became a problem. At first the counties afforded relief, but the burden became too great for local resources, and the legislature in 1863, in response to a recommendation by Governor Francis R. Lubbock, appropriated six hundred thousand dollars for the dependents of soldiers. Very soon the number of dependents assisted by the state totaled seventy-four thousand.

The Confederate army established a regional depot in Sherman in 1861 to receive clothing for soldiers and a commissary to supply food to passing troops and the families and widows of soldiers. Dick Hopson recounted the day that Sherman fell into the hands of a mob of women and tells how Quantrill saved the day:

> The Southern Confederacy, for the last two years of its existence, maintained in the county site of all organized counties a commissary department on the east side of the [Sherman] square, where was kept all kinds of foodstuffs, which that particular county produced. This produce was raised by a sort of tithing process. From these commissaries, rations could be drawn by passing soldiers, and all "war widows" were privileged to draw rations there. The number of "war widows" was very large in Grayson County, and many of them needed the rations badly.

The officer in charge of the Sherman commissary was a major named Blaine, a veteran of the Texas Revolution. Bumper crops meant that the Sherman commissary was unusually well supplied with grain, flour, and meat, and it became well known to all the county's "war widows." But they became dissatisfied with the sameness of the rations they were permitted to draw. By this time, trade between Mexico and Texas had grown to huge numbers. Texas cotton was hauled to the Rio Grande, sold for a good price, and the money was invested in such supplies as the people lacked because of the blockade. One could buy almost anything in the principal towns, if one had enough money to pay for it.

Hopson noted that the war widows of Grayson County believed this trade was being carried on by the government and that many luxury items—such as tea and coffee—had been purchased by the government for the soldiers' families, but the officers in charge were selling them to anyone and keeping the money. The war widows banded together to get what they believed should be coming to them.

One day in early1864, the county seat swarmed with wild-eyed, desperate, hungry women armed with guns, axes, sledgehammers, and clubs. The mob numbered more that 125, and their leader was named Savage. Those who came with her obeyed her every command. The women surrounded the commissary, and Savage told Blaine that she knew a soldier's ration contained sugar, coffee, and tea, and that Blaine had been withholding these things from the rations of the war widows. Pointing to the mob of women, she stated that they had come for what belonged to them and would accept nothing less.

Blaine very gracefully surrendered. Producing the keys, he escorted the ladies through his warehouse, showing them that he had no luxury items such as they imagined. The ladies, however, were not satisfied and argued that what they sought must be in another building. The women determined to find the hidden supplies, and with their axes, sledgehammers, weapons, and clubs, the outraged daughters of the frontier began to search every building in town.

On the east side of the square was I. Heilbroner's general store. Heilbroner was a British subject, and he had quite a stock of Mexican goods, including the luxury items demanded by the women. In time, the mob broke into the store and pillaged the stock, helping themselves to whatever they wanted. And then Quantrill entered the store. He was alone and gave no orders nor made any threats. The sudden appearance of the guerrilla leader and the icy coolness of his voice brought sanity to the mob immediately. He simply advised the ladies to return the merchandise, and asked, "What would your husbands think of you if they could see you? They are at the front, enduring all kinds of hardships, hungry, barefooted, half starved, doing their duty without complaint. What would they think of you?" The women became ashamed, disbanded, and left the goods, nailing up the doors of the store as they left.

Hopson suggested this was likely the only time Quantrill had "ever addressed a 'Sewing Circle' and probably the only instance of an American town being in the hands of a mob of women." One townsperson remembered, "He [Quantrill], by his quiet tones and convincing talk, was able to quiet the women and get them to leave. He and his men were always friendly, and quite often helpful, to the people of this county." Such actions as this brought Quantrill much favorable recognition and established goodwill between him and the residents of Sherman.[2]

In addition to Sherman, Quantrill also assisted the larger area of Grayson County. Gen. Henry E. McCulloch had received numerous pleas from towns throughout the county regarding the havoc and terror being generated by the deserters and draft dodgers who had taken to the brush. Lacking any relief from McCulloch, the townspeople called on Quantrill to quell the criminal element in their neighborhoods.

A resident of McKinney recalled what happened in his community: "[The deserters and draft dodgers] lived in the woods during the day, stealing from the local farms, and robbing passersby. In 1864, the problem had gotten so bad that help was sought from guerrilla leader William Quantrill, who was at that time in Sherman."

Isaac Graves of McKinney was a former resident of Pleasant Hill, Missouri. He addressed his plea for help to Quantrill through his friend Tuck Hill. Quantrill rode into McKinney with about one hundred men—including Tuck Hill, his brother Woot, and their cousins Frank and Jesse James. A history of Collin County reports:

At last the people of McKinney sent an appeal to Quantrill, who was camped at Sherman, Texas, to come down and give them some relief from these bushwhackers. Quantrill immediately arrived with a company of his best men and surrounded the swamp known as Finch Park where the bandits were hiding. As the day progressed, Quantrill's men captured 42 bushwhackers and marched them to the town square. Once there Quantrill's men hung all 42 men from a limb on the southeast corner of the square by the large public well.[3]

This action further widened the breach between Quantrill and McCulloch. Sylvester Akers recalled that the general was so angry with Quantrill for killing the deserters that he "determined to dismount the guerrillas and attach them to an infantry command. This the guerrillas objected to. Quantrill said his men could neither march nor fight afoot, and he refused to go to Bonham as ordered by General McCulloch." In trying to impose this order, another account stated:

McCulloch sent a force to Quantrill's camp to disarm the guerrillas. Quantrill divided his men, placing half of them beyond his camp on the road McCulloch's men were to come in by. He ordered them to fire over the approaching troops and then fall back to the camp where the other half of the force was stationed. If McCulloch's men persisted in coming on, then they were to be met with a fire to kill. But they retreated when fired on outside the camp, and they did not again molest Quantrill.[4]

Besides being upset at Quantrill's men for their harsh actions toward the McKinney deserters, McCulloch began receiving reports of criminal activity other than those committed by newcomers to North Texas. In nearby Hopkins County, a citizen reported, "We hear no news now but accounts of murders done and suffered by the natives. Nothing seems more common or less condemned than assassination. There have been four or five men shot or hanged within a few miles of us within a week. . . . A few evenings ago a captain in the army had just reached home on furlough three hours before when he was shot at through his window. He was killed and his wife dangerously wounded."[5]

In Collin County, Quantrill took sixty men to investigate crimes committed by the local sheriff, James Reed. The guerrillas approached the McKinney Tucker Hotel on the northeast corner of the square and initiated their search for Reed. When the sheriff heard that Quantrill had come for him, he gathered eighteen men and retreated down Tennessee Street, taking refuge in an uncompleted mill. The guerrillas took up positions a short distance away and opened fire. All the horses of the sheriff's men were killed and some of his men were gravely injured. As soon as it was dark, all the men fled except the sheriff and J. M. McReynolds. Reed and McReynolds borrowed horses and briefly eluded capture. The next afternoon, Quantrill's company caught up with the pair and hanged them.[6]

Lawlessness in North Texas had a long history before Quantrill and his men arrived in the winter of 1863/64. But with the guerrillas came their reputations as bold, fearless fighters. Even as they attempted to safeguard the people of North Texas, every outrage committed within one hundred miles of Sherman was laid on them. As far away as McKinney and Dallas, robberies and murders were attributed to Quantrill's men. Since Quantrill held a presidential commission to lead an independent command, he could not be forced to join the regular Confederate army, and so any accusations directed toward his men were solely Quantrill's responsibility—the men in his company were solely accountable to him. Compounding the confusion, many desperados claimed to be Quantrill's men so that no one could claim jurisdiction. When they were captured, deserters, thieves, and criminals quickly asserted their connection to Quantrill's command, playing also on the fears of civilians. Crimes carried out by soldiers claiming to be part of Quantrill's command were reported in the Grayson County newspapers, and these naturally found their way to McCulloch's headquarters. Because of the irregularity of the uniforms used by Quantrill's men, it was very easy for any deserter, bushwhacker, or transient to pass himself off as a Missouri guerrilla.

Quantrill responded by issuing a warning about these criminals and issuing passes to his men; unless a man had a printed furlough personally signed by Quantrill, "they were sailing under false colors." Meanwhile, McCulloch attempted to quell the rampant lawlessness in his district by issuing General Orders No. 33 on December 29, 1863, that restricted all soldiers to their camps and threatening prosecution of anyone who permitted soldiers from the army or enrolled conscripts without proper papers to stay or be fed at their homes or premises.[7]

Andy Walker commented on the identity theft:

It was during this time that a lot of fellows, claiming to be Quantrill's men,
fell to robbing and killing in the country about McKinney and Dallas. General McCullough brought Quantrill to task about them. Quantrill insisted
that they were not his men, but declared that, if the general would commission him to do so, he would undertake to arrest them. The general agreed,
and Quantrill sent George Todd with twenty men, of whom I was one, to
try to apprehend the robbers. They got wind of us though, and had deserted
those parts by the time we arrived. Dick Berry, our orderly sergeant killed a
man however, one of the "Jernigan Thicket men" near McKinney on the
return journey. General McCulloch when he learned of this incident sent
one of his nephews to Quantrill, directing him to have this man Berry sent
to his headquarters at Bonham. Quantrill was out south of Sherman that
day, taking dinner with a friend. However, some of his men who were in
town on a spree directed young McCulloch to him. Quantrill accompanied
the young man, who had very long legs and a very small pony, to camp, and
then to Sherman. He sent McCulloch the message that Berry was out of
camp, but that he would be ordered to report to the general as soon as he
should arrive.[8]

As usual, the guerrillas' actions displeased McCulloch, and so to keep
Quantrill's men from killing any more people, he began assigning them to duties that would keep them out of North Texas. Frank Smith noted, "When a
unit of Federals came through Indian Territory on a raiding party, Quantrill's
men were ordered by McCulloch to go after them. They did so, going as far as
the region of Coffeeville, Kansas where they had a skirmish in which they
killed six of the Federals. They remained there two days, returning to their
camp at Mineral Springs after having been gone for two weeks."[9]

McCulloch next sent some guerrillas to track down a band of Comanches
after a raid on the northwest frontier. Due to the lack of troops, the Comanches had pushed the Texas frontier back one hundred miles to the east
during the Civil War. The Indians at one time even managed to capture
Gainesville. Resident George Newman recalled that he gathered up a group of
boys from around Gainesville and went to recapture the town, but the Indians
had already taken all they wanted and left before either Newman's or Quantrill's men arrived.[10] There were many other military units in the area to which
McCulloch could assign these tasks, but he chose to detail them to Quantrill's
company, depriving them of any rest. McCulloch controlled all the militia

units in North Texas, and it galled Quantrill to be ordered to do all of the general's dirty work.

McCulloch ordered Quantrill to destroy all the stills in the Red River Valley because Gen. Douglas H. Cooper's Indians were getting drunk so often as to be useless. Frank Smith reported that Quantrill's men seized the whiskey from the stills and complied somewhat with McCulloch's order by destroying only one still and killing three operators.[11] McCulloch reported the episode to John B. Magruder: "In one instance the enrolling officer of Grayson County sent them to impress some whiskey at a distiller, under my orders, based upon yours; and they got into a row, killed one man and plundered the still house and dwelling."[12]

WHILE QUANTRILL was busy maintaining law and order in North Texas, many young men joined his command. Several North Texas settlers had relatives in Missouri, and many were related to the guerrillas accompanying Quantrill. Guerrilla James Simeon Whitsett was one who had relatives in the area. Whitsett's cousin, sixteen-year-old James Haden Whitsett, and several other North Texans from Fannin County—including sixteen-year-old Anthony Wayne Van Leer and eighteen-year-old William H. Ragsdale—joined Quantrill's ranks and moved north with his command in the spring. Neighbors recalled. "Everyone was so sad, because the boys were so young."[13]

Many of the men who joined Quantrill's command in Texas were farmers. Texas, the granary of the Confederacy, suffered little in comparison with other Confederate states. There had been no wide-scale destruction of farms, livestock, and homes, as in the states that had been invaded by Northern troops. Money was more plentiful due to Texas's trade with Mexico. Still, sorrow touched almost every family through the deaths of loved ones. The despondency and discouragement of soldiers returning from the front lines, combined with the uncertainty of the future, settled like a pall over all. Indians and Jayhawkers were a principal source of trouble.

With most of the men gone to fight, the people had to adjust to the necessity of providing themselves with the necessities of life. In the field and garden, as well as the home, the women worked. They were now required to do most of the chopping, plowing, carrying, lifting, and moving on the farms. Cutting firewood, milking and churning, feeding the stock, mending clothing and shoes, and doing the normal chores occupied their days and months and years. The spinning wheel and the loom provided the clothing for those at home and for those on the battlefield as well. One Southerner remarked: "Most of the male population would probably (if permitted) elect to remain at their homes, braving the fate that might await them. But the women are more patriotic, and would brave all in following the fortunes of the Confederate States Government."[14]

Privations caused by the blockade were beginning to be felt. and the Southern states were no longer able to trade with and support one another. Women made their own clothes and searched for bark and berries to make different dyes. Hats and bonnets were made of straw or cornhusks. Wheat straw, being most plentiful on the farm, was used for durable outdoor hats. Children's hats were made of inner shucks of Indian corn. Homemade shoes were made of carved wooden soles onto which coarse leather uppers were tacked.

But life for the pioneer settler was not all work and no play. The two were combined. Frontier life was lonely, especially for the women, but there was some opportunity for fun and social contact. Logrolling, house raising, harvesting, weddings, and funerals attracted the neighbors. But as the population was sparse, the crowds were small. There was an occasional candy stew in the older settlements, well-regulated balls, and socials at the Masonic lodge.[15]

As the new year of 1864 progressed, the privations were beginning to affect every Texan. Quantrill noticed that, in comparison to his trip to Richmond the previous winter, in Texas the towns evidenced only a few shortages and patches on clothing. Spinning wheels hummed more busily than ever, and hand-carded cotton was common as clothes became mostly handmade. Coffee was now rare, with parched wheat or barley considered tolerable substitutes. Many people had been substituting barley, corn, okra, peanuts, and sweet potatoes for their coffee. A British visitor reported, "The loss of coffee afflicts the Confederates even more than the loss of spirits; and they exercise their ingenuity in devising substitutes, which are not generally very successful." There was a shortage of lamp fluid. Tallow candles were used by many, but some used smelly sycamore balls soaked in oil for illumination. Prices were perceptibly higher on everything, but far from the peak they would scale. Flour was about fifteen dollars for one hundred pounds, corn sold for two dollars a bushel, cloth went for four to five dollars a yard, and cotton sold for eight cents a pound.[16]

Although Texas suffered less economically than other Confederate states, many adjustments were necessary. Shortages cropped up for many commodities, but salt became so scarce it was treated as precious as gold, and some Texans dug up the floors of their smokehouses and leached the dirt to recover salt drippings. The Confederate government, recognizing the importance of salt in preserving the meat needed to feed the troops in the field, nationalized the salt mines in eastern and coastal Texas. Thorns were used for pins, willow bark extract and red pepper were mixed to substitute for quinine, and pieces of wallpaper served as writing paper. Several Texas newspapers suspended or discontinued operation for periods of time due to lack of paper. Once trade with Mexico was established, goods were more readily available. In return for cotton, Texans received military supplies, medicines, dry goods, food, iron goods, liquor, coffee, and tobacco. Confederate money was no good in Mexico, so goods had to be purchased with gold. One Texan noted: "Shortages have arisen in most commodities. Some are non-existent, or almost so, as coffee from South America and sugar. Grains of corn, parched until almost black, are being used as a substitute for coffee."[17] The supply of sugar to Texas diminished when the blockade ended imports from Cuba and halted altogether as Union troops drove into the Louisiana cane fields, making sugar disappear completely from most Southern kitchens. Another Texan recalled that no one used sugar in coffee and tea since honey was so plentiful.[18]

Despite these privations, good times prevailed in the days after Christmas 1863 and the celebrations that took place on New Year's Day, but tragedy soon struck. In early February 1864 George Butts of Glen Eden was reported to be in Sherman either having sold a large quantity of cotton or being in town at Jim "Crow" Chiles's place in a card game with several of Quantrill's men where he won a large amount of money. On his way home that night, Butts was killed.

EVEN BEFORE Quantrill's arrival in Texas during the fall of 1863, the October 16 *Austin Tri-Weekly Gazette* warned: "We would caution all who may have occasion to go outside our city limits to go well armed as there are Jayhawkers all around us hiding in the hills and who have been seen frequently close by." It is quite likely that some of the violence in Grayson County attributed to Quantrill's guerrillas was committed by others. Several murders around Sherman were blamed on Quantrill's men. A newspaper article stated: "Renegades and deserters from the armies of both the North and South began filtering into this area to prey upon the citizenry through thievery and robbery, often through disguised attempts to pass themselves off as members of Quantrill's band."[19]

Even some of Quantrill's men and those of other Missouri units were preyed upon by the criminal element in North Texas. On January 18, 1864, the *Austin Tri-Weekly Gazette* repeated an account from the *McKinney Messenger* of how "three Confederate soldiers 'on furlough' from General Shelby's command in Arkansas were 'captured' near Farmersville, Texas southeast of Sherman by twelve strange men in soldiers' garb who shot and killed two of the Confederates. The third escaped, but the twelve perpetrators are unknown."[20]

Other Texas military units experienced their share of disciplinary problems. The recruits were often frontiersman and Indian fighters from the western fringes of the settlements, and they were difficult to control. They disliked both drill and discipline. Some commanders issued orders that enlisted man could not leave the vicinity of their camps unless escorted by an officer. These orders were often ignored. Several carefree men of Mosby M. Parson's Texas Brigade, after imbibing too much whiskey, terrorized civilians. Even though the culprits did little damage and authorities soon arrested them, a much-exaggerated account appeared in the newspapers. One eyewitness summed up the incident: "Some of the boys got drunk and run through town firing off pistols and broke into a grocery store and took the man's whiskey and done other things unbecoming a civilized soldier."[21]

Accounts also circulated that soldiers had "seized private property, entered houses of private citizens, brutally practiced extortion and outrage, and with bullying and threatening language and manner spread terror among the people." When men of the Twenty-first Texas rode into Tyler, McCulloch ordered all the liquor stores closed and issued orders holding the officers personally responsible for the actions of their men.[22]

These incidents in McCulloch's district forced him to act. His officers rounded up four hundred stragglers in the area, including deserters from both Northern and Southern armies. McCulloch received a directive on January 29, 1864, from Magruder, urging him to stronger action: "There are doubtless 500 more in the woods and brush, and those at large will certainly increase unless they are put down at once. These men should be shot without hesitation or mercy and should be hunted down with the forces you have. Operating all the time day and night until the work is done."[23] A squad of Grayson County militia responded to Magruder's directive and was detailed to take seven prisoners in chains to Bonham for trial in connection with the attempted hanging of a civilian.[24]

When accounts of outrages against civilians around Grayson County reached McCulloch's headquarters, he immediately blamed Quantrill and the guerrillas. He did nothing to investigate the matter, nor did he support Quantrill's efforts in quelling the rampant crime in his district. McCulloch harbored an animosity toward Quantrill that only deepened when praise was heaped upon Quantrill's command. Nothing, however, highlighted McCulloch's administrative inefficiency more than Quantrill's success in halting the cattle rustling and Indian raids that plagued North Texas. Early in 1863, cattle rustling had reached its apex. Civilians noted: "As soon as Quantrill arrived and set up camp cattle stealing stopped in this section of North Texas and in the southern Indian Territory." It was also reported, "There was a cessation of Indian raids during Quantrill's presence here. Some looked upon his arrival as a source of safety."[25]

Contrary to McCulloch's beliefs, the people of Sherman were quite pleased to have the guerrillas among them. One townsperson spoke for most people in North Texas: "There were some in Grayson County who exceedingly admired the person of the guerrilla chieftain, whereas in North Texas there was almost universal, though unmerited contempt for McCulloch."[26] Dick Hopson, editor of the *Sherman Courier* and a friend of Quantrill, wrote:

> Quantrill is described as [being] below medium height, only about five feet eight inches tall; sandy hair; blue eyes, that seemed to change to violet at times. He was quiet, unassuming, never raised his voice in conversation, never smoked, drank or swore. The fifty or sixty men who composed his band were under perfect discipline. He never spoke to a man but one time, in a low tone of voice and no man was ever known to disobey him. The above is the consensus of opinion of many people interviewed.[27]

Despite Quantrill's success at curtailing the criminal element in North Texas, McCulloch informed his superiors of the opposite. He wrote to Magruder: "The community believes that they [guerrillas] have committed all the robberies that have been committed about here for some time." But then, in a later letter, McCulloch impeached the sources behind this statement, charging them with incompetence: "I have no officers of the line in the districts scarcely who know anything about military affairs, and the enrolling officers, conscript and state, as well as most of the people, exhibit, as a general thing, more ignorance or knavery than any other people in the world."[28]

As more sensational accounts filtered into his headquarters about the guerrillas—mostly pertaining to the chaos and havoc they wreaked in the area and the general atmosphere of fear in which civilians were forced to live—McCulloch became that much angrier with the state of affairs. From time to time, Quantrill's men would ride into Sherman for a lark. One county history summarized:

> It is a matter of record in the history of Grayson County that on occasion they went on drunken sprees and in states of hilarity or mischief tended to shoot up towns. The men in Quantrill's band were mostly young and a

"dare-devil lot." They would come into Sherman, race up and down the streets, shooting and yelling. They would shoot out the lights; shoot off doorknobs and locks, and such little tricks. A gilded ball surmounted the Methodist church on South Travis Street in Sherman, and this was a favorite target for the bullets of Quantrill's men.[29]

Andy Walker recalled:

In particular one glorious lark Bill Anderson's men had come into Sherman the evening previous, and after nightfall some of them stole a demijohn of whiskey from a drug store. After a riotous breakfast, Anderson, muttering heavily, formed his men in platoons, and they made a systematic circuit of the streets and public square shattering with bullets, amid mighty peals of laughter, every doorknob in the district covered. The merriment was no less when they rode into the lobby of old man Christian's hotel. To begin with, the clock was perforated with quite a number of bullet holes. Then two riders at once urged their steeds over a lounge on which Dick Maddox lay. They succeeded in reducing the couch to kindling wood. Then various objects in the room claimed their attention. Bullets passed to either side of Ol Johnson, who was sprawled on the floor upstairs.[30]

Both Maddox and Johnson were friends of Quantrill's. When Christian complained about the damage, Quantrill rode into town with Todd and two other men and forced the perpetrators to apologize and make restitution.

On more than one occasion, Quantrill rode into Sherman to quell disturbances by Anderson's men. Anderson didn't appreciate Quantrill bypassing his leadership and making his men responsible for their actions. The two guerrilla leaders reportedly quarreled on several occasions. Quantrill was a strict disciplinarian when it came to keeping his men in line.

The most upsetting incident to Anderson involved Bill Morgan, who stole a bolt of cloth belonging to one of Quantrill's men and had a pair of pants made from it. Quantrill never tolerated dishonesty in his command. He disarmed Morgan and escorted him to the other side of the Red River, warning him not to return to Texas or he would be killed. But Morgan returned and robbed and murdered an old farmer. Sylvester Akers noted that Morgan "became a murderer and robber and Quantrill condemned him to death."

Quantrill sent William Gaugh, Sylvester Akers, Allen Parmer, and another guerrilla after Morgan with orders to hunt him down and kill him. But some vowed that they would not kill him. Gaugh and Parmer, however, found Morgan. When Gaugh tried to apprehend him, Morgan tried to get his weapon, so he was shot and killed. A short time later, Gaugh and Parmer simply reported that Morgan had been taken care of. Gaugh added, "It was the law of warfare such as we were compelled to wage, but I hated to do it."[31]

Frank Smith recorded that Anderson was furious when he learned the details of Morgan's death. But despite Anderson's fearless reputation, he knew that neither Quantrill nor his men were intimidated by him. So he bided his time.[32]

The status and notoriety of being part of an independent command emboldened many guerrillas, and they developed attitudes of self-reliance and aloofness. Confederate Gen. Paul O. Hébert wrote to Secretary of War George W. Randolph "that it has been found impossible to control these independent corps, raised by persons under direct authority from Richmond and with orders to report to some command or general outside of the Department of Texas."[33]

Additional complaints from McCulloch of the unruliness of Quantrill's men led to a decision to control them. At first, however, McCulloch tried to use his influence to have Quantrill's command transferred to Gen. Theophilus H. Holmes in Arkansas, but Sterling Price intervened by summoning Quantrill to his headquarters. Price knew that this reassignment would fail since several of Quantrill's men had deserted Holmes's army the winter before after tiring of garrison duty and constant inactivity; they would be arrested as deserters if they returned to Holmes's command. After Price consulted with Gen. Edmund Kirby Smith, new orders were issued through McCulloch by way of adjutant P. H. Thomson:

> The lieutenant general commanding directs me to revoke the orders instructing you to report to Lieutenant General Holmes. At the time they were issued active operations against the enemy in Arkansas were contemplated, and it was desirable to have all the re-enforcements possible concentrated. The emergency in that quarter has passed, the lieutenant general directs that you proceed as rapidly as possible to the headquarters of Major-General Magruder with your command, where you will immediately be placed in the face of the enemy. You will start as soon as possible, and acknowledge the receipt of this letter.[34]

Price directed Quantrill to reduce his command to eighty cavalrymen and four officers, per army regulations. He was allowed to remain in overall command as colonel, and he could select three other officers. The balance of his men would be assigned to the regular army. As the commander of all Missouri troops, Price was authorized to commission officers as he believed promotion was appropriate.

Frank Smith noted, "After conferring with General Price Quantrill reorganized his company and 'Quantrill was in general command and had a colonel's commission from Price.'" Quantrill's newly won promotion was also recorded by Lee C. Miller: "Quantrill himself had a captain's commission from General Price, and later a colonel's commission from the Confederate war department. His commission authorized him to operate on the Missouri-Kansas border as a partisan ranger."[35]

From this time on, Quantrill was an operational commander while conducting military maneuvers in Missouri. One of his responsibilities was establishing cohesion among his widely dispersed elements. To do this job successfully, he had to have confidence in his subordinate commanders while cultivating their understanding of their own operating style in the context of his specific campaign intent. Quantrill's responsibility included training his staff as an extension of his personality. This proved easy for Quantrill; he had been fighting alongside his subordinate leaders for almost three years.

On his return from Price's headquarters, Quantrill gathered his company and made the required realignment. Quantrill selected George Todd as captain, William Anderson as first lieutenant, Fletcher Taylor as second lieutenant, and Jim Little as third lieutenant. He chose Isaac Berry as his orderly sergeant. William Gregg was passed over, despite his leadership of Andy Blunt's former company, and Gregg resented this. Todd, however, didn't favor Gregg, and he apparently orchestrated Gregg's removal from command. This was likely due to Todd's grudge against Blunt's company when it had attached itself to Gregg's company instead of his own at the beginning of the winter's march to Texas.

Gregg sought Quantrill's permission to join the regular army and requested a leave of absence; he believed he could only function in the partisan service if he was an officer. The prime distinction between officers and enlisted men was that officers did not have to stand picket duty or night watch. Gregg pondered his future for two days before talking with Quantrill. When he did, Quantrill granted him a ninety-day leave of absence, commenting, "You have been a good soldier and a good officer, and an honest man." Gregg then reported to Gen. Jo Shelby and was assigned to Company I of Shanks's regiment. Gregg was soon promoted to captain in Company H, where he remained until the close of the war. Meanwhile, Gregg's transfer displeased An-

derson, who viewed Gregg's demotion as another instance of Quantrill's fa-
voritism of Todd.

The balance of Quantrill's men not assigned to his realigned command
served as an independent cavalry, with missions assigned by the commander
of the Trans-Mississippi Department. Dave Poole commanded one company,
and Cole Younger joined his brother-in-law, John Jarrette, in the other. Jarrette and Poole reported to Edmund Kirby Smith in Shreveport, Louisiana,
to make arrangements for a winter campaign beyond the Texas border. In
fact, Smith stated, "There are many plantations on the [Mississippi] river
being cultivated by the negroes for the Federals. All such should be destroyed
and the negroes captured."[36]

The Union government, at the insistence of Abraham Lincoln, had
permitted the South to continue its commerce in cotton by issuing special
permits and licenses through the Federal Treasury Department. Lincoln understood the importance of cotton to Northern industries, and a Cotton
Bureau was established early in his administration. Texans sold their cotton
to Confederate agents who then sold it to the national government. But all
along the Mississippi River, and for miles inland, thieves and speculators
dealt with Louisiana planters directly and bypassed the Confederate agents,
working instead with Union officers. Thus, Federal gunboats ensured that
their operations were successful, and Union cavalry and infantry escorted
the shipments of stolen cotton.

John Newman Edwards summarized the benefits of the arrangement:
"They brought into the Confederacy quinine, opium, whiskey, gun caps,
clothing, many necessities, and a few luxuries, but with the speculators came
such an army of spies that [Edmund Kirby] Smith could neither issue a secret
order in safety nor make an important military movement unreported to the
headquarters of the Federals.[37]

Smith assigned Quantrill's former guerrilla companies to combat these
cotton thieves and speculators. The independent cavalry was ordered from
Sherman to Shreveport, from which Jarrette and Poole then headed to an
outpost at Bastrop, Louisiana, for better horses and to refit themselves for the
campaign. They crossed Bayou Roeuf at Wallace's Ferry and pushed on another forty miles to Floyd in Carroll Parish. Then they went across Bayou
Mason the next morning at Tester's Ferry, where they soon found themselves
behind Federal lines.

Just a few miles farther they encountered a cotton train composed of
fourteen six-mule teams and escorted by fifty cavalrymen. The guerrillas
charged the wagon train as soon as they saw it. They were on them so quickly

that the soldiers had no time to unsling their carbines. The column was stretched out over a quarter mile, making the work easier for the charging guerrillas. Only ten Federals escaped; the drivers were shot and the entire wagon train captured. In the rear of the wagon train was an ambulance with four cotton buyers; three were from Illinois and one was from Ohio. They had more than $180,000 with them. Jarrette had the men taken to a nearby cotton mill and hanged from the rafters. The mules, wagons, ambulance, and the money were sent back to Bastrop with William Greenwood; Jarrette pushed his company on, seeking more action.

Jarrette's guerrillas were passing Bayou Tensas when Younger noticed a cotton plantation in the distance. He could see blue dots in the fields and wagons laden with cotton. In guerrilla fashion, he turned and charged without a word. His comrades were soon on his heels. Younger was the first to enter the fray, "galloping about in every direction and firing here at one squad and there at another, until he had killed three and wounded two others."[38] When the smoke cleared, fifty-two black soldiers had been killed and eighteen wagons of cotton were confiscated.

The next action took place five miles from Goodrich's Ferry, along the Mississippi River. Jarrette's lead scout came upon a Federal column guarding a convoy of cotton wagons. He charged and single-handedly killed nine soldiers in less than ten minutes. Jarrette heard the firing and came to his aid at a dead run. But before Jarrette arrived, the Federal escort had fled. The guerrillas turned their attention to the cotton wagons and killed seventy-two teamsters and captured twenty-seven wagons of cotton. A Federal gunboat anchored nearby observed the encounter and shelled the woods close to the guerrillas, ending further action. The guerrillas suffered four men wounded.

When news of Jarrette's success reached Smith in Shreveport, he congratulated him in a special order. But the campaign was far from over. At the little town of Omega, lying close to the Mississippi River, was a Federal camp of two hundred black soldiers under white officers. Behind the levee, breastworks had been built, but on the higher ground in front of the levee was their camp. Jarrette divided up his command into two detachments. He ordered Younger to assault the entrenchments while he attacked the camp. Younger attacked at dawn, shooting four pickets then rushing into the fort before the startled soldiers could emerge from their tents. Meanwhile, Jarrette attacked the camp from the opposite side, trapping the terrified soldiers between them. The result was one hundred black soldiers killed, twenty taken prisoner, and eighty escaped into the nearby swamps where the guerrilla cavalry could not go. Federal gunboats shelled the area but were afraid of firing directly on the guerrillas, because they were in the middle of their own men.

Jarrette continued this campaign for two weeks, patrolling either side of the river. This audacious operation demoralized the Federals so that seldom did a patrol venture farther from the river than the protective canopy of the gunboats. During the campaign, the guerrilla cavalry hanged twenty-two spies: seventeen cotton buyers and five guides known to be working with the enemy. Repercussions from Jarrette's actions were felt back at Smith's head-quarters: cotton speculators sold out their contracts at ruinous discounts. As a result, some Confederate officers who were benefiting from this illicit trade were so alarmed that, together with the cotton planters who saw their profits disappear, they took their complaints to powerful men. The main complaint was that the guerrillas' tactics were "unchristian" and "barbaric," and soon Jarrette was ordered back from the river.

At his headquarters in Bonham, Henry E. McCulloch continued to receive accounts of criminal activity by Quantrill's men even though his command had been reduced. On February 15, 1864, McCulloch wrote to Magruder:

> Quantrill will not obey orders, and so much mischief is charged to his com-mand here that I have determined to disarm, arrest, and send his entire command to you or to General Smith at Shreveport. This is the only chance to get them out of this section of the country, which they have nearly ruined, and I have never yet got them to do any service. When or-ders have gone out to them, they always have some excuse, and are certain not to go.
>
> My plan is to arrest Quantrill's men, send you about 100 deserters for you to dispose of, and then arrest all the balance of the brush crowd. If the true men of this country would swear what they know, I could send several hundred men to the penitentiary for treason, etc.; but they are afraid and will not make affidavits, in any instance, but I think when I get Quantrill and the brush men out of the way, they will have more confidence.
>
> Quantrill and his men are determined never to go into the army or fight in any general battle, first because many of them are deserters from our Confederate ranks, and next they are afraid of being captured, and then be-cause it won't pay men who fight for plunder. They will fight only when they have the advantage and when they can run when they find things too hot for them. I regard them as but one shade better than highwaymen, and the community believe that they have committed all the robberies that have been committed about here for some time. Every man that has money

about his house is scared nearly to death, and several moneyed men have taken all their money and gone where they feel more secure.[39]

McCulloch conveniently forgot that Quantrill had chased raiding Indians out of his territory and saved North Texas citizens from attacks by Kansas Jayhawkers. The guerrillas also had made an honest attempt to rid the area of illegal stills. No matter the outcome, McCulloch was not satisfied with their efforts. Quantrill also cleaned out some camps of deserters in North Texas, but his methods were far from McCulloch's appeasing style. In the end, McCulloch had found an excuse for everything that had gone wrong in his jurisdiction; the laxness and incompetence of his administration was blamed wholly on Quantrill because of the general's personal animosity toward Missouri. After complaining that Quantrill failed to obey orders, he ordered the guerrilla leader to report to Magruder, believing that this would remove Quantrill from his district. Gloating over this apparent accomplishment, McCulloch stated that the move would not have been possible if he had not promised to use his influence to keep the guerrillas in the independent partisan service to which Quantrill was entitled by his presidential commission.

But McCulloch's reports in the *Official Records* are inconsistent. The report he submitted to Magruder chastised Quantrill's command. His tone was far different in a statement he made a week later to Gen. Hamilton P. Bee, who was in charge of a neighboring Texas subdistrict. Where McCulloch had expressed his unequivocal dissatisfaction with Quantrill's command to Magruder, he now related to Bee that he thought Quantrill's command would do the South a great service:

There is no doubt about their being true Southern men, and, no odds what happens, will fight only on our side. They have been bad behaved in some instances, but have not been guilty of a fourth of what has been charged against them. They are in a country filled with the very worst character of men, numbers of whom are hid in the brush and come out at night and rob and steal; and there are plenty of enemies in the country who would have been glad to get up a conflict by telling bad tales upon them besides those that were true, and I really think the people are to a great extent unnecessarily uneasy about them. . . . If kept together under Quantrill they can be controlled. . . . They are superbly armed and well mounted, and there is no reason that they should not do good service. They have not been paid for months; this should be done immediately, and let them see that they are to be treated properly and required to behave themselves.[40]

But before Quantrill could assemble his command and depart for Ma-gruder's headquarters, McCulloch received an urgent message from Gen. Douglas H. Cooper on February 15, 1864, stating that three hundred cavalry-men of the Fourteenth Kansas Jayhawker Regiment from Fort Smith and three hundred Federal Indians from Fort Gibson were within thirty miles of Boggy Depot and heading south. Leading the advance were Companies B, K, L, and M of the Fourteenth Kansas, under Col. J. G. Brown; the Unionist In-dians were commanded by Col. William A. Phillips. The Confederates ascer-tained that the enemy was poorly supplied at their garrisons and were on a raid to capture or destroy the large ammunition and commissary supplies ac-cumulated at Boggy Depot.[41]

The previous September, the enemy had been effectively repulsed on an earlier advance toward the area, but that successful effort had required mus-tering more than four hundred citizen volunteers from the surrounding areas. In addition to the danger of having one of their major supply depots fall into enemy hands, Cooper noted that the Federals appeared to be preparing to at-tack Fort Washita. He urgently requested troops from McCulloch, who had one thousand men, but they were scattered all over North Texas.

McCulloch replied, "I have directed Quantrill from Preston to Fort Washita at once, and Col. James G. Bourland to throw his disposable force to Preston and thence on the Cornage Point as early as possible, while I assem-ble all the companies of Colonel Martin's regiment that I can collect at this place in order to advance from here in case General Cooper has to fall back toward Red River."[42]

This enemy invasion, however, was mostly due to McCulloch's decision to allow state troops to disband for thirty days to plow and plant their fields. The only troops he had at hand were conscripts, whose abilities were ques-tionable. Besides a minor mention in the Kansas adjutant's report, no subse-quent record of this military engagement survives, but one can assume that Quantrill aided in repelling this invasion.[43]

After this incident, Quantrill departed North Texas for Magruder's head-quarters in Houston, and he was gone for several weeks. When he returned to the Mineral Springs camp in March 1864, he received information that led him to suspect that one of his men had been involved in the killing of George Butts. One account claimed that there had been some unpleasantness be-tween his wife, Sophia, and one of Quantrill's men. Some say that a quarrel developed Butts and a guerrilla.

Many officers as well as Quantrill's men frequented Glen Eden just to be near Sophia. Fletcher Taylor and several guerrillas were staying at the estate as guests at the time, and when Butts failed to return home, Sophia and these men went out to look for him. They were unable to find him, and the searched continued for days. His bullet-riddled body was found ten to fifteen days later in a grove of trees close to the road, about a mile and a half north of Sherman. Butts's horse was still saddled and bridled when it was found almost starved, tied to a nearby tree not far from his body. Butts's watch and wallet were missing.

At first it was assumed that Indians were responsible for Butts's murder, but several people commented, "The major had many enemies as he had been instrumental in drafting men for military service." He had worked hand-in-hand with Henry McCulloch in Bonham to get as many men as possible into the military. Sometimes this required the threat of force to round up these men and force them back into the ranks. Gen. Edmund Kirby Smith had instructed McCulloch that any conscripts who returned voluntarily would be allowed to select which state regiment they would serve in, but if they were compelled to come in, they would be sent to a regiment of McCulloch's choosing or assigned to the infantry. Both McCulloch and Butts were very zealous in seeing all conscripts brought into the service.

Both George Butts and Sophia were ardent in their devotion to the Confederacy. They invited transients and local men whom they regarded as slackers into their home and served "refreshments" till the guests were in a state of mellow acquiescence. When these evaders regained their senses, they found themselves duly sworn recruits in the Trans-Mississippi Department of the Confederacy.[44]

Everyone knew that Butts had been very active in trying to have every able-bodied man in the county forced into the ranks of the army. He also favored the induction of all able-bodied officeholders. Almost every town was full of stout, hearty, able-bodied young men, either wealthy men or their sons. Many people "knew" that rich men and their sons were "either in the Quartermasters Department, the Commissaries Department, the Transportation Department or some other department, simply to keep them out of the 'bullet department.'" Citizens were disgusted when they learned that F. P. Alexander, a wealthy thirty-year-old, held the office of tax assessor.[45]

Reports indicated that Fletcher Taylor, one of the men who had gone with Sophia Butts to search for her husband, had been wearing Butts's watch; thus, many believed he had something to do with the murder. In fact, Sophia had seen Taylor wearing her husband's watch, and she flatly accused him of the crime. An outcry from the townspeople of Sherman demanded that McCulloch act decisively in the matter, and resulted in a great deal of pressure on

Quantrill's company. One indication of this is that Sophia no longer extended her hospitality to Quantrill's men after the murder of her husband. And she said that she would gladly play Salome to Quantrill's John the Baptist.

Shortly after George Butts's death, Sophia departed Glen Eden for Waco, with a large number of faithful slaves. She stayed there until the end of the war.

After the war, Sylvester Akers acknowledged that Taylor and John Ross had killed Butts. Akers explained: "George Todd went up to Ross and jerked [Butts's] watch out of his [Ross's] pocket and pointed to [Butts's] name on it. Ross tried to say he had bought the watch, off some stroller he did not know, but Todd had so much evidence that Ross and Taylor had to admit that they were guilty.[46]

In the spring of 1864, the evidence of Taylor's guilt must have been convincing to Quantrill. He immediately arrested Taylor and sent word to McCulloch at Bonham, informing him of the arrest and requesting authority to court-martial Taylor. Other men were also arrested on other charges. But while this correspondence was still going on, guards allowed the prisoners to escape, and they left camp with horses and supplies. Frank Smith recalled, "The guards made no attempt to stop him as he [Taylor] was very well liked." An official record added, "Quantrill himself had nothing to do with these outrages and desired to bring the offenders in the band to court-martial. Bill Anderson however defending the men who had leaned toward his authority, refused to permit it."[47]

When Quantrill discovered Taylor and the others had escaped, he ordered his men into formation and addressed them. He said that if any man had robbed anyone in Texas, he should confess his crimes and promise to refrain from any further criminal activity. If any guilty parties did this, they could remain in his command and he would prevent any punishment for the crimes to which they confessed. At the same time, he vowed if anyone was guilty of a criminal act and did not acknowledge it, and if it was later proved that a guerrilla had violated the law, then he would be expelled from Quantrill's command and punished to the full extent of the law. In response to this offer of amnesty, not one of the guerrillas admitted any guilt. So Quantrill told them that if anyone did not like his style of command, or if any of them wished to withdraw from his command, they could take their horses and weapons and leave.

William Anderson rode out of the ranks, protesting that he had not broken any Texas laws, but he did not like Quantrill's leadership and wanted to quit his command. With Quantrill's permission, he gathered his belongings and left the camp, staying in town with Jim Chiles. The only constraint Quantrill exercised was that Anderson could not take any of his men with him.

But as soon as Anderson left, approximately ten other men quit the command and headed for Sherman, making their camp near the present intersection of College and Broughton streets. Anderson posted guards on the outskirts of town in case Quantrill might raid the former men of his command. No conflict materialized, however.[48] Anderson's anxiety was not allayed; he gathered his men and rode to McCulloch's headquarters in Bonham.

After the break between the two leaders, Anderson followed a deliberate course of action to discredit his former commander. One guerrilla recalled that Anderson communicated several times with McCulloch, alleging that various crimes in Grayson County had been ordered directly by Quantrill. Among the statements submitted to the general, Fletcher Taylor—who had recently joined Anderson's group—confessed to the murder of George Butts. W. L. Potter recalled that this happened in late March 1864; he said that Quantrill and Anderson were never on friendly terms again.[49]

A few days later, McCulloch informed Quantrill that Taylor had been arrested in Bonham and ordered Quantrill to his headquarters, along with his command as well as any witnesses against Taylor. The court-martial was to be conducted at his headquarters, on the second floor of the town courthouse.

Quantrill surmised that Anderson and Taylor had probably given McCulloch all the false information the general wanted to hear. On the morning of March 28, Quantrill and sixty men departed the Mineral Springs camp for McCulloch's headquarters, leaving George Todd and ten men to guard the camp. Arriving in Bonham just before noon, Quantrill—being naturally cautious—ordered his men to remain in the saddle and to be alert for any trouble. He hitched his horse to a post in front of the courthouse and went inside. Quantrill approached McCulloch with a military salute and stated that he was reporting as ordered.

Both Andy Walker and W. L. Potter were present, and they recalled what followed: "Being a very genteel man, Quantrill took off his pistols and laid them on the center table. Then he sat down for a cordial chat with the general." McCulloch informed Quantrill that Taylor had admitted to killing Butts, but he claimed that Quantrill had ordered him to do so. Therefore, Quantrill should consider himself under arrest. Two armed privates of Martin's Fifth Texas Infantry immediately stepped into the room with their guns in their hands. McCulloch added, "I am going to arrest your whole command, and investigate, and find out who he is that has been doing all this robbing. Colonel Martin is on his way to your camp, with orders to seize [the rest] of your command."[50]

McCulloch then relaxed and stated that Quantrill's parole would be immediately accepted, that he would not be imprisoned before his trial, and he could remain at McCulloch's headquarters until the court-martial convened. The general added, "Now, nobody but you can do anything with these men of yours out there, and I want you to go out and tell them to surrender. I'll give you quarters, provisions and forage for your horses." McCulloch checked his watch and then invited Quantrill to eat with him, saying that afterward they would discuss the matter further.

Quantrill calmly replied: "I consider this a strange way of doing business General McCulloch. I do not understand your manner of doing business. I have preferred a criminal charge against one of my officers. I have placed him under guard as you well know. He made his escape from my camp, and now you place me under arrest on his word and undertake to try me for the crime that he acknowledges that he has committed. No Sir! I will not go to dinner. I do not care if I never eat another bite in Texas!"[51]

McCulloch left Quantrill in his office with the two guards. There was a water cooler in the corner of the room, and Quantrill crossed the room to get a drink. He raised the dipper and then, before the guards knew what was happening, threw it on the ground and sprang for his weapons. Drawing his pistols from their holsters and cocking them with his fingers on the triggers, he said, "If you make a move, I'll kill you." He then ordered the guards to lay down their weapons and step across the room. After buckling on his pistol belt, he backed out of the room, locking the guards in and taking the key with him. At the foot of the stairs he encountered two more guards. He ordered them to drop their weapons and step outside.

On getting to the street, Quantrill shouted to his men, "Mount your horses men, we are all prisoners here!"

Some of the guerrillas were still on their horses, but some were dismounted and idly talking with some of Anderson's men across the street. But as soon as they heard Quantrill's order, they gave a shout and leaped to their saddles, racing out of town, leaving only a cloud of dust in their wake.

One bystander stated, "On South Main Street they met McCulloch's men, who politely parted, and gave them a wide berth."[52]

The guerrillas were soon on their way to Colbert's Ferry, with Quantrill in the lead. One of the guards reported the escape to McCulloch, who dispatched men from Martin's regiment to overtake Quantrill and bring him back to Bonham dead or alive. Bill Anderson and his men joined the pursuit.[53]

As Quantrill raced out of Bonham, he sent a man to Todd with word to come quickly and meet them five miles east of Sherman, along the Bonham to Sherman road. Todd was to bring nothing but ammunition with him, as much as he could carry. As soon as the courier relayed Quantrill's message,

Todd and his men were on their horses. His quick compliance with the order let him join up with the guerrillas at a ford over Caney Creek just in time; Quantrill's men were then hard pressed by Martin's regiment.

Todd formed his men in the timber east of the ford on either side of the creek, where the pursuers would have to cross. This allowed him to hold the lead element of Anderson, Taylor, and fourteen men, including some of Martin's men, in check while Quantrill headed toward Kentuckytown for fresh horses. As soon as Todd's men were entrenched, the skirmishing began.

During a lull in the firing, Anderson yelled out to Todd, "If you're not such a damn set of cowards come out of the timber in the open prairie and fight like men."

Todd replied: "You have the most men. If you are not a damn set of cowards come in here and take us out."

Each side had one man slightly wounded. In the meantime, Quantrill headed north, skirting the creek and doing some long-range skirmishing with some of Martin's men who were trying to swing north to outflank him. Todd heard the firing and kept moving along the timber of the creek, trying to stay close enough to Quantrill so he could reinforce him if necessary. The skirmishing kept up until nightfall. Realizing that Quantrill had made it to safety, Todd slipped away from Anderson and raced off to join his leader on the way to Colbert's Ferry.

It was dark when Todd rejoined Quantrill. Todd was ordered to take some men and scout the area while Quantrill kept the main group moving toward the ferry crossing. Todd came upon ten soldiers huddled around a campfire in a small clearing. He called out, "Who are you?" The men replied that they were Confederate militia. At that moment, a pistol of one of Todd's men discharged accidentally, the bullet striking the left arm of Jim Little. But the militia believed they were being fired upon and quickly mounted their horses and fled. Todd's patrol investigated the camp and decided they had little to fear from the militia. With this in mind, Quantrill swung his men away from the ferry crossing and back toward the Mineral Springs camp. When the guerrillas rode into camp, Quantrill issued orders to quickly load provisions. Some were assigned to pack up their belongings and to be ready to ride at a moment's notice.

Under the cover of darkness, as Quantrill and Todd were busy in the camp, Anderson's men sneaked in and took Andy Walker prisoner. But Walker soon escaped and rejoined Quantrill. Anderson also tried unsuccessfully to steal Ol' Charley, Quantrill's horse, but the animal reared and created such a ruckus the attempt was abandoned.

In the morning, Todd was ordered to scout ahead as the guerrillas pulled out of camp. He soon encountered a company of Texas militia and inquired about its mission. The militia commander replied, "We have been sent down by General McCulloch's orders to get Quantrill."

Todd replied, "Well, don't you know that you're not going to get him? Now you listen to me, captain. You had better get your men together and go back to Bonham and you tell General McCulloch that Quantrill said that if he was molested any further he would turn his bushwhackers loose on Texas and he would not be responsible for anything that might happen for what his men did."

The captain, visibly shaken, pulled his men back and returned to McCulloch's headquarters.[54]

After the militia captain abandoned his pursuit of the guerrillas, Quantrill leisurely broke camp and crossed to the north side of the Red River to establish a new camp beyond McCulloch's jurisdiction. But as they were advancing toward the Red River, they saw they were being pursued by four hundred regular soldiers, the balance of Martin's Fifth Texas. It looked like the guerrillas were not going to get out of Texas without a fight. Martin skillfully kept his men just out of range of the Missouri guerrillas. When Quantrill sensed that the Texans were about to charge, he arranged his men in formation along the north bank of the river. Just as the guerrillas drew and cocked their revolvers, Martin appeared on the Texas side of the river with a white flag. Since the river was at a fordable depth, Quantrill met Martin at midriver and told him that he would not permit any officer to arrest a single man of his command; any attempt to do so would cause the guerrillas to kill every man Martin had.

"I'm not fighting the Confederates, but if you try to arrest us I'll certainly fight you," Quantrill said, adding that if Martin's command crossed the river after him, his colors would not be respected. If Martin wanted to fight, Quantrill would oblige him and fight as long as he had a cartridge to burst and a man left with strength to pull a trigger.[55]

Martin stated that he had no jurisdiction in Indian Territory and neither did McCulloch, and thus he had no authority to follow the guerrillas out of Texas. When the conversation ended, Martin led his men back to Bonham. Cautiously, Quantrill waited until the Texans were out of sight before he pulled his men out of formation. When Martin reported to McCulloch, he was asked why he hadn't brought Quantrill back. The colonel responded, "It wouldn't do to fool with that man."[56]

Even though the guerrillas had pulled out of Texas, their families were forced to remain behind. North Texas newspapers reported that after the

Missouri guerrillas returned to the battlefields in their home state, "Their families remained here out of necessity for food and shelter, their homes in Missouri having been destroyed in 1863 when several counties were depopulated."

Most of the civilians hated to see the guerrillas go. Dick Hopson noted, "Sherman will never be knit together again by the universal bands of friendship and hospitality it had then."[57]

Quantrill set up camp on the north side of the Red River in Gen. Douglas H. Cooper's district. Cooper later acknowledged that McCulloch had asked him to let Quantrill return to Kansas or Missouri. He said that he sent for Quantrill and asked if he could send him to the west of Fort Gibson, which was occupied by Federal troops, to "stampede those Kansas Indians and run them into Kansas."[58]

On April 3, 1864, a captain named Kaufman, in charge of a Federal company at Fort Gibson, in the northeast part of Indian Territory, received an order: "Let none of your command straggle as Quantrill is around."[59]

The winter of 1863/64 was uncommonly bitter, and a foot of snow covered the ground in mid-March. So rather than proceed immediately toward Missouri, Quantrill waited for grass and forage to become available before heading north.

Guerrilla John McCorkle recalled, "We broke camp on Red River and started back north, with around 50 to 60 men left in the command."[60] Frank Smith recalled, "Quantrill started back to Missouri with 64 men and it rained practically all the way. They traveled most of the way through mud and water."[61]

The unrelenting rain swelled the rivers. All the streams were full, so the horses had to swim their riders across. Thus the animals were much worn, more so since the guerrillas found no grain on the way.

Because there was not ample time to pack provisions before their hasty departure from Mineral Springs, the guerrillas had little food for either themselves or their animals. Hiram James George and twenty-two guerrillas left Quantrill to join Shelby's Brigade, then stationed in Washington, Arkansas. The small band stopped on the way at Clarksville, Texas, to have their horses shod by Zachary Cooper, a refugee from Jackson County. They reached Shelby's camp on April 2, 1864.[62]

Even after Quantrill's departure from North Texas, Henry E. McCulloch's headquarters still received reports of robberies and other depredations in the area. District commander John B. Magruder was not aware that Quantrill was no longer in Texas when he wrote to McCulloch on March 31, 1864:

There are a number of men roaming about in your district, dressed in Federal uniforms, who represent themselves to belong to Quantrill's command. The major general commanding is informed that all kinds of outrages are being committed by the devils in the northern districts and by persons wearing uniforms. You will at once cause all of these men to be conscripted and placed in the service, unless you can prove satisfactory that they belong to Quantrill's command, in which case they will be ordered to join their command forthwith. You will then ascertain from Captain Quantrill whether these men are borne on his muster rolls, and all who are not borne will be conscripted without delay.[63]

McCulloch replied on April 6:

The brush battalion behaved badly everywhere, committing petty depredations on the property of the people about all their camps. . . . Until I have a good cavalry regiment sent to me from some other portion of the state, I will not be able to get this country cleared of the bad men in it, and it will be very difficult to do it anyway. . . . Many robberies, thefts, and murders have been committed in this country principally by men with Federal overcoats on, some of which have been traced to Captain Quantrill's company proper and others to some of the men who came here with him last fall, and to renegade Missourians and Arkansans who have left our army in Arkansas and Missouri and have been lurking about this country all the winter in spite of my best efforts to rid the country of them; and I assure you that Captain Quantrill's command has been a terror to the country and a curse to our land and cause in this section. I have never been able to control them because I have not had troops that had the moral and physical courage to arrest and disarm them less than which never would have done any good.

As to those other blue coated gentry lurking about the country, they have been able generally to evade the scouts by keeping out of their way or scare them off by declaring they were Quantrill's men, whom they were afraid to arrest, having my orders at the same time to arrest Quantrill's men if found absent from camp, as well as any others similarly circumstanced. Some of the robberies lately committed have been traced to certain parties who have been arrested by some of the minutemen in Grayson County.[64]

But with Quantrill gone, McCulloch could no longer blame the Missouri partisans for every misdeed perpetrated in his jurisdiction. As late as December 29, 1864, months after Quantrill's departure, the general alleged: "Recent thefts, robberies, and murders committed in this area by lawless men renders it necessary that this area should be cleared of all men who do not properly belong here."[65]

McCulloch assigned Gen. James W. Throckmorton to investigate recent robberies reported around Kentuckytown. In the end, McCulloch had to acknowledge that Col. Robert S. Gould's Thirteenth Texas Cavalry had stolen horses and forage and committed other indiscretions as well.[66] That spring, Maj. Gen. Sam Bell Maxey exceeded his authority by restricting soldiers to their military districts, unless they procured proper passes or furloughs, and trying to make Texas off-limits to all non-Texans.[67]

ON THE trek north, several regular army officers accompanied Quantrill on April 22 to Gens. Douglas H. Cooper and Stand Watie's headquarters at Boggy Depot. Col. Jeremiah Vardeman Cockrell, a brother of U.S. Senator Francis M. Cockrell of Missouri, rode with the guerrillas back to Jackson County. The guerrillas stayed at Boggy Depot for two days. Col. Daniel McIntosh and five hundred men from the Indian Brigade accompanied them as far north as the Canadian River.[68]

Before leaving Texas, Quantrill had talked with Andy Walker about the possibility of leaving the country. He said that surrender was out of the question and stated that if they did, "They would hang every one of us." Shortly after his discussion with Walker, Quantrill sent a letter to district commander Magruder requesting a pass for himself and five others to cross the Mississippi and travel to Canada. A short time later, Magruder replied that he would only issue passes for two men, leaving Quantrill to reject the idea for the present.[69]

The guerrillas traveled mostly at night, riding up to sixty miles a day. They skirmished with Federal patrols whenever they encountered the Union troops. But incessant rains hampered their river crossings. At the Arkansas River, Quantrill halted his command for two days, waiting for the water to subside. With his provisions getting low, he decided to attempt the crossing. A letter from Gen. Stand Watie stated, "Quantrill crossed the Arkansas River near the Creek Agency and killed eight men."[70] With each passing day, these river crossings became more difficult and dangerous for both men and horses. Many times a horse and rider were swept downstream and never seen again. To minimize casualties, Quantrill allowed only two men to enter the water at a time. As an example, Quantrill and Todd were the first to ford every river.

As soon as Quantrill crossed the Red River, he saw two abandoned cabins and discovered two rummaging hogs inside one of them. Quickly trapping the animals inside the cabin, he rode back to the river and called out to the men on the other bank: "Hurry up, boys! I've got a good supper for you over here." After all had safely crossed the river, they killed the hogs, built a roaring fire in the cabin, and enjoyed their first warm meal in days.[71]

From Indian Territory, the guerrilla column slipped back through the southwest corner of Missouri and headed for Neosho, crossing the Neosho River at Gilstrap's Ferry. West of Neosho, the advance guard was ambushed, and Colonel Cockrell suffered a severe arm wound. Quantrill ordered John McCorkle to stay with Cockrell, but McCorkle argued against being separated from the command. Cockrell settled the matter by claiming to be able to ride. After Quantrill and Todd swam their horses across the Osage River in Vernon County, they lit fires on the bank as a guide for the rest of the company.

It wasn't long before the guerrillas approached the outskirts of Lamar. Hoping to overcome the stigma from their defeat here the preceding autumn, Quantrill and Todd decided to attack the Union outpost. For a short time, a rumor had been circulating that Quantrill was planning to attack Neosho, and this led to a redeployment of a large portion of the Union command to Newton County. The shifting of troops left Lamar largely undefended. Only a small contingent of the Seventh Missouri Provisional Cavalry remained in Lamar under the command of Lt. George N. Adler. Most of the soldiers were militiamen quartered in their own homes.

Quantrill attacked at dawn as the troopers were having breakfast and feeding their horses. The surprise assault caused many to abandon their posts. Those who could reach their horses fled to Fort Scott or nearby Greenfield, while others hid in the timber around Muddy Creek. Nine of the cavalrymen were trapped in town. A few men under Sgt. Jefferson Cavender found protection behind the gutted walls of the courthouse, where their rifles were stored for emergencies such as this.

After the initial volley, Quantrill called on the Federals to surrender. Cavender sent out a sergeant named Montgomery to parley with the guerrilla leader while his men loaded their weapons. Cavender refused to surrender, and after two fruitless assaults on the bullet-scarred courthouse, Quantrill withdrew and continued his journey. Exaggerated accounts claim that the guerrillas left thirty dead and wounded behind. In fact, all the Federal defenders survived the attack.[72]

The guerrillas continued north until they came to the raging Grand River. They could not have crossed the waterway had it not been for a rickety bridge they happened to find in the dark. Once they were on the other side, the guerrillas took shelter in some abandoned cabins. They next moved through the region of Dayton, in Cass County, before finding themselves back home in Jackson County. Here they captured some Federal soldiers, whom they shot on Quantrill's orders.

Since the Lawrence raid, the Federals were ever fearful of another attack somewhere in Kansas. After he had received reports of Quantrill's return to Jackson County, Union Gen. Samuel R. Curtis, newly assigned departmental commander for the District of Kansas, issued a warning to Fort Leavenworth: "Dispatch from Kansas City says 80 rebels, crossed Grand River near Dayton, Cass County, this morning, going toward Rose Hill, Shawnee, and Olathe. Get ready to protect the terrified towns."[73]

6

A Dying Breed

Always outnumbered—never outfought.
—QUANTRILL GUERRILLA MOTTO

HE FOLLOWING DAY THE guerrillas turned east, stopping for a breakfast of biscuits and bacon at a large farmhouse near Chapel Hill in Johnson County. After the meal, Quantrill told his men to break into small groups of three or four and scatter while he and George Todd rode into Jackson County to look over the situation. Many of the guerrillas needed horses, equipment, and rest, so Quantrill took twelve men whose horses were still in good condition and made a broad trail for the Federals to follow, leading them away from the unmounted men in camp. He swore that he would strike at the first Union force he encountered regardless of its size.

After skirting Warrensburg on the west, Quantrill came upon eight Federals led by Lt. James E. Couch of Company C, First Missouri State Militia.[1] Couch and Quantrill halted their men and rode out to identify themselves. Quantrill claimed to be leading some Colorado troops to the West on special duty. After Couch identified himself as a Federal, Quantrill saw no need to parley further: the guerrillas charged. Quantrill shot Couch and another trooper while his men emptied the saddles of the remaining soldiers.

During the winter of 1863/64 the Union command structure in the West was completely reorganized. Thomas Ewing was replaced as the commander of the District of the Border due to his ineptitude in solving the guerrilla problem along the border and for his unpopular decision to banish all relatives of guerrillas, incurring untold Federal casualties in the process. Ewing

was transferred to a small post near St. Louis. Gen. Egbert B. Brown of the
Missouri State Militia succeeded Ewing and was given command of the
newly established District of Central Missouri. Unlike the previous year
when Quantrill returned from Texas and shocked Federal authorities with his
audacious lighting attacks, in 1864 the Federals confronted him with a different plan of attack. While waiting to counteract Quantrill's first move, the
Federals were prepared with twice as many men as they had the year before.
Whenever they learned of Quantrill's presence, they initiated massive patrols
across the countryside, searching out the guerrillas and their camps. These
patrols took a tremendous toll on some of Quantrill's best fighters.

In addition to increasing his forces, Brown brought in troops from Colorado who were better trained than the Missouri and Kansas militias. John
Newman Edwards described the Coloradoans as

> slashing fellows, fond of a grapple and fond of a melee. They were grave,
> quiet, middle-aged men, the most of them, rarely influenced by sentiment
> and not at all by any romantic folly. They volunteered to fight, and they did
> it as they would follow an Indian trail or develop a silver mine. Most of the
> Colorado troops were old mountaineers, cool, middle-aged and wiry as an-
> telope. Neither were they lacking in that essential quality of a soldier, stead-
> fastness. They could be whipped, and they were whipped; but such fighting
> as would do for the militia would not do for them. Man to man, the best of
> the border knew that to drive them required close work and steady work.[2]

As soon as word spread of the annihilation of Couch's patrol, a company
of Colorado troops was soon on Quantrill's trail. They persistently dogged his
heels as he sought a safe place to camp in Jackson County. It was nearly
nightfall when Quantrill discovered two companies of Federal infantry entrenched and awaiting his arrival. The infantry was set up as a blocking force,
trying to catch Quantrill in the middle as the Colorado troops pushed him
from behind. Ascertaining that he could neither penetrate their line nor
flank their position, Quantrill decided to reverse direction and counterattack
the Coloradoans. Because Quantrill's force was so much smaller than the
Colorado unit, the Federal commander did not expect any resistance; he had
planned only to follow the guerrillas' trail until he could catch up and bring
on an engagement.

THE FEDERALS were strung out on the road and lacked unit cohesion.
Quantrill surprised them by personally leading the attack down a narrow

lane against their advance column. Nine cavalrymen were in the lead. Guerrilla Andy McGuire shot down the first three before he was thrown from his horse. The rest of the Coloradoans quickly closed up and joined the engagement.

Turning off the road and finding some cover in the nearby timber, Quantrill and twelve men held more than one hundred Federals at bay. All but two of Quantrill's men were wounded. As darkness fell on the battlefield, Quantrill pulled back farther into the timber. He finally found safety in one of his former camps in Blue Springs, and there he rested while waiting for his separated commands to report. Those guerrillas who had remained in Jackson County during the winter season and some small squads of men who were still making their way north from Texas were spread out across the county. It would take a little time for them to return to their former campsites and link up with Quantrill.

Quantrill and Todd were alarmed at the number of Federal troops in Jackson County. And word was beginning to spread among the Union commands that "the lion had been heard roaring about his Jackson County lair again."[3] Quantrill decided that the situation was "too squally" for concerted guerrilla action. George Shepherd rode into camp at midnight, bringing all the guerrillas he had found in Johnson County and reporting that seven hundred Federals had been tracking him. He surmised that they would probably discover the camp and bring on an engagement in the morning. During the night, Quantrill moved his men to another location. Frank Smith recalled, "During May the Federals chased the guerrillas around from here to there and he began to think there was no fight left in them."[4]

The rain continued for days, and the Federals lost Quantrill's trail in the muddy roads. Quantrill and Todd discussed moving their men to Lafayette County, where guerrilla operations seemed more promising. Quantrill told Todd that he would be riding to Howard County with his wife, Kate, and a few handpicked men. He had previously discussed this plan with Andy Walker, who recalled that the guerrilla leader said, "Andy, it's a lost cause. We'd better make preparations to get out of the country. We ought to manage to get some money together to take us out of the country."[5]

Some accounts indicate that Quantrill and Todd quarreled over Quantrill's plans. Todd was determined to fight as long as possible in Jackson County, but even he knew it was an almost impossible task. Some guerrillas recounted an earlier episode of bad blood between the two men. Guerrilla John Tatum recalled, "The bad feeling began at Spring River, as they returned from Texas in the spring of 1864. They swam the river and were wet and cold. Quantrill by some chance got a piece of beef and boiled it. When he was eating Todd came by and without saying 'by your leave' cut off a large part of it and took it away. Quantrill was angered and said some very harsh things to Todd, and they were never again friends."[6]

Meanwhile, Quantrill gathered his most trusted men and prepared for the long march to Howard County. There would be safety as well as sanctuary in what was referred to as "Little Dixie." Other Southern refugees had preceded Quantrill to Howard County and reported, "We met with many good warm-hearted people who were very kind and helpful to us."[7]

After discussing his decision with Walker, Quantrill asked Jim Little, John Barker, Tom Harris, Dave Hilton, Tom Evans, George Shepherd, John Ross, William Toler, and eight others to accompany him. He asked Warren Welch to act as their guide through the cordon of Federal posts and unfamiliar territory. After two days they arrived at Arrow Rock in Saline County. Quantrill obtained provisions from friends who were living nearby after they were run out of Jackson County as a consequence of Ewing's General Orders No. 11. Here Quantrill stayed for several days.

Some said that Quantrill was suffering from old wounds and in poor health. A letter from Ruth A. Bomar reported that the guerrilla leader was wounded and hiding in the Blackfoot Hills around Boonsboro.[8] Most of Quantrill's battle wounds were never recorded, but it is known that he received serious wounds on at least four different occasions. John Newman Edwards states that Quantrill's reason for going on to Howard County "was not so much to fight as to rest, not so much to hide himself as to be at peace. He was sick, wounded, barely able to ride, and worn from long pain and exposure."[9] An edition of the *Huntsville Citizen*, reprinted in the *Columbia Missouri Statesman* on August 5, 1864, recorded that after William Anderson attacked Huntsville on July 15, he stated that he was a captain under Quantrill, "who is at present sick on the south side of the river."

Quantrill instructed Warren Welch to return for him in two weeks, time he needed to rest and regain his strength. Then he would find a way to cross the river from Arrow Rock into Howard County. But Welch was soon seriously wounded in a skirmish. When he failed to return, Quantrill found another way across the river. Once he was on the other side, he found an ideal site for a camp well hidden in heavy timber, with no inhabitants closer than a small log cabin a short distance away. Here he set up camp near a spring in a secluded hollow up a branch of a small creek three miles south of Boonsboro and five miles west of the town of Franklin. Quantrill erected a tent for himself and Kate, with a kitchen built into it, making it as comfortable as possible.

He probably chose this area because most of the people in the river hills around Boonsboro were Southern sympathizers. Other Confederate military units were operating in the area as well. Col. W. S. Jackson, son of Governor Claiborne Fox Jackson, commanded a unit in Cooper and Howard counties. Local Southern officers Capts. Clifton D. Holtzclaw and William Steward, who had been Quantrill's first company commander in the Missouri State Guard at the start of the war, carried on intensive guerrilla activity throughout this area. The home of Col. Stephen Cooper, a Confederate colonel in a Missouri brigade, was only a mile away.[10]

During Quantrill's time in Howard County he had few encounters with Jayhawkers or Federal patrols. A few days before his arrival on July 2, 1864, the *Boonville Weekly Monitor* reported that two hundred yards of telegraph wire was cut in Howard County about three miles from the river and carried off. On the same day, Clifton Holtzclaw's guerrillas had a skirmish with troops of the Ninth Cavalry, Missouri State Militia, garrisoned in Fayette. Area commander Gen. Clinton B. Fisk wrote to Maj. Gen. William S. Rosecrans and requested five hundred well-armed mounted men for a ten-day campaign against the guerrillas in Howard and Boone counties, where he reported that the bushwhackers were increasing daily.[11]

In late June 1864, Gen. Sterling Price sent Capt. John Chestnut to Jackson County with instructions for the guerrillas to harass Union troops by raiding outposts, ambushing patrols, cutting telegraph wires, burning bridges, and tearing up track. Meanwhile, a large number of Colorado troops from Independence were still patrolling the hills of the Sni and the Blue in search of Quantrill's camps. Among these were sixty-five men of Company C of the Second Colorado led by Capt. Seymour Wagner, who boasted that he would catch and defeat the guerrillas. In Jackson County, George Todd led a group of sixty-four guerrillas, and they heard of Wagner's claim.

For several weeks both companies sought one another. On a hot July 6, seven miles south of Independence, in the valley of the Little Blue, the two units came together. The valley was wide and long, well suited for maneuver warfare. At three hundred yards, the commanders formed their men into a battle lines and each took his place in the center of his respective line. There was no hesitation; Todd and Wagner hollered out the order to charge simultaneously. As the two forces came together, the sound was like a steel trap snapping shut. Both commands were well mounted, and none were skittish. The contest would have been evenly matched but the Federals had inferior arms. All of Todd's men carried double-barreled shotguns and a double brace of Colt Navy revolvers; Wagner's troops carried Spencer carbines and inferior Savage revolvers. A subsequent Federal report stated: "The foe came rushing on until the combatants were mingled together, fighting a hand-to-hand encounter midst the fallen dead and dying until gallant Wagoner fell, mortally wounded."[12]

The action was brutal and bloody. Guerrilla training made short work of the encounter. Horsemanship combined with marksmanship and the experience of untold skirmishes quickly ended the engagement. Todd shot down three Federals in the first charge. Guerrilla Dick Kinney and Wagner signaled each other out during the fray. Wagner fired three times at Kinney and missed; Kinney did the same, but then his fourth shot struck the Union commander in the chest.

The guerrillas' horses instinctively knew their role, while many of the Coloradoans' horses became unmanageable, forcing many to dismount and fight on foot. The dismounted troops died where they stood. After seeing their captain killed, the Federals lost heart and broke into a mad dash for Independence; some tried to escape into the timber. The guerrillas killed twenty-seven and captured twenty-four horses, thirty revolvers, and thirty-two Spencer rifles. Two of Todd's men were wounded.[13]

After the skirmish with Company C, Todd saw that his position in Jackson County was tenuous at best; there were just too many Federals in the area. Realizing that Quantrill's assessment of the military situation was correct, Todd's only choice was to transfer his operations to another county farther east and wait for Sterling Price to advance from Arkansas in another attempt to free the state from Federal occupation. To accomplish this redeployment, Todd divided his command into smaller units.

Warren Welch took ten men—Jim Johnson, Frank Ketchem, Dick Kinney, John Koger, Jacob Meade, Sam Moore, Joseph Smith, Bob Thompson, and Mar Warner, and another—east to Moniteau County. They made their way into Boonville dressed in Federal uniforms, claiming to be part of Col. James McFerrin's command on a thirty-day furlough. They skirmished with local militia, and Thompson was killed.

Throughout the summer of 1864, Todd's command of forty men and Dave Poole's command of eighty men skirmished with Federal troops in every county from Jackson to Saline, a distance of sixty miles. After the garrison commander at Arrow Rock captured and executed guerrillas Jim Janes, Charles Bochman, and a man named Perkins, Todd and Poole decided to attack the Arrow Rock garrison in Saline County. Arrow Rock was situated at the intersection of the Santa Fe Trail and the Missouri River. The garrison was manned by a small detachment from the First Cavalry, Missouri State

Militia, commanded by a captain named Sims. Todd and Poole's plan of attack on July 19 was for Todd to surround the town and close all avenues of escape; Poole would attack the town directly. Poole's guerrillas wore Federal
uniforms when they entered Arrow Rock, Sims's men were leisurely passing
the time in the street, completely unaware of the approaching danger. Guerrilla Simeon Whitsett was in the advance and remarked to his comrades,
"Boys, I will knock the middle man out for you." After Whitsett's first shot,
the guerrillas unleashed a withering fire until the Federals surrendered after
just a few minutes. Ben Morrow and Harrison Trow captured Sims in an upstairs hotel bedroom and shot him in the head. The guerrillas killed 25 soldiers and wounded 35 others; they captured 150 militiamen and paroled
them out of the service.[14]

Only one guerrilla was wounded in the action, Richard Yeager. Turning
back from Arrow Rock, Todd took Yeager to a guerrilla camp in a cornfield
owned by a man named Gilliam in Cambridge Township near Marshall and
asked a friend to hide him. Sixteen-year-old Laura Jane Flanery and other
Southern women brought Yeager food and cared for his wounds, but spies in
the neighborhood discovered his whereabouts, and a company of seventy soldiers soon found his camp. Due to his wounds, Yeager was unable to stand. A
friend propped him up against a tree and placed his revolvers in his hands. As
the Federals charged the camp, this man stood over Yeager's body and defended him until he was shot down. Yeager killed three of his attackers and
wounded two more before he was killed. Gilliam was arrested and charged
with harboring a guerrilla. He was released after Laura Jane Flanery confessed
to having cared for Yeager; she was imprisoned.

Other Southern women were similarly abused. Federal soldiers discovered
a letter addressed to a seventeen-year-old Boone County girl with the expression, "God bless the bushwhackers." The girl was arrested and incarcerated in
the female prison in St. Louis, where she was kept for months and then released after taking a loyalty oath and filing a three-thousand-dollar bond.[15]

With so many spies in the neighborhoods, the guerrillas were forced to
change their tactics. Federal commanders issued warnings that any civilian
not reporting guerrillas camped on their property within twenty-four hours
would be executed, their property would be confiscated, and their homes
would be destroyed. Still, many Southern sympathizers bravely helped the
guerrillas and paid for their patriotism with their lives. Their widows were
forced to burn their homes, and their families were made destitute after being
exiled from their neighborhoods. As a result, the guerrillas protected their
friends by forcing well-known Union sympathizers to feed them.

Todd's and Poole's commands headed east toward Wellington. Along the way, a Federal militia unit mounted an ambush and claimed to have wounded John Thrailkill and Fletcher Taylor. In the fight, Taylor's right arm was badly mangled by a blast from a double-barreled shotgun, and he was carried to a camp in the woods. Todd sent some men to kidnap a country doctor and escort him to camp; Taylor's arm was amputated.

On August 9, 1864, a Federal dispatch reported the discovery of guerrilla camps in Lafayette County, but the guerrillas had scattered. The guerrillas were estimated to be from two hundred to five hundred strong, with the ability to concentrate in less than twenty-four hours. They were reportedly waiting to join Gen. Jo Shelby when he advanced from the south.[16]

After clashing with the Federals all summer, Todd decided to follow Quantrill to Howard County. He sent word to his men to muster at Bone Hill in eastern Jackson County by mid-September. On September 13, he crossed the Missouri River into Clay County then made his way east into Ray County, where he engaged with a militia company. Todd's thirty men were joined by Poole's forty men, and together they attacked Federal garrisons whenever they came across them. After making a circuitous route from the counties north of the river into Moniteau County, south of Boonville, they killed forty militiamen in Tipton. Riding toward Boonville, the guerrillas crossed the river into Howard County and began searching for Quantrill.

Quantrill had been in Howard County since July 10, 1864. With only sixteen men in his command, and being accompanied by his wife, Quantrill's respite was short lived. He continued his military operations, but his maneuvers were mostly small scale.

After Todd and Poole joined forces with Quantrill in late September, other guerrilla units united and decided for an all-out assault on the Federal outpost in Fayette. On September 20, 1864, six miles south of the town, near Franklin, the combined forces of William C. Quantrill, Bill Anderson, George Todd, Tom Todd, and Dave Poole met to discuss the attack. Anderson was given overall command.

Riding into Fayette from the south, along the Rocheport to Fayette road, the guerrillas came within one hundred yards of the square without raising the alarm; then one of Anderson's men fired at a black soldier. This opened a wild rush toward the courthouse and the blockhouses north of town. Fifty determined Federals were barricaded inside the buildings. The soldiers were concealed well; only muzzle flashes from the portholes of the buildings indicated their positions.

For the guerrillas, it was a foolhardy adventure. Anderson led the charge, and many of his best men were killed or wounded. George Todd joined the attack and also suffered numerous casualties. Jim Little was shot twice and only able to stay in the saddle with Quantrill's assistance. Quantrill held back his men when he saw the assault was a fruitless endeavor; he refused all pleas from Anderson to send in his men. Guerrilla Hampton Watts agreed that Anderson's charge was foolhardy: "Leading men, armed only with revolvers, charging an invisible enemy in blockhouses, to simply embed bullets in logs, with no possible chance to either kill or inflict injury on the foe, was both stupid and reckless."[17]

After eighteen guerrillas had been killed and forty-two had been wounded, Anderson and Todd pulled back and retreated down the Glasgow road toward Randolph County. Quantrill led his men to his former camp near Boonsboro.

RICHARD KIMSEY, a citizen of Howard County, had a reputation for plundering the homes of Southern sympathizers. He told his victims that he was one of Quantrill's men. Citizens complained to Quantrill, who was staying nearby at the time. The guerrilla leader warned Kimsey to stop his depredations, but his warnings were ignored. So Quantrill and Thomas Harris began a search for the marauder. Kimsey should not have underrated Quantrill's warning. Many guerrillas reported that, with one or two exceptions, Quantrill was the "fastest draw," best shot, and finest horseman of all the bushwhackers.[18] On October 8, Quantrill and Harris found Kimsey and Robert Montgomery on a pillaging expedition near the Clark's Chapel United Methodist Church. The four men met in the middle of the lane. Quantrill told Kimsey he was under arrest, but Kimsey went for his gun instead. Quantrill was quicker and shot Kimsey and Montgomery out of their saddles. Quantrill was also credited with killing John West, a notorious Jayhawker, near Lisbon, seven miles from the guerrillas' camp in Boonsboro.[19]

After the murder of a number of female relatives of Quantrill's men the preceding summer, two of the survivors—fourteen-year-old Mattie Anderson and nineteen-year-old Molly Anderson, sisters of William Anderson—went to live with friends in Lafayette County. Here they looked after a wounded Warren Welch for four or five weeks until he recovered. At the same time that Quantrill was establishing his headquarters in Howard County, the Anderson girls moved near Fayette and lived with Porter Jackman, an elderly Southern friend. After the failed Fayette battle, the girls were arrested on November 20, 1864, for giving encouragement to bushwhackers. They were sent to St. Louis, where they remained for several months. After Bill Anderson's death, their brother Jim took them to live with Bill Anderson's widow in Sherman, Texas.

After the bold attack on Fayette, Federals in Mexico, Missouri, feared a similar attack from Quantrill's men and began reinforcing their commands. While the Federals maneuvered through the countryside, a rear party of sixteen militiamen swept through the area and plundered the homes of Southern sympathizers. But their escapades did not go unnoticed.

Alex Bomar, a local citizen, was in the Confederate army and far from his family. His home was stripped of everything of value. His wife reported the theft to the Federal provost marshal in Mexico. She recalled: "He caused a search, and the stolen goods were found in the quarters of those sixteen men. They were put under arrest and taken away on the North Missouri Valley train to St. Joseph to be tried by a military court for stealing and making war on women, children and non-combatants."[20]

Meanwhile, the guerrillas scattered and backtracked through the area to throw off the Federal pursuit after the Fayette fight. Quantrill led his few men to the vastness of western Howard County, while Todd and Anderson joined forces and headed for Huntsville. Anderson sent a dispatch to the Federal commander in town to surrender the garrison or be attacked. Within a half hour the officer responded, "If he wants us, to come for us."

But Anderson chose not to attack the outpost. Still reeling from the stinging defeat at Fayette, Anderson turned east and bivouacked in Monroe County. Then Anderson and Todd moved southeast, into eastern Boone County, and camped outside of Centralia on September 26, 1864.

Anderson rose early on the morning of September 27, taking thirty men into nearby Centralia to get a newspaper, check for military news, and look for supplies. He learned that there were several crates of much-needed boots at the railroad depot. Shortly after entering the town, Anderson's men woke some people and demanded breakfast at Sneed's hotel, one of two hotels in town. The other buildings were a saloon and a couple of commercial stores. The guerrillas knew that Centralia was a Northern enclave, so they amused themselves by robbing a few townspeople. Reportedly, one resident was killed. Before leaving town, Anderson's men torched the railroad depot. In the distance, a whistle signaled the arrival of the westbound train.

When the train pulled into the burning station, the guerrillas immediately surrounded the cars, firing their pistols into the air to discourage any resistance. Twenty-five Union soldiers were on board, including the sixteen militiamen from Mexico, who were being escorted to St. Joseph for court-martial. The other nine soldiers were from the First Iowa Cavalry and were commanded by a lieutenant named Peters; some were reporting for duty up the line and the rest were recently returning on furlough from Gen. William T. Sherman's army.

Some guerrillas reported gunfire from the coaches as the train approached. An Iowa soldier was alleged to have fired from the train, setting the stage for the retaliation that followed. George T. Scholl, one of Anderson's men, described what happened when the train pulled into the station: "We rode into town with no intention of taking a trip around town. Some time later a train came in filled with Federal soldiers. The company lined up outside the coach and began a fusillade. We answered and started to clean them."[21]

Fifteen-year-old J. Frank Dalton rode with Anderson too and offered this account: "Fighting under Captain Bill Anderson, he had captured a passenger train and got a lot of money, most of which was being sent South to pay the Union troops. On the train were thirty-four Union soldiers who were being sent South to join the Union army. As the soldiers showed fight when we ordered them to leave the train, we had to dispose of them. The Yankee troops saw us and lined up to give battle."[22]

One guerrilla recognized a Federal soldier who had testified against him in court. The soldier was dragged from the train and shot.

The rest of the soldiers surrendered and were taken from the train, lined up alongside the station, and questioned by Anderson. Recent atrocities against captured guerrillas played a role in what happened next, especially since some of Anderson's best men had been shot and then scalped by Federals in Howard County. He recounted this story for the soldiers in front of him: "You Federals have just killed six of my men, scalped them, and left them on the prairie. I will show you that I can kill men with as much skill and rapidity as anybody. From this time on I ask no quarter and give none." He added, "You are Federals, and Federals scalped my men, and carry their scalps at their saddle bows. I have never allowed my men to do such things."

Sgt. Thomas Goodman was called out of line and spared for an exchange for one of Anderson's recently captured men. The sixteen militiamen from Mexico were taken off the train, and they were stood up alongside the others and shot. Their bodies were shipped back to Mexico for burial; one of them was buried in Alex Bomar's wedding suit, which had been earlier stolen.[23]

After Anderson returned to camp, he told Todd what had happened in town. By midafternoon, the guerrillas learned that Federal troops had mounted a pursuit. These Union soldiers had ridden hard for Centralia as soon as they saw smoke rising from town. Maj. A. V. E. Johnson and 150 men of the Thirty-ninth Missouri Militia had been in pursuit of the guerrillas since learning of the attack on Fayette. As soon as Johnson viewed the scene at Centralia, he hoisted a black flag at the head of his column and started toward the guerrilla camp, leaving only a handful of men behind to guard the town.

Todd saw Johnson coming, and with ten men he rode out to ascertain the Federals' strength. The odds appeared favorable to him, so he left a squad to lure Johnson into a trap and rode back to form his remaining men into a battle line.

When Johnson saw a line of guerrillas facing him five hundred yards away, he approached within effective rifle range. At two hundred yards, the Federal commander dismounted his men to fight on foot; this single act en- sured their destruction. The Federals formed a line, with every fourth man holding the horses for the rest. They were spread out almost a quarter mile; the guerrillas covered slightly more ground.

Todd called out the order to advance, and the guerrillas started off at a slow walk; men and horses instinctively knew what would be expected in the next few minutes. When the distance between them closed to a little more than a hundred yards, Johnson's men fired a volley. Most of the rounds went over the guerrillas' heads, but Sam Shepherd and Dick Kinney were killed. The guerrillas responded with a volley from their carbines then flipped the weapons across their shoulders, drew their revolvers, and spurred their horses into a run. At the sight of hundreds of heavily armed guerrillas, many of Johnson's men broke and ran. Those Federals left in line frantically tried to reload as the guerrillas charged them, their deadly pistol fire wiping out all re- sistance. One soldier tried to bayonet Todd, but he only managed to thrust the cold steel through the back of the guerrilla leader's saddle; Frank Smith shot the soldier as he rode by.

Whatever soldiers were not shot were knocked off their feet by a solid wall of horseflesh. The guerrillas quickly wheeled their mounts for another pass, but Johnson's opposition was soon ended. Smoke hung heavily in the air. Wounded horses ran frantically around the countryside. David Poole dis- mounted and counted 123 Federal dead. Several more were shot from their saddles while trying to escape back to town.

J. Frank Dalton noted that Jesse James carried a watch and had timed the fight. The battle lasted exactly five minutes.[24]

After the battle, the guerrillas withdrew toward Boonville. When word of the battle reached Union headquarters, more than six hundred cavalrymen were dispatched to find and destroy the guerrillas.

Todd's men continued west toward Lafayette County. Because the guer- rillas still wore Federal uniforms they were able to ride up to the Union pa- trols and wipe them out at close range. On one occasion, two of Poole's men acted as advance scouts and came running back to the main body with an entire Federal company in pursuit. Todd naturally ordered a charge, and Frank Smith claimed that the guerrillas killed thirty to forty Federals in the ensuing fight. Only those able to outrun the guerrillas survived.

After Quantrill's return to his hideout in Howard County, some neighboring Putnam County militia rode into nearby Glasgow and began stealing, shooting, and burning. When they continued to move south, they discovered Quantrill's camp near Boonsboro and made a quick charge. Quantrill barely had time to launch himself into the saddle and take up James Little, still recuperating from his wounds from Fayette, behind him and fall back behind John Barker and five other of his veterans, who withdrew fighting, holding their own for fourteen miles.[25] They were forced to move their camp until they received news of Sterling Price's return to Missouri.

IN OCTOBER, from his headquarters in Arkansas, Price was given instructions for another campaign in Missouri. He crossed the border with three thousand cavalrymen and joined Jo Shelby, who was also moving north from Arkansas. Accompanying Shelby was Missouri Governor Thomas Reynolds, who left his capital in Marshall, Texas, and served on the general's staff as a volunteer aide-de-camp.[26] The combined force numbered around twelve thousand men. Price did not anticipate in spending the winter in Missouri but rather was making a large raid to draw off Union forces in order to relieve the pressure on Robert E. Lee's army in northern Virginia and especially from William T. Sherman's destructive path through Georgia. Southern accounts carried the news of Price's upcoming campaign: "General Price, at the head of 20,000 men, is in Missouri. To expel him, many troops will be required; and this may relieve us a little in the East."[27] In addition to drawing manpower away from the eastern theater of the war, Price was also directed to destroy as much of the enemy's military stores and supplies as he could.[28]

To counter Price's maneuver, the Federals drew Gen. Andrew J. Smith's Sixteenth Corps from Memphis and Gen. Benjamin Henry Grierson's cavalry from Mississippi, leaving Confederate Gen. Nathan Bedford Forrest to operate at will in northern Georgia. Price's campaign compelled the Federals to concentrate forty thousand to fifty thousand men in Missouri and diverted reinforcements that would otherwise have been sent to Sherman.

After fighting a brief but costly skirmish at Pilot Grove, Price made his way through the state toward the Missouri River, establishing his headquarters in Boonville. Here he met with Quantrill and Todd. Anderson rode in a day later. Price ordered the guerrilla leaders to destroy portions of the railroads north and south of the river to keep the Federals from sending reinforcements from St. Louis.

After the war, a Confederate officer stated that Price specifically directed the guerrillas to destroy the Perraque Bridge on the North Missouri Railroad as he began his move toward Kansas City. The officer added that the orders "were given to Colonels Anderson and Quantrill. They were the most distinguished partisan leaders, and were the terror of the enemy in that section and accustomed to operating on railroads."[29]

While resting in Boonville, Price ordered Gens. Jo Shelby and John B. Clark to Glasgow to seize a large ammunition cache reportedly stored in the city hall. Early in the war, Glasgow had been a Confederate recruitment and training camp. This caused the Federals to send a force to run off the recruitment effort and occupy the town for the duration of the war. Price assigned Quantrill's command to scout the city for Shelby's twenty-nine hundred troops. Eight hundred Federals garrisoned the town, and they occupied heavily fortified positions.

At dawn on October 15, Confederate artillery opened on the Union fortifications. The Confederates advanced by various routes, forcing the defenders into their second line of defensive trenches on Hereford Hill, high above the city. When he saw the futility of further resistance, the Federal commander, Col. Chester Harding, surrendered shortly after noon.

Clark gave Harding generous terms: Harding's men would be treated as prisoners of war, private property would be respected, and officers would be permitted to keep their sidearms. Quantrill informed Clark, whom he had known in Arkansas, that he had been the first man in the trenches after the Federals surrendered. Union Capt. G. A. Holloway remarked after the battle: "I must testify to the uniform kind and gentlemanly treatment we received at the hands of the Confederate officers among whom were General J. B. Clark, Brig. Gen. Joseph Shelby, Colonels Green, Quantrill, [Sidney D.] Jackman, [Dick?] Kitchen, [William L.] Jeffers, [John Q.] Burbridge, [W.O.] Coleman, and Nichols; all Missourians and most of the subordinates to Major General [John S.] Marmaduke."[30] Even though Harding tried to destroy some Federal stores before capitulating, Clark's men found a great deal of much-needed supplies: captured 1,200 rifles, 1,200 overcoats, 150 horses, and large quantities of clothing. The Confederates paroled their prisoners after remaining in town for three days.

As soon as the shooting stopped, Quantrill took the bank manager into custody and confiscated twenty-one thousand dollars from the bank. The manager was released unharmed.

Unionist Benjamin Lewis, a wealthy tobacco farmer, was a resident of Glasgow. He had offered a six-thousand-dollar reward for Bill Anderson, dead or alive. Anderson searched Lewis out and told him to give him six thousand dollars or be killed. Lewis raised the amount from his neighbors. He was released after he was beaten.[31]

DURING THE time Quantrill and Todd were fighting at Glasgow, Anderson received a special request from some of his men. Three brothers—Isaac, Richard, and James Berry—had ridden with Anderson since the Lawrence raid. Their home was in nearby Callaway County. While they had been away, Federal militia from the neighboring town of Danville had raped their four sisters. They received Anderson's permission to ride to Danville and avenge their sisters' honor, but Anderson did not want them to go alone. He also sent the Hill brothers—Tom, Tuck, and Woot—along with Ben Broomfield, Theodore Cassell, Archie Clements, Moses Huffaker, John Maupin, Gooley Robertson, William Stuart, Richard West, and a handful of others.

At ten o'clock on Friday evening, October 14, a bright moon shown down as the guerrillas rode unobserved into Danville, their horses' hooves muffled to silence their approach. The guards were changing shifts for the night. Some of the soldiers stationed here for the last few months were detailed five miles away to protect the railroad. A log fort stood in the center of the town square, but the suddenness of the guerrilla attack prevented the pickets from reaching safety there, instead driving them into nearby buildings. To flush out the soldiers, the buildings were set on fire. The guerrillas killed a number of the guilty militiamen, among them Henry L. Diggs, Michael A. Gilbert, and Merrill S. Simmons of Company C. Robertson was the only guerrilla killed.

Students at the Danville Female Academy reported that Tuck Hill and some guerrillas demanded the keys to the chapel because they believed Union soldiers were hiding there. The school's principal was known to be a Unionist, and he had already escaped to a safer place. When the students saw what seemed to be every building in town in flames, they panicked out of fear that the guerrillas were going to harm them and set fire to their school. Tuck Hill shouted at the scholars, "Be quiet. Not one of you shall be harmed." As he started to ride off, the girls grabbed the reins of his horse and began pleading for the life of their principal. Hill rode into town and escorted the gentleman back to the school with an admonition to stay out of sight.

After accomplishing their mission, the guerrillas departed, riding off as quietly as they had arrived. From Danville they rode five miles and burned the railroad depot and tore up the track before rejoining Price in Boonville.[32]

WITH SHELBY'S men leading the way, Price advanced toward Kansas City. Regarding the orders he had given the guerrilla leaders, he wrote that they had not been fully executed and that the guerrillas had affected little damage to the railroads. After the Southern victory at Glasgow, there was little resistance until Price reached the outskirts of Lexington, where he easily pushed back units of Kansas militia. Real resistance wasn't encountered until Price confronted the Second Colorado Cavalry east of Independence in what became known as the battle of the Little Blue.

George Todd's men accompanied Shelby as scouts and rapidly pushed back the Union defenders with each attack. Riding next to Shelby, Todd paused to raise himself in his stirrups to look over a slight rise when a sniper's bullet struck him in the neck, inflicting a mortal wound. Morgan T. Maddox and another man dragged Todd to safety. Another Federal volley killed Todd's horse, which had been given to him by John Barnhill in January 1862.[33]

As Price followed the old route south of the river toward Kansas City, he ordered Anderson to parallel his course north of the river, with instructions to keep any Union force from crossing and coming up behind his army. Approaching Independence from the east, Price's army easily pushed back the Federal defenders, first from the Little Blue River and then to the Big Blue.

On Sunday, October 23, 1864, nearly thirty thousand Union and Confederate troops clashed south of Kansas City in what became known as the battle of Westport. After several bloody stands by the Confederates, Union Gen. Samuel R. Curtis's army overwhelmed Price's troops with superior numbers, forcing the Confederates back into Arkansas. Price's army was pushed south along the Kansas-Missouri border, ending the last major Confederate military action in Missouri.

Price anticipated that if he were compelled to retreat from Missouri, he would do so by way of Kansas and the Indian Territory, sweeping the countryside of mules, horses, cattle, and military supplies and bringing back as many recruits as possible.[34] On November 8, 1864, Price pronounced the campaign at an end and began the long winter march to Texas. The withdrawal from Missouri was described in detail by some of his men. One trooper wrote that his unit subsisted for four days on parched acorns, while another told how he and his comrades butchered and devoured a fat pony along the way. A cold wind cut through their rags, freezing the water in their canteens; coyotes trailed the army, terrifying men too weak from hunger or dysentery to keep up with the column. Hundreds fell out.[35] Some of Price's best officers had been captured, including Gen. John S. Marmaduke and most of his brigade, but as Price withdrew, remarkably, he gathered more recruits and supply wagons than he had initially brought on the raid.

During this last campaign, Price's men marched 1,434 miles and fought forty-three battles and skirmishes. They had captured three thousand Federals and destroyed property worth about ten million dollars, including bridges and railroads. Attempting to minimize his defeat after the battle of Westport, Price did not report the degree of demoralization in what was left of his army. In his report on Price's campaign, Gen. Edmund Kirby Smith wrote: "I consider General Price as having effected the objects for which he was ordered into Missouri and the expedition a success. I am informed he has crossed south of the Arkansas with his command largely increased."[36]

Price proceeded through Indian Territory, picking up much-needed supplies at Boggy Depot as he made his way toward Texas. As soon as the Missourians crossed the Red River, Jo Shelby set up his headquarters at Bonham, while Governor Thomas Reynolds returned to Marshall.

After hearing of Price's defeat, Bill Anderson continued to operate north of the river. On October 26, 1864, near Richmond, Missouri, Anderson found three hundred Federals under the command of Maj. Samuel P. Cox. Anderson led a charge, but he was cut down as he passed through the Federal line with his pistols blazing. Afterward, while searching his body, the enemy found a letter from his wife and a small Confederate flag with the inscription, "Presented to W. L. Anderson by his friend, F.M.R. Let it not be contaminated by Federal hands." F. M. Richardson was the thirty-three-year-old carpenter who had built the house for Anderson and his wife in Sherman the previous year.

The Federals took Anderson's body to Richmond, where they photographed it before cutting off his head. Then they severed his finger to get at his wedding ring. He was buried in an unmarked grave. The next morning the soldiers found flowers on the grave. Despising any acts of compassion or respect for the Missouri guerrillas, the Federals spat and urinated on the grave then rode their horses over the spot in an attempt to hide it.

Charlie Baker, a black man who served as Anderson's hostler, said: "I want to say that Mr. Bill was a good master. He treated me very well and I looked after his horses and family after his tragic death." Baker spent the next year after the guerrilla chieftain's death with Bush Smith Anderson in Sherman, Texas.[37]

WITH TODD and Anderson now both dead, Quantrill gathered about him many of the remaining guerrillas. Sylvester Akers said, "He [Quantrill] told his men that he had gotten them into the war and he would get them out all right if they would go with him to Virginia. His judgment was correct." Akers and the other guerrillas confirmed that Quantrill went to Kentucky or in that direction because the war was about over: "He intended to get into Virginia and attach himself to General Lee's army. He believed he could surrender with Lee, and he said Lee would soon have to surrender."[38]

By November 13, 1864, Quantrill and George Shepherd each formed a company and headed south. Quantrill's group included Sylvester Akers, John Barnhill, John Barker, Bill Bassham, Dick Burns, Tom Evans, William Gaugh, Joe Gibson, Richard Glasscock, Jack Graham, George Hall, Isaac Hall, Robert Hall, Tom Hall, Thomas Harris, Dave Hilton, Clark Hockingsmith, William Hulse, Frank James, Foster Key, Jim Little, Payne Jones, James Lilly, Peyton Long, John McCorkle, Andy McGuire, Lee McMurtry, Henry Noland, William Noland, Allen Parmer, Bud Pence, Donnie Pence, Henry Porter, Chat Renick, George Robinson, John Ross, Randolph Venable, George Wigginton, Jim Williams, and James Younger. This group followed Quantrill toward Virginia, while Shepherd's group, including Jesse James (still suffering from a wound received at Centralia), headed south to Grayson County, Texas.

Shepherd had been a close friend of Quantrill's throughout the war. In a display of admiration and comradeship while accompanying Quantrill into Howard County the previous summer, Shepherd and his twenty-one-year-old brother Oliver had their picture taken with Quantrill.[39] Cole Younger wrote of Shepherd after the war: "I have no doubt that he had more ups and downs during the war than any other man connected with Quantrill. I have been in some very close places with him myself. He is the quickest man on earth; a stranger might take him for a coward, but in that he would be mistaken, for Shepherd is a brave man."[40]

So as to reduce the shared risks inherent in combat, Henry Akers separated from his brother Sylvester and followed Shepherd to Texas while his brother followed Quantrill to Virginia. Frank James and his brother Jesse decided to do the same. Jesse would return to Texas to look after their sister, Susan, in Sherman, and Frank would follow Quantrill.[41] Hopefully one brother would survive and return home to take care of the family. Some of those following Shepherd were accompanied by their wives, while others simply wanted to return to relatives they left behind the previous spring. Those in Shepherd's group included Jack Bishop, Theodore Cassell, John Chatman, Archie Clements, James Cummins, James and Alfred Corum, Arthur Devers, Joshua Estes, William Gregg, James Hendrix, Jesse James,

John Jarrette, a man named Kelly, Silas King, Richard Maddox, John and Thomas Maupin, John Norfolk, Jack Rupe, Perry Smith, Bud Story, Harrison Trow, Samuel Wade, Preston Webb, Jack Williams, Matt Wyman, and Cole Younger. Gregg, Hendrix, and Maddox brought their wives.

But the trip south was a constant skirmish. At the Neosho River, a large party of Federals attacked Shepherd's column. Gregg chased one Federal officer whom he shot in the back nine times without killing him. During the heaviest part of the fighting, Jarrette's horse was killed. His brother-in-law Cole Younger came to his rescue.[42]

A noteworthy skirmish took place on November 22, twenty to thirty miles north of Cane Hill, Arkansas, near Cabin Creek in the Cherokee Nation. Shepherd came face to face with thirty-two Federals of Company M of the Fifteenth Kansas Jayhawker Regiment; they were led by Lt. Emmett Goss. Before enlisting as a Jayhawker, Goss had been a neighbor of farmer Marcus Gill. It was said that Goss's share of the plunder taken from raids on Missouri homes was spent on alcohol and prostitutes. As soon as Shepherd's men saw Goss's command, they charged. Twenty-nine Jayhawkers were killed. One escaped, two were captured, and one of these was released. The guerrillas lost four killed and several wounded.[43]

Before reaching Texas, the guerrillas encountered a fifteen-man Federal patrol that was escorting a mail shipment and included several pack mules with provisions. The guerrillas killed all but one soldier and made good use of the provisions. As soon as word of the attack reached the closest Federal outpost, they were on the guerrillas' trail, forcing them to leave the main road and take to the woods. Federal Pin Indians joined in the chase as they closed in on the guerrilla column.

The guerrillas were not alone in their fight against all comers; their families joined in the action as well. William Gregg tried to get the wives to remain safely in the background, but his efforts were not completely successful. The horse of Dick Maddox's wife, Martha, was shot in the skirmish with the Pins. Jesse James and James Cummins captured a horse and gave it to her, and Martha Maddox insisted on getting in on the fight. During the battle she "commenced to shoot at the enemy and had a lock of her hair shot off just above the ear."[44]

Shepherd's small band finally crossed over into Texas on December 2. Some stayed at their old haunts in Grayson County, some sought out Sterling Price and rejoined his command, and Shepherd and Gregg led the remnant of Missouri guerrilas to Waco. Those remaining in Texas shared the great hardships brought on by the war. A February 20, 1865, letter from George W.

Newcome to G. H. Bringhurst described conditions in the state: "The county is full of soldiers, mostly Missourians quartered about in Northern Texas, or on furlough going where they please. There are hundreds of families, mostly women and children from Missouri and Arkansas, besides our own absent soldiers' families thrown on the county for support. Where the bread is to come from God only knows."[45]

Gen. Henry E. McCulloch added to the alarm, writing from his head-quarters: "The enemy having driven many from Arkansas, Missouri, and Louisiana into Texas for safety, it adds greatly to the demand upon us for bread, and, as the enemy press us back from the valleys of the large streams in Louisiana and Arkansas, the area of grain-producing land is diminished, and the demand upon it increased."[46]

QUANTRILL'S FORTY handpicked men continued to seek support from South-ern families as they made their way toward Virginia. They intended to join Lee's army, hoping to receive honorable terms once the war ended. But many historians have said that Quantrill planned to assassinate Abraham Lincoln. Author William Elsey Connelley interviewed several of Quantrill's surviving guerrillas after the war and concluded, "The guerrillas at Independence all said Quantrill had no thought to assassinate President Lincoln even though irresponsible writers still perpetrate this falsehood today."

All of Quantrill's men wore Federal uniforms in order to make it through Tennessee disguised as a Union patrol, a ruse that had worked well in the past. Quantrill intended to start his journey north of the Missouri River, crossing the river at Arrow Rock in Saline County, but when they approached the river, they found it so full of ice they were unable to cross. Quantrill left his men for a short time, telling them that he would return in a few days in order to take his wife to St. Louis to stay with friends.[47] His men foraged for themselves, killing geese and deer and getting support from sympathetic farmers. Within a few days, Quantrill rejoined his command near Dover, Missouri, and resumed his journey. Going through Lafayette, Saline, Cooper, Moniteau, and Miller coun-ties, heading in a southeasterly direction, the guerrillas continued to identify themselves as a Federal scouting party on special duty.

At Tuscumbia, on the Osage River, the guerrillas captured a militia com-pany and paroled them without having to fire a shot and acquiring some new uniforms and blankets. From here they followed the Current River south into Arkansas. Joe Hall contracted small pox along the way. For a while, Quantrill left Joe's brother Ike Hall in charge of him near Pocahontas, Arkansas. After bidding the Hall brothers farewell, the guerrillas crossed the Black River at

Crawley's Ridge in Greene County, Arkansas, headquarters of southern Missouri guerrilla leader Sam Hildebrand.

Quantrill's small band reached the Mississippi River and attempted to cross opposite Memphis. Twenty-five miles upriver, at Shawnee Village on Devil's Bend, they found an old boat that they repaired on New Year's Day and successfully crossed the river, swimming their horses beside them. Once in Tennessee, they stopped at various plantations along the way for food. John McCorkle remembered that they once found a Southern gentleman who graciously fed them; Quantrill trusted him enough to confide that "he was Colonel Quantrill and was taking his command through to Virginia."[48] Shortly afterward Quantrill learned that he would not be able to pass through the Federal lines in East Tennessee. From this point Quantrill led his men into Kentucky, cutting across the northwestern portion of Tennessee. Just before entering Kentucky the guerrillas were approached by people they learned were relatives of Thomas Harris, John McCorkle, and George Wigginton. After a brief visit, the guerrillas continued on to Canton, Kentucky. From there, their next stop was Greenville in Muhlenberg County.

The guerrillas had few skirmishes, but in one skirmish they were surrounded in a farmhouse by a group of Federals. During the fight, Jim Little was shot in the leg and died a few days later. Guerrilla William Bassham found a relative and stayed with them until he was discovered and killed.

As part of their charade, Quantrill passed himself off as Captain Clark of the Second Colorado Regiment. Quantrill had shot Clark in an earlier skirmish in Missouri, and he still wore the man's uniform.

In Houstonville, Kentucky, the guerrillas stopped at a Union post for a change of horses. As Quantrill's men commandeered new mounts from the stables, the Federals became suspicious. Events led Allen Parmer to shoot the Union commander. Sylvester Akers stated that the Federals demanded that Quantrill give Parmer up; Akers and some of the guerrillas agreed because the affair was going to wreck the whole expedition. But rather than surrender one of his men, Quantrill chose to protect Parmer and reveal their true identities. Once his identity was known, the chase was on, and an alarm spread quickly.

From Houstonville, the guerrillas rode to Danville, camping eight miles from Harrodsburg. They split into two groups to look for food and shelter. While seventeen guerrillas were getting something to eat at a local farmhouse, a Federal patrol under Col. J. H. Bridgewater surrounded the building, and a sharp skirmish ensued. Several guerrillas were killed, and ten were captured. Only two of the guerrillas managed to shoot their way out and escape. When

Quantrill learned of the defeat, he was furious at the thought of losing so many men in one skirmish. Among those killed were John Barker, Foster Key, and Henry Noland; Sylvester Akers, John Barnhill, Dick Burns, Tom Evans, William Gaugh, Richard Glasscock, Jack Graham, Andy McGuire, George Robinson, and James Younger were captured. Akers had been wounded in the left shoulder.

Quantrill sent Allen Parmer, Frank James, Peyton Long, and Chat Renick to see if they could rescue any of the men. Renick was killed in the attempted rescue. The captured guerillas were taken to Lexington, Kentucky, and threatened with hanging. All except Tom Evans were transferred to Louisville, where, with the assistance of some civilians, they managed to escape, and several rejoined Quantrill. Akers escaped from custody after the end of the war.

Quantrill led his remaining men to Mayfield, Kentucky, always managing to find friends along the way. McCorkle reported that they found two families there who had been driven out of Missouri by Ewing's General Orders No. 11, one by the name of Saunders and a widow by the name of Cooper. Some of the guerrillas rode into town and visited with the refugees. Relatives of George Wigginton were discovered in Spencer County. On a tip from a Southern friend, the guerrillas changed direction and rode toward Taylorsville. Quantrill had been apprised that a regiment of black soldiers would be marching down the road toward the town. Using the same tactics previously employed by the patriots at Lexington and Concord in 1775, Quantrill concealed his men in the timber and fired into the ranks of the black soldiers as they marched past. The guerrillas kept this up until the regiment finally reached the town badly mauled and with diminishing numbers.

The guerrillas were preparing to cross the Salt River and head back to Nelson County when a resident handed Quantrill a newspaper informing him of Lincoln's assassination. Several of the men began to cheer, thinking that the South might still have a chance at victory, but then they learned that Lee had surrendered the previous week at Appomattox Court House, and the war was virtually over.

The same excitement occurred when news of Lincoln's assassination reached the remnant of Price's army in Texas. Maj. Jacob F. Stonestreet recalled the moment: "We were down in Texas when we got news of Lincoln's assassination. The men were on review and the intelligence went down the line like a flash. Some of them foolishly cheered. 'Boys,' said General Shelby, sitting erect on his horse with one hand raised in the air and his head barred, 'This is the heaviest blow yet dealt to us. Lincoln's slaughter was the act of a madman. If he had lived he would have been just and generous to the South.'"[49]

Meanwhile, Quantrill's command decided to separate and seek the best terms of surrender they could. Quantrill and a few handpicked men decided to ride back to Taylorsville. Since his command was not recognized in Kentucky as part of the regular Confederate army, the guerrillas planned to join up with local Southern commands and surrender as new recruits. Sylvester Akers commented that Frank James did not ride with Quantrill to Taylorsville. John Barnhill, Tom Harris, John McCorkle, and George Wigginton were told to meet Quantrill in two days at the Cooper farm near Mayfield. Quantrill had left some money with Mrs. Cooper and planned to reclaim it after he found a Union force to which he could surrender.[50] Others of Quantrill's company stayed behind at the farmhouse of a man named Thurman.

Quantrill's last act was a noble gesture by protecting those who had supported him and with whom he had formed a close relationship. A local citizen, an old man by the name of Jones, claimed that one of Quantrill's men had robbed him. Quantrill was taking this man to Jones's house, and if he turned out to be the thief, Quantrill was going to have him shot. As he entered the road leading from Taylorsville to Bloomfield, a heavy rain commenced. Quantrill turned in at James Heady Wakefield's house, a farmhouse in which he had previously stayed. The guerrillas settled in the barn to wait out the rainstorm. Unknown to them, a Federal scouting party led by Capt. Edwin Terrill, under orders from Gen. John M. Palmer to drive Quantrill from Kentucky, had been following their tracks.

Along the Taylorsville Pike leading from Bardstown, Terrill's men stopped at a blacksmith shop operated by Almsted Jacobs, a free black, to get their horses shod. A trooper recalled that Jacobs shouted: "Great God! Geminy! Don't stop here to get yo horses shod, fo' de guerrilla Quantrill and twenty men went by here not half an hour ago and are over dah in de ba'n now."[51] Upon hearing this, Terrill wheeled his men down the lane for an immediate attack on the barn.

When the Southern pickets cried out, "The bluecoats are coming!" Quantrill's men reached for their pistols and scrambled for their horses. William Hulse, Allen Parmer, and Henry Porter were the only guerrillas able to mount their horses and get away by leaping a fence in the corner of the barn lot. The other guerrillas—Robert Hall, Thomas Harris, Dave Hilton, Payne Jones, James Lilly, Andy McGuire, Lee McMurtry, Bud Pence, John Ross, and Randolph Venable—managed to escape on foot to the nearby timber. Quantrill held the Federals at bay until his men made it to safety, then he tried to escape with the aid of Richard Glasscock and Clark Hockensmith. Quantrill and Hockensmith were riding double; a Federal volley killed Hockensmith and mortally wounded Quantrill, pinning Quantrill under their fallen horse. Pvt. John Langford of Company B, Fifteenth Kentucky Infantry, claimed to have fired the mortal shot. Glasscock was killed as he turned back to help Quantrill.

The Federals carried Quantrill on a blanket into Wakefield's house. They plundered the dwelling then departed. Some of Quantrill's men returned for their leader, but his injuries were too grave for him to be moved. As soon as Terrill discovered Quantrill's identity, he returned and transported him to the military hospital in Louisville, where Quantrill died on June 6, 1865.

Before Quantrill died, Mrs. Neville Ross of Independence, Missouri, visited him in the hospital. She was the mother of John Ross, one of Quantrill's men, and carried messages to Quantrill's friends in Missouri. She respected his wish that his identity not be revealed and that he be given a quiet burial.

Quantrill's death stunned and shocked his men. They had served with him through unnumbered battles and skirmishes. They remembered that he always had their interests at heart; his faithfulness endeared him greatly to them. Kate Quantrill recounted their devotion to him. She said that he seemed to have a hypnotic influence over them, and they were ready to lay down their lives for him. The people of Jackson County recalled how Quantrill came to the homes where the wounded were being treated to check on his men after the August 10, 1862, battle of Independence. Others of Quantrill's men had their own remembrances of Quantrill. Henry Noland, a black soldier serving with Quantrill, said that he admired Quantrill because the guerrilla leader trusted and depended on him. Jim Little was devoted to Quantrill and rode next to him in battle, never letting him go into a tight spot alone. After the war, when hard feelings were eased, Fletcher Taylor commented that Quantrill was always well liked by his men. James Campbell said that Quantrill never endangered the lives of his men. All his men remembered that he never once ordered them into battle but rather led his men from the front, shouting, "Come boys, let's get 'em." Both William Gregg and Hiram George wrote that Quantrill usually restrained the ardor of his men in combat and never sacrificed a man needlessly. Gregg went on to remark that "[Quantrill] was simply a tiger with the brains and the bearing of a gentleman," and paid his former leader the utmost compliment by simply saying, "He was a Confederate soldier."[52] Hiram George summed it up by foretelling what was soon to transpire: "As yet he is, however, relatively unknown outside the immediate areas in Kansas and Missouri, but he is destined to be known, feared, and maligned by his enemies, and to be loved and honored by his friends and comrades in arms, especially the latter, many of whom are to love and respect and honor his memory long after he is dead."[53]

ON SEPTEMBER 26, 1865, Capt. Henry Porter rounded up what remained of Quantrill's command, and they surrendered at Samuel's Depot and received their paroles. Fewer than twenty were left alive: Isaac Hall, Robert Hall, Thomas Harris, Dave Hilton, William Hulse, Frank James, Payne Jones, James Lilly, John McCorkle, Andy McGuire, Lee McMurtry, Allen Parmer, Bud Pence, John Ross, Randolph Venable, George Wigginton, and a few unnamed men. Most managed to return to Missouri when the war ended but found that they were not welcomed because they had fought with Quantrill. After Federal vigilantes drove them from their homes, many found refuge in other states, mostly in their former homes in Texas. It was here they had sought comfort even while engaging in numerous military and peacekeeping actions, but even here the situation was tenuous.

With Quantrill's assistance, the Texas army of the Trans-Mississippi was credited with keeping Federal troops out of the state even when Federal armies occupied much of Arkansas and Louisiana. As the war drew to a close, Gen. Henry E. McCulloch at Bonham had only a skeleton force; if he had had a difficult time previously keeping civil order and protecting the citizens, he was finding it impossible to attempt to maintain order with the disintegration of the military. The countryside entered a savage state when neither the civil authorities nor the reduced military authorities could cope with the rampant crime. A home guard of vigilantes was organized. It was especially needed in Grayson and other counties of North Texas, from which the governor's office was receiving constant petitions for help.

The surrenders of Robert E. Lee in Virginia and Joseph E. Johnston in the Carolinas virtually put an end to the war west of the Mississippi. McCulloch gathered about him a regiment of Confederate soldiers at Bonham for protection. Under a previous order, one-tenth of what the people had, other than real estate, was taken by McCulloch for military purposes, which turned out to be a legalized system of robbery. Eventually the government seized half of all cotton produced, teams were sacrificed by their owners, and corn cribs were measured, leaving only the bare necessities for families. After the war, much of this seized property lay unclaimed at various commissaries. One of McCulloch's men recounted, "It was several weeks after Lee laid down his sword at Appomattox, before news of the surrender reached us, when it did and the question was settled beyond peradventure, the military headquarters at Bonham were broken up."

McCulloch asked to be relieved of his position.[54] Seeking to overcome earlier charges by Gen. Edmund Kirby Smith of willful disobedience of orders, McCulloch went home to Seguin, Texas, with an armed escort for protection against deserters who had sworn to kill him. W. L. Potter claimed that McCulloch took with him several wagons filled with the most valuable Confederate supplies.[55] McCulloch became superintendent of the Texas School for the Deaf. His lax and inept administrative policies brought about a legislative investigation that made him resign his position in 1879. He died on March 12, 1895.

7

Heading Home

The history of war is the history of warriors; few in number, mighty in influence.

—GEORGE S. PATTON, 1926

O N MAY 9, 1865, EXACTLY ONE month after Lee's surrender at Appomattox, Gen. Edmund Kirby Smith, commander of the department west of the Mississippi, with headquarters in Shreveport, rejected a dispatch from Gen. Ulysses S. Grant ordering the surrender of the armies under his command, which totaled sixty thousand men. The proffered terms were the same as those that Lee had accepted. Confederate president Jefferson Davis had abandoned the capital and was heading west with a hope to continue the war with Smith's forces from Texas. There was still strong sentiment among the high-ranking military leaders and the governors of Arkansas, Louisiana, and Texas to carry on the war in the belief that additional thousands of men could be added to those already in service before Grant would have time to move his forces and mount an offensive west of the Mississippi. There was also the hope that France and Mexico would become embroiled in the war on the side of the South if the war continued; at the least, they hoped for better surrender terms than those currently being offered.

As a result, Smith on May 18, 1865, issued orders to move his headquarters from Shreveport to Houston as a gesture of his determination to fight out the war in Texas. One citizen wrote, "General Smith in my opinion will hold on if possible a month or two yet, until the hopelessness of further resistance is apparent to the world, before he will yield the contest. From all that I learn his army will fall to pieces."[1]

At the time of Lee's surrender, the rank-and-file soldiers and the civilian population of the Trans-Mississippi Department knew that the war was lost. Entire detachments, including their lower-ranking officers, had simply walked away and gone home to their families, where they were sorely needed for the spring planting. None looked upon these departures as desertions. Patriotic appeals from military and civil officers alike went unheeded. The cause was lost, and a great many of the soldiers who had bravely endured hardships during the war now adopted the rule of every man for himself. Confederate soldiers in Texas disbanded without orders, and as they had not received pay for months, they took whatever public property they could carry as payment for services rendered. It was impossible to maintain an army without supplies or rations. The description of the Confederacy in Texas was "disorder and confusion." All courier lines had been destroyed, the outposts were without rations, and all means of government transportation had been stolen. Military units still intact intended on deserting, and those that didn't disband became Home Guard units guarding against banditry. When Smith arrived at his headquarters in Houston, he was without an army to command.[2]

Under these dire prospects, the governors of the Trans-Mississippi Department urged Smith to surrender. Absent from this appeal was Missouri's governor; Thomas Reynolds had fled the country with Jo Shelby. Eventually, Smith informed the Federal officer conducting the surrender that, save for the Missourians and some Arkansas troops, his army was disbanded and the department was open to occupation.[3] Smith eventually surrendered the Trans-Mississippi Department to Gen. Edward R. S. Canby on May 26, 1865. On June 2, 1865, Smith boarded a Union frigate at Galveston and signed documents surrendering all remaining Confederate troops. When the last vestige of Confederate authority vanished, rumors circulated that those who had played any prominent part in the affairs of the state or the Confederacy would be punished. Many former Confederate officials panicked, and others declared they would not live under Yankee rule.

France had recently seized Mexico, and inasmuch as the United States, under the Monroe Doctrine, was opposed to French plans in connection to that seizure, the Federal government feared that France might join forces with the Confederacy and complicate the war. For this reason, many former Confederates thought of joining the French forces of Maximilian of Austria, who controlled Mexico. Jo Shelby took the remnants of his cavalry brigade—three thousand men—and marched into Mexico rather than surrender to Union forces. In return, the French-supported government of Emperor Maximilian offered land in Mexico. Protests by the Federal government eventually influenced the French to withdraw their support of Maximilian. When Shelby stood before the Austrian in Mexico City, he was told that his services could not be accepted. Shelby's men either joined the French army or drifted back home. Shelby himself remained in Mexico until 1867, when he returned and was later appointed U.S. marshal for the western district of Missouri, a post he held until his death in 1897.

Accompanying Shelby to Mexico was his former commander, Sterling Price. Price settled in Cordova, Mexico, where Maximilian granted him a tract of land. His plan to establish a colony of former Confederates failed after the fall of Maximilian's government. Price returned to Missouri in 1866; he died in St. Louis on September 29, 1867.

Many of the former guerrillas, like John Thrailkill and brothers Ike and Dick Berry, traveled with Shelby to Mexico. Thrailkill had been captured in Clinton County in July 1863 and imprisoned at the Myrtle Street prison, the Gratiot Street prison, and the Alton, Illinois, prison. In June 1864 he escaped and returned to Quantrill's command. Rather than take the oath of allegiance, Thrailkill proudly boasted, "I am not ashamed to say that I am a Rebel and if I am shot in the defense of my country I will die in a glorious cause. And if I live through, I will never be ashamed to own up to the fact that I have been in the Rebel ranks."[4]

Others also found their way to Mexico with Shelby, including Governor Thomas Reynolds and Missouri senators Trusten Polk and William M. Gwin and Gens. John Bankhead Magruder and John B. Clark, who had fought alongside Quantrill at the battle of Glasgow. Prominent Texans also went to Mexico, including governors Edward Clark and Pendleton Murrah. Within a few years, most of the former Confederates drifted back to Texas or to their former homes in Missouri.

JOHN NEWMAN EDWARDS observed, "Some Confederate soldiers dared not return home, and many guerrillas fled the country. It was dark everywhere, and the bravest held their breath, not knowing how much longer they would be permitted to remain peacefully at home, or suffered to enjoy the fruits of their labor."[5]

George Shepherd led a group of guerrillas to Texas in the winter of 1864/65, anad Archie Clements led the remnant of Anderson's command to the Lone Star State for the winter. Anxious to return to Missouri in the spring of 1865, Clements departed from Sherman in early March 1865 with a number of Anderson's men and ten guerrillas led by David Poole. They passed through Bonham and Marshall, stopping for a few days in Mount Pleasant, Arkansas. From Mount Pleasant they traveled north along the Arkansas border and Indian Territory, arriving in Missouri on April 14, where they learned of Lee's surrender. Clements and Poole discussed the possibility of surrender. There was much discussion of continuing a guerrilla war with the disbanded forces from the regular Confederate army. Most preferred a wait-and-see attitude. Some guerrillas refused to surrender and joined Shelby in Mexico. Those who wished to surrender knew they must do so to an official authority that they could trust in order to get honorable terms.

One group of guerrillas, including Archie Clements, Jesse Hamlet, Jesse James, Willis King, Jack Rupe, and John Vanmeter decided to surrender to Col. Chester Harding Jr. in Lexington, Missouri. They hoped to get favorable terms from Harding, who formerly had been given favorable terms himself from the Confederates when he surrendered at the battle of Glasgow the year before. Maj. J. B. Rogers, the provost marshal of Lexington, sent word to Clements to have his command ride into town by a certain day.

After officially surrendering to the Federal commander, an agreement was made that allowed them to keep their horses and sidearms. But upon leaving town under a flag of truce, the guerrillas were fired upon at point-blank range by an advance guard of eight Federal soldiers. The guerrillas returned fire, killing four Federals and wounding two. The main column of sixty cavalrymen of the Johnson County militia and the Second Wisconsin Cavalry followed up the attack and soon overtook the guerrillas. Vanmeter's horse was killed, and Jesse James was wounded, while the other guerrillas made their escape.

As a result of the Federals' duplicity, Archie Clements and James Anderson asked for more favorable surrender terms, stating that they needed extra protection and guarantees. A number of guerrillas who refused to surrender were shot down.

In Jackson County on April 21, David Poole rounded up 129 guerrillas from the hills of the Sni and Little Blue and surrendered. Harrison Trow noted, "A good many of my men surrendered with Dave Poole, while others planned to go to Old Mexico with me and not surrender at all." Trow said he was persuaded to surrender after being promised that he would be protected and allowed to keep his sidearms and horses.[6]

After assisting the Federal authorities in persuading the remaining guerrillas along the border to give up the fight, Poole and his two brothers, Dick and John, went back to Sherman, Texas, and started a cattle ranch. Poole returned to Jackson County, Missouri, in 1878 to marry; he and his wife went back to Texas. John Poole settled in Coleman County, Texas. He moved to Presidio County, Texas, in 1884. In his pension application to the state of Texas, Annie James, Frank James's wife, signed an affidavit certifying John Poole's wartime service. Dave and John's brother, Christopher Columbus Poole, served with Company E of the Ninth Texas Cavalry, Partisan Rangers, then transferred to Shelby's Missouri Cavalry until the war's end. Christopher also moved to Texas after the war and lived the rest of his life there.

Gen. James Spencer Rains had commanded the regiment William C. Quantrill had joined at the beginning of the war. Rains also settled in Texas, where he died on May 19, 1880.

A few of the guerrillas who accompanied Quantrill into Kentucky chose to remain there after the war. Seeking honorable terms of surrender, they tried to make the best of their lives. Donnie Pence and his brother Bud stayed in Kentucky after their surrender. Some say that Donnie Pence fell in love with one of the local girls from Samuel's Depot and later married her. He was originally from Clay County, Missouri. During the war he was wounded several times. Once he had been shot and pinned beneath his horse. As a hundred Federals were closing on him, Frank James appeared and rescued him. The two men remained close friends after this, and Frank often visited him after the war and stayed in his home. Frank was even credited with teaching Sunday school at the New Salem Baptist Church down the road from Samuel's Depot. In 1868, the Pence brothers built homes in Nelson County, near Samuel's Depot, and farmed the land. Donnie was elected sheriff in 1871 and remained in office until his death in 1896. His brother Bud served as his deputy. Donnie's neighbors remarked on his character: "He has never during his time of office had the slightest discrepancy in his accounts with the county or the auditors, but on the contrary has been the recipient of many letters from different heads of State departments and Circuit and County judges, praising him in high terms as a capable, efficient and prompt official. In social life he is kind, affable and at all times gentlemanly, and numbers among his friends people from all grades of society.[7]

The four Hall brothers—George, Isaac, Robert, and Tom—all rode with Quantrill into Kentucky. Isaac had joined Quantrill in May 1862 after Jayhawkers had burned down his house. The Hall brothers fought at Lawrence, Baxter Springs, and most of the notable battles under Quantrill. Robert was one of the first to join Quantrill's company; his name appears on Quantrill's muster roll under the date of July 6, 1862. The Hall brothers surrendered at

Samuel's Depot, and Isaac and Robert reportedly settled there after the war, becoming neighbors with Donnie and Bud Pence.

Allen Parmer was one of Quantrill's youngest recruits at the age of fourteen. He fought in several notable battles, including the Lawrence raid, the battle of Baxter Springs, the Fayette fight, and the battle at Centralia. He was wounded five times during the war. After being one of the last men to see Quantrill alive, Parmer surrendered at Bardstown, Kentucky, on July 26, 1865. While in Texas with Quantrill, Parmer had met and fallen in love with Susan Lavinia James, Frank and Jesse's sister. They were married on November 24, 1870. Parmer first settled in Grayson County but moved in 1873 to a seven-hundred-acre farm in Wichita Falls. Susan was one of the founders of the Wichita Falls Baptist Church and was listed as a respected church leader. Near the end of his life, Parmer moved to Alpine, Texas, and entered the railroad construction business, becoming the general manager of the J. Stone Land and Cattle Company. He could not escape his past, however, and he was unjustly arrested in Texas, charged with robbing a train as a member of the James gang, and jailed in Missouri. When the charges were proved false, he was released. In 1914 Parmer attended a reunion of Quantrill's men in Sherman hosted by Samuel Kimberlin, and in 1916 he attended a reunion hosted by Tuck Hill in McKinney. Parmer retired in 1920. He died in Alpine of a heart attack on October 27, 1927.[8]

Frank and Jesse James were frequent visitors in Sherman after the war. When Jesse married Zerelda "Zee" Mimms, the newlyweds honeymooned in Grayson County for six months with Susan and Allen Parmer. They also visited Dave Poole, who was living in town. Frank and Jesse also stayed with their cousin Tuck Hill in nearby McKinney.

Francis Marion "Tuck" Hill and his brother James "Woot" settled in McKinney and joined the First Christian Church, where Tuck became a deacon. The well-respected brothers raised livestock and traded mules. Tuck was a civic leader and a city councilman. They married the daughters of Albert Graves, a refugee from Cass County, Missouri, and attended many of the Quantrill reunions after the war. Tuck had been born in Kentucky in 1843, the fifth child of a family of thirteen. During the war, he had initially served for three months under Sterling Price before receiving an honorable discharge so he could join Quantrill's company. Brothers Tuck, Thomas, and Woot served as his lieutenants. Tom settled in Okmulgee, Oklahoma. Another brother, John, was killed during the war. The Hills were in a number of battles with Quantrill's company, including the Lawrence raid, the battle of Baxter Springs, the Fayette fight, the battle of Centralia, and the attack on Danville.

Tuck was described as an excellent horseman and an unerring marksman. It was said that, with his reins between his teeth and a pistol in each hand, he could shoot a ring around a tree. Tuck died in McKinney, Texas, on February 2, 1920.[9]

Lee McMurtry was a sergeant under Quantrill and was with the guerrilla leader in Kentucky. McMurtry took part in the Lawrence raid and numerous other battles and skirmishes with Quantrill's band. Born in Clay County, McMurtry had a ten-thousand-dollar reward on his head courtesy of the Federal government for his service with Quantrill's company. After the war, McMurtry moved to Wichita Falls, Texas, and became the county sheriff. Local citizens praised his work: "At Wichita Falls he made the best sheriff the country thereabouts had ever known. He was absolutely fearless and enforced the law to the letter." During the war, he once saved the life of Sen. Stephen B. Elkins, a schoolboy friend. Of his guerrilla service, McMurtry said, "The company was raised of fearless and daring men of the frontier who were accustomed to ride and shoot and was intended as a light horse attachment of the Confederate army. I fought under the Black Flag for two years and I tell you it's a mighty dangerous business."[10]

Another guerrilla who became a lawman after the war was Newton "Plunk" Murray. He joined Quantrill's company because he was too young to join the regular Confederate army. Like Alan Parmer, he was fourteen when he donned a guerrilla shirt. After the war he settled in Blanco County, Texas, and became a Texas Ranger.

Boone T. Muir was originally from the Brooking Township of Jackson County but moved to Texas after the war. In addition to riding with Quantrill, Muir was part of Jo Shelby's escort and accompanied him to Mexico after the war rather than surrender. Following the overthrow of Maximilian, Muir returned to Texas.

Another member of Quantrill's company to settle in Texas was John S. Kritser. Nineteen-year-old Kritser and his seventeen-year-old brother, Martin, were also from the Brooking Township. Their family were Unionists, but when war broke out, Federal horsemen rode up to the farm and demanded to be fed and have their horses cared for. While the brothers were leading the soldiers' horses from the barn, the soldiers began beating them with heavy leather straps and cursing them for being "damned Secesh." After this, John and Martin wanted no part of a blue uniform. They rode away from home to join the Confederates, both armed with double-barreled shotguns. John Kritser went to Mexico with Shelby and then returned to Texas. He died in Taylor.[11]

Harrison Trow rode with Quantrill for the entire war. He was credited with writing the much-publicized account *A True Story of Charles W. Quantrill and His Guerrilla Band,* in which he intimately describes the fights in which he participated, narrow escapes, and the stories of the James brothers and the Youngers when they were with Quantrill during the war. Trow identified Jesse James when he was killed at St. Joseph. He was also the last man to surrender in the state of Missouri. Trow died on February 24, 1925, in Hereford, Texas.

After Jim Younger was captured in Kentucky in April 1865, he was incarcerated in Lexington then transferred to the Louisville prison. Following his release, he returned home and tried to farm with his brother, but it was impossible to do so because, as Harrison Trow recalled, "Western Missouri was then full of disbanded Federal soldiers, organized squads of predatory Redlegs and Jayhawkers, horse thieves disguised as vigilance committees, and highway robbers known as law and order men."[12] Jim and Cole Younger left the country and headed for Texas, looking for a new home for their mother and younger siblings. In their absence, Federals raided the Younger home and abused Bursheba Fristoe Younger and her children, causing her emotional and physical trauma that led to her premature death. When the brothers returned, they took their mother and family to Texas to settle in Dallas County, where Jim became the deputy sheriff in 1870.

After his brother Bill's death, Jim Anderson gathered his surviving sisters and took them to Sherman. They were still suffering from wounds inflicted by the Jayhawkers who attempted to murder them when their prison building was undermined during the summer of 1863. Molly Anderson married after the Civil War and moved back to the Kansas City area. Jim Anderson allegedly killed Isaac Flanery, a nephew of George Shepherd, on April 12, 1866, near Rocheport, Missouri, in order to gain an inheritance that Flanery supposedly carried on him. Just as George Todd had married his brother's widow, Jim Anderson married his brother Bill's widow on October 21, 1868. Bush Smith married him under her legal name, Mary Erwin Anderson, and they resided in the same home on East Cherry Street that Bill had built for her in the spring of 1864. Bush's first child with Bill died in infancy, and with Jim, she bore a daughter, Jimmie Maude Anderson, on August 21, 1870. The daughter lived in Sherman for many years and was employed by Marks Brothers Dry Goods on North Travis Street. Her name was still in the city directory in 1926. Townspeople described her as "a popular, refined and highly respected sales lady who resided at the home until her death." She died at the age of ninety-six in 1966 in Dallas. Her obituary incorrectly lists her father as Bill Anderson.[13] Jim Anderson was slain sometime after November 1869 in Sherman. George Shepherd admitted to Harrison Trow that he killed Anderson in retaliation for the killing of Isaac Flanery.

After Jim Anderson's death, Mary Erwin Anderson married fifty-year-old Burrell P. Smith Jr., son of Sherman's first mayor, in 1872. They had a daughter whom they named Bush Smith; Bush was the maiden name of Burrell Smith Sr.'s wife. Records indicate that Mary Erwin Anderson Smith died sometime before 1918. The results of the Bushes' and Smiths' probate records show them to have prospered in Sherman.[14]

Another Quantrillian who settled near Texas after the war was John Rice Maupin. He moved to a house on the Red River at Colbert in the Chickasaw Nation. John was the son of John Harris Maupin and Margaret M. Thompson. He was born on September 15, 1843, at Nicholasville, Kentucky. His family settled at Westport, Missouri, in 1858. Maupin took part in most of the major battles along the border. In 1872, Benjamin Colbert rented out a half interest in his ferry across the Red River to Maupin. John's brother, William, also served in Quantrill's company, later joining his brother in 1880 in operating the ferry. They soon found that as southern immigration increased, one boat was not sufficient to do the work. So the brothers added another boat. Each vessel could carry six or seven two-horse wagons. Many notable individuals visited and stayed in their homes on their way to Texas. Frank and Jesse James were frequent visitors, and Frank worked for Maupin for two years in the early 1870s under the name Frank Rapp.[15] The Maupin brothers also owned a mercantile business offering groceries, dry goods, whiskey, and tobacco and also traded with the Indians for horses.

Many guerrillas decided to make the long trip to Texas. James Madison Bedicheck first met Quantrill when they fought together in the same division of the Missouri State Guard at the battle of Wilson's Creek. He later rode into Lawrence at Quantrill's side. After the war he moved to Texas and founded the Bedicheck Institute for Scientific and Literary Education. One of the earliest members of Quantrill's company was James A. Hendricks. He became the sheriff of Lewis and Clark County in Texas before moving to Montana, where he later died. The names of Michael Houx and his brother Robert appear on the July 16, 1862, roster of Quantrill's company, Both settled in Texas and later died in the city of Gordon. John S. Watson fought alongside Quantrill and as a major in the Missouri State Guard. He settled in Lamar County, just a few miles east of Quantrill's Mineral Springs camp in Grayson County. He died in Paris, Texas. The Marchbanks—Robert and

William—fought alongside Quantrill and settled just east of their old camp-site; Robert settled in Kiomatia and William in nearby Paris.

On August 24, 1865, former guerrilla Marcus Aurelius Ayres relocated to Kentuckytown, Texas. He built a new home with his wife, Mary K. Batsell, two and a half miles north of town, right next to the old camp. Ayres had been born on May 23, 1842, in Saline County, Missouri. He first joined Company D of Dorsey's Missouri Cavalry under Sterling Price and took part in the battle of Pea Ridge, where he was taken prisoner and discharged on August 26, 1863.[16] He then joined Quantrill's company. Ayres participate in the Lawrence raid and went south with Quantrill in the fall of 1863, during which he also took part in the battle of Baxter Springs. After settling in Kentuckytown, some Federals believed he had bought the land because gold was rumored to be hidden on it. As a result, his home was repeatedly burned. In 1870, Jesse James often stayed at Ayres's home.

Silas M. Gordon handled the funds for Quantrill's company. He remained in Grayson County after the war and operated a trading post close to the Mineral Springs camp that later developed into a town that was named after him—Gordonville. J. Frank Dalton settled in Granbury, Texas, just south of Fort Worth. He had been born in Goliad, Texas, on March 8, 1848. Dalton joined Quantrill on March 8, 1863, when he was fifteen years old. He died in Granbury on August 15, 1951. William Henry Ogden moved to Texas after the war and died in Wichita Falls in 1875. Guerrilla Jack Reinhardt also settled in Texas and was killed in 1874.

Another famous Missouri guerrilla chose Texas after the war due to harassment for his wartime service. Southern Missouri guerrilla leader Sam Hildebrand had a price on his head and was chased by Pinkerton detectives across Arkansas and Missouri before taking his family to Sherman. Richard Samuel Kimberlin and his four brothers joined Quantrill after their father was hanged in his barn and the barn burned down over him. They decided to remain in Texas. Kimberlin organized three Quantrill reunions: two in Sherman and Clarendon, Texas, and one in Chickasaw, Oklahoma.[17] Another guerrilla who chose to stay in Texas after the war was James Overton Hinde. He served in Todd's company with cousins Boone and George Scholl. He died on November 14, 1928.

After fighting in the most notable battles along the border, Jacob Franklin Gregg, Arthur McCoy, Benjamin Moore, James Poisal, John and Harvey Rupe, Bud Story, Daniel Vaughn, and Mack Wilson all moved to Texas. These former guerrillas sought desperately to settle down, get married, start families, and live in peace with their neighbors.

Quantrill's good friend Andy Walker went to Mexico with Shelby and stayed there for nineteen months before returning to Jackson County trying to resume farming. But old animosities and prejudices forced him to move to Texas. He attended the Quantrill reunions and died in Weatherford on February 26, 1911.

Jack Bishop stayed in Texas after the war, taking refuge in the Pecos River country, where he was often visited by the James brothers. The last living Confederate veteran in the United States was Walter Williams; he rode with Quantrill during the war and died in Houston, Texas, on December 19, 1959.

It took several years for the area of North Texas to return to normal after the war. Following the murder of George Butts, his wife, Sophia, went to live in Waco, and soon after the close of the war she married Judge James Porter. Porter was from Missouri and had served as an officer in the Confederate army. They returned to Glen Eden, and again this noted plantation became a social center, preserving the traditions of Southern hospitality. During the 1870s, Sophia and Porter built Glen Eden into a cotton and cattle empire. Historic Glen Eden lies now beneath the waters of present-day Lake Texoma; only a memory remains of the gracious hospitality that once was. After the war, Sophia converted to Christianity and joined a local church during a revival meeting held by Sherman's retired Methodist pastor Jacob Binkley. James Porter died on September 10, 1886; Sophia Suttenfield Aughinbaugh Coffee Butts Porter died at the age of eighty-one on August 27, 1897. She was buried beside Porter in a small cemetery at Glen Eden.

Epilogue

TEXAS ENDURED carpetbaggers and scalawags and discharged Union soldiers who were attracted by the prospect of taking over the land and property of former Confederate soldiers. Scalawags were Southerners who joined the most unscrupulous of the Northern carpetbaggers in pillaging state treasuries and acted as the pawns of the Radical Republicans in Congress. Resentment grew as Texans saw their state overrun by these opportunists. For several years after the war, former Confederates were barred from holding office by the Reconstruction Act. In order to check out a man's status, he was asked probing questions. Many asked any stranger they met, Where are you from? Where were you born? How long have you resided in the South?

Andrew Johnson instituted Lincoln's plan of reconstruction for the South, but its implementation drew sharp opposition from the Radical Republicans in Congress, who believed such lenient measures would simply restore the old planter aristocracy to power. As late as 1867, Congress declared that the Southern states were still in a state of rebellion. The South was divided into five military districts and occupied by Federal troops. Texas and Louisiana fell under the Fifth Military District, which was headed by Gen. Philip H. Sheridan.

Another restriction posed by the Reconstruction Act denied the right to vote to former Confederates; voters were required to take an "Ironclad Oath" by which they swore that they had never been involved in any activities against the Federal government. Under the iron fist of the Radical Republicans, Reconstruction policies were far more severe than Lincoln's design to rebuild the country. The Johnson administration disenfranchised all former military and civil leaders of the Confederacy and all who owned property worth more than twenty thousand dollars; in some instances, large estates were liable to confiscation. The president then appointed provisional governors for the states of the former Confederacy. Congress refused to seat senators and representatives from the Southern states whom they believed were not agreeable to their radical philosophy. By the end of 1865, every former Confederate state—except Texas—had reestablished its civil government.

In Texas, heavy taxes were assessed by the Reconstruction government. Former Confederates had only worthless Confederate script, so thousands of acres of their land were either sold or seized to pay the tax bill. Federal troops were stationed at Sherman and Bonham to enforce the orders of the Union occupation forces in the Lone Star State. Newly elected Governor James W. Throckmorton was removed from office, and a Reconstruction governor was appointed in his place. The government's action intensified the enmity between Southern sympathizers and Unionists. Anyone who tried to curry favor with the new administration was publicly condemned as a turncoat. But many of them were appointed to office, and they bore the label *scalawag* for the rest of their lives. Judges were displaced, sheriffs were ousted, new justices of the peace were appointed. In some counties, men refused to take office until they received a vote of confidence from their constituencies.

White Southerners resented their exclusion from the "healing" process that Lincoln had formerly called for. Texans saw the vanquished South as dominated by outsiders and uneducated freedmen and supported by corrupt state governments bought and paid for by unscrupulous carpetbaggers and scalawags. After the passing of some of the most strident abolitionists, proof of the Radicals' ill-conceived policies came to light with the revelations of wide-scale corruption. Reconstruction came to symbolize both misgovernment and a misguided attempt to use state power to lift up the lower classes of society.

In this environment, wartime rivalries festered long after the war was over. Disorder prevailed as social chaos and political hatreds rooted in wartime actions overcame the sensibilities of the people. Federal vigilantes, know as the Union League, continually harassed former Confederates. Provisional Governor Edmund J. Davis proclaimed Texas "a state filled with desperate characters intent on avenging those that had formerly opposed them."

One of these desperate characters in the eyes of the Federal authorities was Bob Lee, a captain in Nathan Bedford Forrest's cavalry, who returned to Texas after the war and then was driven from his home. He built a hideout in the timber of Wildcat Thicket. This thicket was a solid mass of undergrowth of trees, briar bushes, thorn vines, and thick grass. Unionist Lewis Peacock led the campaign against Lee and his followers. After evading the Federal vigilantes for several years, Lee was gunned down in 1869. His followers continued their feud until June 1871, when Peacock was killed and his gang left the county.[1]

After many years, Federal troops were finally withdrawn from the South. Texas was readmitted to the Union on March 30, 1870, but local civilian control was not fully reestablished until January 14, 1873. Not until 1874 did Democrats for the first time since the Civil War win control of the House of Representatives.

Who knows when the last chapter of the Civil War will be written? In 1975 full citizenship was finally restored to Robert E. Lee. The following year Sen. Mark Hatfield of Oregon introduced a resolution to reinstate Jefferson Davis's citizenship to right a "glaring injustice in the history of the United States." Hatfield quoted the words of Chief Justice Salmon P. Chase: "If you bring these leaders to trial, it will condemn the North, for by the Constitution secession is not rebellion. We cannot convict him of treason." In his memoirs, Davis declared that his purpose was to "keep the memory of our Southern heroes green, for they belong not to us alone: they belong to the whole country: they belong to America." On October 17, 1978, Hatfield's resolution passed unanimously by voice vote and was signed into law by President Jimmy Carter.[2]

And in Missouri, where the bodies of Confederate soldiers rest in Confederate cemeteries across the state, the flag they fought under to protect the guarantees of the Constitution is not tolerated. Even though the symbol of the Confederacy had flown over state property for decades, politicians bowed to political correctness in an effort to gain a handful of selected votes. Recent efforts have been made to mollify the situation. Where once state politicians pressured and manipulated government agencies to conform to their will, Missouri House Bill 999 prohibits state agencies from interfering in historic markers. Recent actions such as these make the quote by author T. S. Eliot even more poignant today: "The Civil War is not ended: I question whether any serious Civil War ever does end."

Appendix
Notes
Selected Bibliography
Index

Appendix

Provenance Used for Photographs

AS WITH any Civil War–era photographs that surface for first-time publication, questions arise as to their origin and authenticity. Photos that are found without provenance bring little remuneration or historical benefit. The most desired provenance occurs when the source is a family member. These can readily be identified and, when obtained by another party, can be easily authenticated.

Ideally, the most preferable provenance occurs when both the photo and subject are documented and the picture notarized from the day it was taken, as well as having a documented notarized ownership linage. One of the most reliable alternatives occurs when photos and their documentation remain within a single family and are passed down from member to member. Image collectors keep a keen eye out for photos that can be substantiated by actual provenance. When family origin is missing, provenance can be confirmed by antique appraisers or collectors whose experience justifies the demand for authenticity.

When comparing photos of the same subject, physical appearances may change when photos span a number of years. Collectors and appraisers look for an individual's features that do not change over time, such as the shapes of ears, eyes, eyebrows, or chin line. Does the subject have full or narrow lips, a wide or narrow nose? Do the ears have attached or unattached earlobes? All these help to identify a subject through other known images of the same person.

Besides looking at an individual in a photo or the photo's actual appearance, collectors make an exhaustive attempt to collect all information when purchasing images. Also important is whether a photograph is identified on the front or back or bears the photographer's name or the date in period ink. Authentic stamping on the photos helps to document provenance. Though not needed for most photos, documentation of provenance can be important for expensive photos or photos where ownership is an integral part of its value. Important provenance can increase a photograph's value.

Provenance does of itself authenticate a photograph, but it can be an integral part of authentication. Other factors include whether a photo looks authentic, appears to be the right age, bears the correct stamping, and an authority agrees that it looks authentic or that it was sold by a credible dealer or appeared in a reputable auction. When photos are purchased at auction, expert collectors maintain all receipts and postal confirmation, which also gives provenance accreditation.

If there is no stamping or other identification marks, provenance might be essential in order to identify the photo's issuer and photographer. A practical example of good provenance might involve purchasing a rare or obscure photo from a respected and well-known dealer. This would be a first step in making your own provenance. The fact that a top dealer believes the photo to be genuine is significant. Saving the receipt or other documentation of sale will help if you resell the photo. In this way, you will have documentation that it came from a reliable source.

Documentation of provenance can include sales receipts, letters about ownership and history, magazine and newspaper articles, auction catalogs, and similar documents. Provenance can include an expert's letter of authenticity or other testimony about the item's identity. The best way to maintain provenance when purchasing a photo from an individual or collector is to keep the mailing envelope with the seller's name and address.

Collectors as well as historians need a critical eye since most individuals argue that their photographs are authentic. So experts must discern period objects and dress to ensure they are genuine. Books, magazines, and Web sites are full of bogus images to satisfy self-interests. Collectors often limit their purchases to those they know to be honest. When an object is traded between collectors, this is another step toward establishing provenance.

The photos used in *Quantrill in Texas* were all donated by reputable sources. The photo of Marcus Gill was obtained from Byron Shutz, Gill's maternal great-great grandson. The photos of Joel Bryan Mayes, Benjamin and Henry E. McCulloch, Daniel McIntosh, Douglas H. Cooper, Johnny Fry, Sophia Butts and husband, and Kate Clarke King were obtained from university archives, county historical societies, and museums.

The 1865 photo of Robert S. Stevens was obtained from his grandson, Robert C. Stevens of New York. The photo of James B. Pond was obtained from his grandson, James B. Pond III.

The photo of Charles Jennison and the carpetbagger photograph came from the Greg Walter collection. Walters obtained his collection from his late brother, a collection of more than 450 Civil War–era carte de visites and daguerreotypes. Walter's brother purchased many of these images from a prominent San Diego collector and dealer in the late 1970s, including an album with about 46 carte de visites of Kansas cavalry during the Civil War. The photograph of Charles Jennison is by Scholten Photographer of St. Louis, Missouri. The Jennison photograph was included in the album obtained from a family member of the paymaster with the Kansas Volunteer Cavalry.

The postwar photo of Dave Poole from the Emory Cantey collection came from a prominent collector in Missouri who found it in an album belonging to the Hudspeth family, whose members also served with Quantrill. The image was identified in the album as Dave Poole. It was purchased for the Cantey collection with a documenting letter. Also included in Cantey's collection is a photograph of guerrilla Riley Crawford. The Crawford photograph came from a Kansas collector who wishes to remain anonymous; it was purchased from the Crawford family in the 1940s and is identified on the back "For Mother, Riley Crawford." Many years later it was purchased by well-known collector and dealer Rick Mack, who sold it to Cantey with a documenting letter. The photographs of Tom, Tuck, and Woot Hill also comes from the Cantey collection directly from the Hill family in the late 1940s. All three carte de visites were possibly made 1865/66. They were purchased by a collector who many years later sold them to Rick Mack. Each image is identified in period ink on the front and back. Mack sold them to the Cantey collection and included a documenting letter.

The photograph of Payne Jones in the Cantey collection also came from the collection of Rick Mack. It was subsequently identified by Jones's great-nephew as identical to one in the family's possession. It is identified in period ink in the case as "A Missouri Ruffian." It was sold by Mack to the Cantey collection. The photo of Bill Anderson in the Cantey collection came from an elderly collector who wishes to remain anonymous. It was purchased between 1940 and 1950 from descendants of Molly Anderson, Bill Anderson's sister. Molly Anderson married after the Civil War and lived in the Kansas City, Missouri, area. It is a tintype with a contemporary identification on the front and back and dated 1864. Years later it was sold to Rick Mack, who later sold it to the Cantey collection with a documenting letter. The photograph of Jim Anderson mounted in a mourning pin in the Cantey collection also came from the same source. The mourning pin was worn by Molly Anderson after Jim's death in 1869.

The photograph of Sylvester Akers and John Barnhill in the Cantey collection came from the Rick Mack collection and was subsequently sold to the Cantey collection with a documenting letter. The image has a contemporary identification on the back: "Vess Akers and Barnhill, Quant KY 1865." The photograph of guerrilla Bob Thompson in the Cantey collection came from a collector in Kansas who wishes to remain anonymous; the image was purchased in the early 1940s from the Thompson family. It is identified in period ink inside the case. Years later the image was purchased by Rick Mack, who subsequently sold it to the Cantey collection with a documenting letter. The photograph of Nate Teague in the Cantey collection came from the Mack collection via a reputable Missouri dealer. It is identified in period ink on the front of the image. It was subsequently sold to the Cantey collection with a documenting letter. The photograph of Jesse Hamlet in the Cantey collection came from an elderly collector who wished to remain anonymous; the image was purchased from the Hamlet family in the 1940s. It is identified in period ink inside the case. It was purchased by Rick Mack and later sold to the Cantey collection with a documenting letter.

The circa 1861 ambrotype of Frank James is the earliest and only known photograph of Frank as a Quantrill guerrilla. It was purchased from the James family in Missouri in the early 1940s by a collector who wishes to remain anonymous. He was a friend of Robert James when Robert lived on the James farm in Kearney, Missouri. The image is identified in period ink inside the case "Frank James, Carney, Mo." Years later it was purchased by Rick Mack, who sold it to the Cantey collection. The photo of Frank James and John Jarrette was discovered by a Missouri dealer recently in Missouri; it was purchased by Rick Mack and sold to the Cantey collection. It is identified in period ink on the back of the tintype. Oll Shepherd is a carte de visite found in an early family album along with another image of Shepherd taken in 1867. Both images were identified in period ink under each image in the original album. They were purchased by Rick Mack and later sold to Emory Cantey. The image of Hi and Hicks George is an ambrotype discovered fully cased by a dealer several years ago in Missouri. The identification came from comparison with other images of both men. It was formerly in the Rick Mack collection then sold to Emory Cantey. The Jim Cummins tintype, circa 1865–70, was found in an early family album along with a carte de visite of Cummins. Both images were identified in the album and identified on the images as well. The image of Cummins used in this book has contemporary handwriting just to the right of Cummins's arm holding his hat. It was in the Rick Mack collection and was later sold to Emory Cantey.

The photograph of guerrilla George Scholl and the pistol used by him and his brother Boone that was given to Boone by William Clarke Quantrill came from Claiborne Scholl Nappier, great-grandson of George Scholl. George Scholl gave the pistol to his son Charles Scholl on his twenty-first birthday while they were attending a Quantrill reunion in Independence, Missouri. Charles kept the pistol and all of his Quantrill memorabilia until his death in 1965. At that time Charles's wife gave the items to her daughter, Shirley Ann Scholl Nappier, who in turn passed them on to her son, Claiborne Scholl Nappier.

The photograph of Lee McMurtry, his brother, and Dick Poole was obtained from a defunct Texas museum that had obtained the photo from the McMurtry family before it was acquired by collector Patrick Marquis.

Notes

Full bibliographical data may be found in the Selected Bibliography.

CHAPTER 1: THE TRIP SOUTH

1. Eakin and Hale, *Branded as Rebels*, 447–48.
2. *Blue and Grey Chronicle* 6, no. 1 (October 2002): 1.
3. Eakin, *Recollections of Quantrill's Guerrillas*, 9.
4. *Kansas City Times*, May 12, 1872.
5. Palmer, "The Time of Quantrill and the Jayhawkers," 31.
6. Trow, *Quantrell*, 118.
7. Eakin, *Recollections of Quantrill's Guerrillas*, 9.
8. Byron Shutz (great-great-grandson of Marcus Gill) to Paul R. Petersen, January 25, 2004.
9. Rankin, *Texas in 1850*; Lucas Collection, Sherman Public Library, Sherman, TX (hereafter cited as Lucas Collection).
10. Bonnewitz and Allen, *Raytown Remembers*, 2.
11. Eakin, *Recollections of Quantrill's Guerrillas*, 9–10.
12. Bonnewitz and Allen, *Raytown Remembers*, 1–2.
13. Lucas and Hall, *History of Grayson County*, 154.
14. *The Old West* (New York: Time, 1974), 142–43.
15. Rogers to Jesup, October 1, 1844, Quartermaster General files, "Hall of Records," bk. 25, 6.
16. Hoffman and Hoffman, "The McKee's Move to Texas," 296.
17. Attributed to Philip H. Sheridan, commander, Fifth District, 1867.
18. Gunn, *First United Methodist Church, Sherman*; Lucas Collection.
19. Lucas Collection.
20. Grayson County Historical Commission, Selected Papers, vol. 7, 114.
21. Lucas Collection, box 4, file 78; *Frontier Times*, 22, no. 9 (June 1945): 258–62.

22. Lucas Collection, box 4, file 78.

23. Hefen, *Overland Mail.*

24. Grayson County Historical Commission, Selected Papers, vol. 7, 108.

25. Ibid., vol. 7, 109–10.

26. Masterson, *Katy Railroad,* 165; Gunn, *First United Methodist Church, Sherman;* Lucas Collection, box 5, file 140; *Frontier Times,* 22, no. 9 (June 1945): 258–62.

27. Pickering and Falls, *Brush Men and Vigilantes.*

28. Lucas and Hall, *History of Grayson County,* 97–98.

29. Boswell, *Quantrill's Raiders in Texas,* 8.

30. Lucas and Hall, *History of Grayson County,* 94.

31. Ibid., 98.

32. Ibid., 100; Henry Vaden, Lucas Papers, Sherman Public Library.

33. *Early Military Forts and Posts in Oklahoma,* transcribed by Sandi Carter and Marlene Clark; Ware, "Indian Territory," 104; U.S. War Department, *The War of the Rebellion,* ser. 4, vol. 1, 360 (hereafter referred to as *OR*).

34. Bevier, *First and Second Missouri Confederate Brigades,* 317; Castel, *Price and the Civil War in the West,* 34.

35. Heidler, "'Embarrassing Situation,'" 48.

36. Lucas and Hall, *History of Grayson County,* 108; Lucas Collection, box 5, file 140.

37. *Dallas Herald,* July 10, 1861.

38. Landrum and Smith, *Illustrated History of Grayson County,* 68.

39. *OR,* ser. 4, vol. 1, 785.

40. National Historical Company, *History of Clay and Platte County,* 195–99.

41. Moore, *Missouri in the Civil War,* chap. 4.

42. Bevier, *First and Second Missouri Confederate Brigades,* 317; Castel, *Price and the Civil War in the West,* 34.

43. Eakin, *Recollections of Quantrill's Guerrillas,* 10.

44. Anderson, "General Stand Watie."

45. *OR,* ser. 3, 611.

46. Ibid., ser. 3, 745.

47. Ibid.

48. Ibid.

49. Edwards, *Noted Guerrillas,* 51.

50. Snead, *Fight for Missouri,* 293–94.

51. McCulloch to Walker; C. F. Jackson to Sterling Price, August 10, 1861, *OR,* ser. 3, vol. 53, 612, 721–23.

52. *Daily Southern Crisis,* March 3, 1863.

53. *Liberty Weekly Tribune,* September 13, 1861.

54. *OR,* ser. 3, 720; Snead, "The First Year of the War in Missouri," 273–74; Snyder, "Capture of Lexington," 8–9.

55. Jones, *Rebel War Clerk's Diary,* 2:14.

56. Bailey, *Between the Enemy and Texas,* 146.

CHAPTER 2: MEN OF VALOR

1. OR, ser. 1, vol. 8, 57.
2. Edwards, *Shelby and His Men*, 338–39; George, *The Georges*, 2:465–66, Jackson County Historical Society, Independence, MO.
3. George, *The Georges*, 3:786–95.
4. Ibid.
5. *Kansas City Times*, July 15, 1935.
6. Maddox, *Hard Trials and Tribulations*, 9.
7. *Kansas City Times*, September 30, 1941.
8. George, *The Georges*.
9. OR, ser. 1, vol. 8, 611–12.
10. *Leavenworth (KS) Conservative*, March 28, 1862.
11. Elvira Ascenith Weir Scott, Diary, 1860–1887, Western Historical Manuscript Collection, University of Missouri, Columbia.
12. *Kansas State Historical Society* 11 (1909–10): 284.
13. *St. Louis Republican*, July 12, 1862.
14. *Oak Grove Banner*, October 8, 1898.
15. George, *The Georges*, 3:735.
16. McCain Library and Archives, University of Southern Mississippi, M243, box 1, folder 22.
17. Appler, *Younger Brothers*, 102–4.
18. Norton, *Behind Enemy Lines*, 80; General Orders no. 19, July 1862, OR, ser. 1, vol. 13, 506; Castel, *Quantrill*, 87.
19. *Lee's Summit Journal*, February 2, 1900.
20. George, *The Georges*, 3:765.
21. Lucas Collection.
22. OR, ser. 1, vol. 8, 46.
23. McCorkle, *Three Years with Quantrill*, 66.
24. OR, ser. 1, vol. 13, pt. 1, 782.
25. William Gregg Manuscript, Western Historical Manuscript Collection, University of Missouri, Kansas City.
26. Ibid.
27. OR, ser. 1, vol. 13, pt. 1, 782.
28. Van Gilder, *Story of Barton County*, 11.
29. *Dallas Herald*, October 4, 1862.
30. Trow, *Quantrell*, 103–4.
31. McCorkle, *Three Years with Quantrill*, 66; Trow, *Quantrell*, 103–4.
32. National Archives, microfilm M322, roll 193.
33. George, *The Georges*, vol. 3.
34. National Archives, microfilm M322, roll 193.
35. Lucas Collection.

36. Grayson County Historical Commission, Selected Papers, vol. 4; David Chumbley, *Kentuckytown History*, Lucas Collection.

37. Millennial Harbinger 13:238, Bethany, Virginia.

38. Kentuckytown Baptist Church Records, 81, Lucas Collection; *Sherman Democrat*, July 4, 1876; Chumbley, *Kentucky Town and Its Baptist Church; Handbook of Texas Online*.

39. Kentuckytown Baptist Church Records, 75; Lucas Collection.

40. Pickering and Falls, *Brush Men and Vigilantes*.

41. Burns, "Illinois, the Railroads, and the Civil War."

42. Rhodes, *History of the Civil War*.

43. *Missouri Historical Review*, 58:37–47.

44. Jones, *Rebel War Clerk's Diary*, 1:200, 2:16.

45. Ibid., 1:191.

46. OR, ser. 3, 729–30.

47. *Washington (AR) Telegraph*, January 15, 1862.

48. Jones, *Rebel War Clerk's Diary*, 1:182.

49. Trow, *Quantrell*, 29.

50. McCorkle, *Three Years with Quantrill*, 76.

51. *Liberty (MO) Advance*, April 1, 1910, quoting the *Lexington News*.

52. Young, *Confederate Wizards of the Saddle*, 549.

53. National Archives, microfilm M322, roll 193.

54. U.S. War Department, *Organization and Status of Missouri Troops*, 308; Connelley, *Quantrill and the Border Wars*, 281.

55. OR, ser. 1, vol. 22, pt. 1, 45–47.

56. *Sherman Herald-Democrat*, May 6, 2001.

57. *Independence Examiner*, September 30, 1927; Edwards, *Noted Guerrillas*, 161; United Daughters of the Confederacy, *Reminiscences of the Women of Missouri*, 249.

58. Woodson, *History of Clay County*, 130–31.

59. McCorkle, *Three Years with Quantrill*, 77.

60. *Oak Grove (AR) Banner*, December 21, 1906.

61. Edwards, *Shelby and His Men*, 118.

62. McCorkle, *Three Years with Quantrill*, 84–85.

63. *Daily Southern Crisis*, March 19, 1863, Jackson, MS.

64. Trow, *Quantrell*, 105.

65. Lucas Collection.

66. Edwards, *Noted Guerrillas*, 159.

67. Trow, *Quantrell*, 122–23.

68. Ibid., 107.

69. Ibid., 121.

70. Eakin, *Recollections of Quantrill's Guerrillas*, 49.

71. Ibid., 50.

72. Frank Smith MS, author's collection, hereafter cited as Frank Smith MS.

73. Trow, *Quantrell*, 193.
74. Jacob Hall Family Papers, Jackson County Historical Society, Independence, MO; United Daughters of the Confederacy, *Reminiscences of the Women of Missouri*.
75. Frank Smith MS.
76. Jacob Hall Family Papers, Jackson County Historical Society, Independence, MO.
77. Frank Smith MS.
78. Trow, *Quantrell*, 139, 141.
79. *Confederate Veteran*, 18 (June 1910): 279.
80. Mansfield, *History of Tuscarawas County*, 463–64.
81. William Gregg Manuscript, Western Historical Manuscript Collection, University of Missouri, Columbia.
82. McCain Library and Archives, University of Southern Mississippi, M243, box 1, folder 22.
83. Jacob Hall Family Papers, Jackson County Historical Society, Independence, MO.
84. Trow, *Quantrell*, 125–27.
85. Ibid., 171.
86. Ibid., 127–28.
87. Castel, *Frontier State at War*, 83.
88. Trow, *Quantrell*, 132–34; William Gregg Manuscript, Western Historical Manuscript Collection, University of Missouri, Columbia; Woodson, *History of Clay County*, 132–33.
89. Missouri Historical Company, *History of Saline County*, 314.
90. Edwards, *Noted Guerrillas*, 169–70.
91. Charles Scholl letter (son of George T. Scholl), Emory Cantey Historical Archives Collection.

Chapter 3: One Man with Courage

1. OR, ser.1, vol. 13, 455.
2. *St. Louis Republican*, September 1863; Jones, *Rebel War Clerk's Diary*, 2:68.
3. Jones, *Rebel War Clerk's Diary*, 2:25.
4. *Confederate Veteran*, 18 (June 1910): 278–79.
5. Woodson, *History of Clay County*, 134.
6. *Confederate Veteran*, 18 (October 1910): 472–73.
7. Mansfield, *History of Tuscarawas County*, 463–64.
8. Ewing to Schofield in OR, ser. 1, vol. 22, pt. 1, 584.
9. *Liberty (MO) Advance*, April 1, 1910, quoting the *Lexington News*.
10. George Caleb Bingham to editor of *Missouri Republican*, February 22, 1877.
11. Thruston, *Echoes of the Past*, 275.
12. Voss, "Town Growth in Central Missouri," 199–200.
13. Cave, "Biography of Benjamin Potter," 44–55.
14. *St. Louis Republican*, September 1863; Jones, *Rebel War Clerk's Diary*, 2:68–69.

15. Cave, "Biography of Benjamin Potter," 54.

16. Missouri Historical Company, *History of Saline County*.

17. Jacob Hall Family Papers, Jackson County Historical Society, Independence, MO.

18. *Missouri Republican*, February 22, 1877.

19. *OR*, ser. 1, vol. 22, pt. 2, 525, 619.

20. *Kansas Historical Collection* 13 (1913–14): 448.

21. Trow, *Quantrell*, 158, 167.

22. National Archives Microfilm Records; Eakin and Hale, *Branded as Rebels*, 279.

23. Frank Smith MS.

24. Hiram George to William Elsey Connelley, McCain Library and Archives, University of Southern Mississippi, M243, box 1, folder 22.

25. George, *The Georges*, vol. 3; McCain Library and Archives, University of Southern Mississippi, M243, box 1, folder 28.

26. Frank Smith MS.

27. *History of Vernon County, Missouri*, 392.

28. *OR*, ser. 1, vol. 22, pt. 2.

29. *OR*, vol. 34, pt. 4, 315; William A. Hall, letter, June 11, 1864, box 5, Schofield transcription; Wood, "Truman," 214.

30. Eakin, *Recollections of Quantrill's Guerrillas*, 78; *(Houston) Tri-Weekly Telegraph*, January 20, 1864; Frank Smith MS.

31. *(Houston) Tri-Weekly Telegraph*, January 20, 1864.

32. *OR*, ser. 1, vol. 22, pt. 1, 688.

33. McCorkle, *Three Years with Quantrill*, 140.

34. Lindberg and Matthews, "'It Haunts Me Night and Day,'" 42–53; Robert Schauffler, "Biographical Notes on Captain William Sloan Tough," Kansas State Historical Society, Topeka.

35. Eakin, *Recollections of Quantrill's Guerrillas*, 78.

36. *OR*, ser. 1, vol. 22, pt. 1, 696.

37. *OR*, ser. 2, vol. 4, pt. 1, 721–22.

38. *OR*, ser. 1, vol. 22, pt. 1, 692.

39. Connelley, *Quantrill and the Border Wars*, 430.

40. *Louisville Post*, April 2, 1897.

41. Frank Smith MS.

42. *OR*, ser. 1, vol. 22, pt. 1, 699.

43. *Oak Grove Banner*, October 8, 1898.

44. Connelley, *Quantrill and the Border Wars*, 427.

45. *Freedom's Champion*, October 22, 1863; A. C. Ellithorpe, Papers, Kansas State Historical Society, Topeka.

46. *OR*, ser. 1, vol. 22, pt. 1, 689–91.

47. Jesse Smith, Co. I, Third Wisconsin Cavalry, January 26, 1866, Amnesty Files, Washington DC.

48. Frank Smith MS.

49. McCorkle, *Three Years with Quantrill*, 95; Eakin, *Recollections of Quantrill's Guerrillas*, 79; OR, ser. 1, vol. 22, pt. 1, 689.

50. Patsy Berryman in Baker and Baker, *WPA Oklahoma Slave Narratives*, 315.

51. Hicks, "Diary of Hanny Hicks."

52. Titchenal, *Titchenal Saga*, 241; chap. 16, vol. 1, sec. 1; Eakin, *Recollections of Quantrill's Guerrillas*, 79.

53. McCorkle, *Three Years with Quantrill*, 96.

54. Eakin, *Recollections of Quantrill's Guerrillas*, 80.

55. Ibid.

56. OR, ser. 1, vol. 22, pt. 1, 700–701.

57. OR, ser. 1, vol. 22, pt. 2, 1045–46.

58. OR, Report of Maj. Gen. James G. Blunt, U.S. Army, Headquarters District of the Frontier, Fort Scott, Kansas, October 1863; Boswell, *Quantrill's Raiders in Texas*, 27.

59. Jones, *Rebel War Clerk's Diary*, 2:75.

60. OR, ser. 1, vol. 53, 908; vol. 26, pt. 2, 339–40; *Kansas City Western Journal of Commerce*, September 26, 1863, quoting *Richmond Examiner*.

61. OR, ser. 1, vol. 22, pt. 2, 715.

62. U.S. War Department, United States, *Organization and Status of Missouri Troops*, 312.

63. OR, ser. 1, vol. 22, pt. 2, 715.

64. Chumbley, *Kentucky Town and Its Baptist Church*, 66, Sherman Public Library, Sherman, TX.

65. *Daily Southern Crisis*, January 6, 1863.

CHAPTER 4: PROUD TO BE A SOLDIER

1. E. F. Jones, "Early Days in Texas History," Lucas Collection, file 101–102, Sherman Public Library, Sherman, TX.

2. Farber, *Fort Worth in the Civil War*, 88.

3. Lucas and Hall, *History of Grayson County*, 115–16; Gallaway, *Texas, the Dark Corner of the Confederacy*, 110.

4. Landrum and Smith, *Illustrated History of Grayson County*, 66.

5. Lucas and Hall, *History of Grayson County*, 123.

6. Lucas Collection, box 6, file 149, Sherman Public Library, Sherman, TX.

7. *(Houston) Tri-Weekly Telegraph*, December 30, 1863.

8. Gunn, *First United Methodist Church, Sherman*.

9. Lucas Collection, box 4, file 101, Sherman Public Library, Sherman, TX.

10. Lucas Collection.

11. *Houston Daily Telegraph*, February 22, 1864.

12. Lucas and Hall, *History of Grayson County*; Steele, "Jesse James," 12–14.

13. "Quantrill, James Brothers Used Early Colbert Ferry," Lucas Collection, Sherman Public Library, Sherman, TX.

14. Bonnewitz and Allen, *Raytown Remembers*, 7–8.
15. Lucas Collection, Sherman Public Library, Sherman, TX.
16. Farber, *Fort Worth in the Civil War*, 27; newspaper clipping, June 29, 1924, Lucas Collection Sherman Public Library, Sherman, TX.
17. McCorkle, *Three Years with Quantrill*, 97.
18. Frank Smith MS.
19. *Dallas Morning News*, October 31, 1926.
20. Grayson County Frontier Village, *History of Grayson County*, 1:51.
21. Hefan, *Overland Mail*.
22. Lucas and Hall, *History of Grayson County*, 89–90.
23. Titchenal, *Titchenal Saga*, vol. 1, chap. 16, sec. 1, 241.
24. *Sherman Weekly Journal*, July 11, 1861; Gunn, *First United Methodist Church, Sherman*.
25. Gunn, *First United Methodist Church, Sherman*.
26. Lucas and Hall, *History of Grayson County*, 108–9.
27. White, *Red River Valley*.
28. Landrum and Smith, *Illustrated History of Grayson County*, 66.
29. Lucas and Hall, *History of Grayson County*, 108–9.
30. Lucas Collection, box 3, file 32, Sherman Public Library, Sherman, TX.
31. Frank Smith MS.
32. Eakin, "Will the Real Jim Crow Chiles Please Stand Up?"
33. Richard Lawrence Miller, "Truman: The Rise to Power," Truman Library Archives, Independence, MO; Joanne Chiles Eakin and Betty Strong House (great-granddaughter of Jim Crow Chiles), "Walter Chiles of Jamestown," in Eakin, *Tears and Turmoil*, 52–55.
34. Eakin, "Will the Real Jim Crow Chiles Please Stand Up?"
35. *Kansas City Star*, May 12, 1929; Larkin, *Bingham*, 210; Lew Larkin, "Bingham: Fighting Artist," *Blue and Grey Chronicle* 7, no. 4 (April 2004): 10–12; *Dallas Herald*, January 26, 1865.
36. *Sherman Daily Democrat*, 7, col 1–6, 1937; Lucas Collection.
37. *The Texas Public Employee*, August-September 1967, 13.
38. *Dallas Morning News*, April 11, 1942; Lucas Collection.
39. Lucas Collection.
40. *Sherman Democrat*, February 6, 1994.
41. *Dallas News*, January 11, 1920; Lucas Collection.
42. Lucas Collection; "Frontier Story of Romance and Tragedy in Life of Sophia Coffee," Newspaper Collection, various articles, n.d., Glen Eden, Sherman Public Library.
43. *Denison Herald*, August 24, 1979; *Dallas Morning News*, April 1, 1942.
44. *The Texas Public Employee*, August-September 1967, 13.
45. Lucas Collection; *Dallas Morning News*, April 11, 1942.
46. *Dallas Morning News*, April 11, 1942.

47. *Biographical Souvenir of the States of Georgia and Florida.*

48. *Denison (TX) Herald,* August 24, 1979; Lea Ellen Lawlis, "Memories of Glen Eden Recalled," Lucas Collection.

49. *Northern Standard,* Clarksville, Texas, October 10, 1846.

50. *(Van Buren) Arkansas Intelligencer,* November 28, 1846.

51. Lucas Collection.

52. E. S. C. Robertson to Mary Robertson, October 24, 1863, Sutherland Collection, Department of Special Collections, University of Texas at Arlington Library.

53. Newspaper clipping, August 21, 1920, Lucas Collection.

54. OR, ser. 1, vol. 26, pt. 2, 348.

55. Thomas A. Coleman to parents, April 23, 1862, in Thomas A. Coleman Letters, Missouri State Historical Society, Columbia.

56. Sylvester Akers to William E. Connelley, McCain Library and Archives, University of Southern Mississippi, M243, box 1, folder 22.

57. Ford, *Rip Ford's Texas,* 332–33; Wooster, *Texas and Texans in the Civil War,* 116.

58. OR, ser. 1, vol. 26, pt. 2, 382.

59. Lucas Collection.

60. OR, ser. 1, vol. 26, pt. 2, 383.

61. *Clarksville (TX) Standard,* October 10, 1863.

62. McCulloch to E. P. Turner, January 6, 1864, OR, ser. 1, vol. 53, 923–25; McCulloch to J. B. Magruder, January 23, 1864, OR, ser. 1, vol. 34, pt. 2, 909.

63. OR, ser. 1, vol. 26, pt. 2, 383.

64. OR, ser. 1, vol. 26, pt. 2, 401.

65. OR, ser. 1, vol. 26, pt. 2, 430.

66. OR, ser. 1, vol. 22, pt. 2, 1072–73.

67. Hall and Hall, *Collin County,* 296.

68. Evault Boswell, "The Disintegration of Quantrill's Raiders and Its Effect on Grayson County of Texas in 1863–1864," East Texas Historical Association, Fort Worth, February 1, 2001, 5; Lucas Collection.

69. Sylvester Akers to William E. Connelley, McCain Library and Archives, University of Southern Mississippi, M243, box 1, folder 22.

70. Lucas Collection, book 4, box 101.

71. OR, ser. 1, vol. 26, 526.

72. Lucas and Hall, *History of Grayson County,* 129; Boswell, *Quantrill's Raiders in Texas,* 89; Tony Swindell Archives Collection, Sherman, TX.

73. McCorkle, *Three Years with Quantrill,* 97.

74. Lucas Collection.

75. *Sherman Herald-Democrat,* May 6, 2001.

76. Mary E. Davidson, "Cedar Mills, Texas History," 51, cited in Grayson County Frontier Village, *History of Grayson County.*

77. Frank Smith MS.

78. *Dallas Morning News,* April 11, 1942; *Sherman Daily Democrat,* 1937.

79. W. L. Potter to W. W. Scott, in Connelley, *Quantrill and the Border Wars*, 440–45.
80. Frank Smith MS.
81. Lucas and Hall, *History of Grayson County*.
82. McCorkle, *Three Years with Quantrill*, 97; Lucas Collection.

CHAPTER 5: TROUBLED WATERS

1. Frank Smith MS.
2. Lucas and Hall, *History of Grayson County*, 118–21; Landrum and Smith, *Illustrated History of Grayson County*, 67; Anderson, *History and Business Guide of Sherman and Grayson Co.*, 11; "Quantrill, James Brothers Used Early Colbert Ferry," Lucas Collection.
3. Hall and Hall, *Collin County*, 296; Martha Hill Davis (great-great-granddaughter of Woot Hill) to Paul Petersen.
4. Sylvester Akers, interview with William E. Connelley, August 20–21, 1909, McCain Library and Archives, University of Southern Mississippi, M243, box 1, folder 22.
5. Gallaway, *Texas, the Dark Corner of the Confederacy*, 153.
6. Hall and Hall, *Collin County*, 296.
7. OR, ser. 1, vol. 22, pt. 2, 1081; OR, ser. 1, vol. 48, pt. 1, 1311.
8. Eakin, *Recollections of Quantrill's Guerrillas*, 80–81.
9. Frank Smith MS.
10. E. T. Jones, February 24, 1934, Lucas Collection.
11. Frank Smith MS.
12. Lucas Collection.
13. Van Leer Papers, Chester County Historical Society, Philadelphia, PA.
14. Jones, *Rebel War Clerk's Diary*, 2:418.
15. Gallaway, *Texas, the Dark Corner of the Confederacy*, 57.
16. Farber, *Fort Worth in the Civil War*, 28–39.
17. Lucas Collection.
18. Jones, *Rebel War Clerk's Diary*, 2:418.
19. Kentuckytown Baptist Church Records, 83, Lucas Collection.
20. Lucas Collection, Sherman Public Library, Sherman, TX.
21. James J. Frazier to R. F. Frazier, December 5, 1861, Frazier Family Papers; journal entry of Henry Orr, October 1861, in Anderson, *Campaigning with Parson's Brigade*, 8.
22. Thomas O. Moore to George W. Randolph, July 8, 1862, OR, vol. 15, 773–74.
23. OR, ser. 1, vol. 34, pt. 2, 936; Lucas Collection.
24. Lucas Collection.
25. Lucas Collection; Landrum and Smith, *Illustrated History of Grayson County*, 66.
26. Landrum and Smith, *Illustrated History of Grayson County*.
27. Lucas and Hall, *History of Grayson County*, 118–19.

28. McCulloch to J. B. Magruder, February 3, 1864, *OR*, ser. 1, vol. 34, pt. 2, 943.

29. Landrum and Smith, *Illustrated History of Grayson County*, 67–69; Lucas Collection.

30. Eakin, *Recollections of Quantrill's Guerrillas*, 81–82.

31. *Kansas City Journal*, July 9, 1908; Sylvester Akers, interview, William Elsey Connelley, August 20–21, 1909, McCain Library and Archives, University of Southern Mississippi, M243, box 1, folder 22; Frank Smith MS.

32. Chumbley, *Kentucky Town and Its Baptist Church*; Lucas Collection.

33. P. O. Hebert to George W. Randolph, October 8, 1862, *OR*, ser. 1, vol. 15, 822.

34. *OR*, ser. 1, vol. 34, pt. 2, 853.

35. Frank Smith MS; *Lexington (MO) Advance*, April 1, 1910, quoting the *Lexington News*.

36. *OR*, ser. 1, vol. 22, pt. 2, 856–57.

37. Edwards, *Noted Guerrillas*, 221–22.

38. Ibid., 223.

39. *OR*, ser. 1, vol. 34, pt. 2, 941–43.

40. *OR*, ser. 1, vol. 34, pt. 2, 957–58.

41. *OR*, ser. 1, vol. 34, pt. 2, 970, 994.

42. *OR*, ser. 1, vol. 34, pt. 2, 969.

43. Kansas, Adjutant General's Office, *Report*, 228.

44. Lucas Collection.

45. W. L. Potter to W. W. Scott, March 11, 1896, quoted in Connelley, *Quantrill and the Border Wars*, 440–45.

46. *Dallas Morning News*, April 11, 1942; Elizabeth Lucas, "Glen Eden," Lucas Collection; McCain Library and Archives, University of Southern Mississippi, M243, book 1, folder 22.

47. "Quantrill, James Brothers Used Early Colbert Ferry," Lucas Collection.

48. Chumbley, *Kentucky Town and Its Baptist Church*; Lucas Collection.

49. Connelley, *Quantrill and the Border Wars*, 440–445; Landrum and Smith, *Illustrated History of Grayson County*, 66.

50. Eakin, *Recollections of Quantrill's Guerrillas*, 82.

51. Connelley, *Quantrill and the Border Wars*, 441; Frank Smith MS; Eakin, *Recollections of Quantrill's Guerrillas*, 82–83.

52. Fannin County, box 1, file 22, Lucas Collection.

53. Eakin, *Recollections of Quantrill's Guerrillas*, 83; W. L. Potter to W. E. Connelley, March 11, 1896, in Connelley, *Quantrill and the Border Wars*, 444.

54. Frank Smith MS.

55. Fannin County, box 1, file 22, Lucas Collection.

56. W. L. Potter to William Elsey Connelley, March 11, 1896, in Connelley, *Quantrill and the Border Wars*, 440–445; Eakin, *Recollections of Quantrill's Guerrillas*, 83.

57. Lucas Collection, box 3, file 32; *OR*, ser. 1, vol. 34, pt. 3, 329.

58. *OR*, ser. 1, vol. 34, pt. 3, 747.

59. Kentuckytown Baptist Church Records, 97, Lucas Collection.

60. McCorkle, *Three Years with Quantrill*, 145.
61. Frank Smith MS.
62. B. James George Sr., "Hiram James George: Man of Many Faces," 1959, Jackson County Historical Archives, Independence, MO.
63. *OR*, ser. 1 vol. 34, pt. 2, 1107.
64. *OR*, ser. 1, vol. 34, pt. 3, 742.
65. Kentuckytown Baptist Church Records, 106–7, Lucas Collection.
66. *OR*, ser. 1, vol. 34, pt. 3, 742–43.
67. *OR*, vol. 48, pt. 1, 1310.
68. George, *The Georges*, vol. 3.
69. Eakin, *Recollections of Quantrill's Guerrillas*, 84.
70. Stand Watie to Mrs. Stand Watie, April 24, 1864, in Watie, "Some Letters of General Stand Watie," 46–47.
71. McCorkle, *Three Years with Quantrill*, 145–46.
72. Van Gilder, *Story of Barton County*, 11.
73. *OR*, ser. 1, vol. 34, pt. 3, 273, 329.

CHAPTER 6: A DYING BREED

1. *OR*, vol. 35, pt. 2, 56–67; vol. 34, pt. 2, 476, 478, 489, 490–91, 493; vol. 34, pt. 1, 902–4; vol. 41, pt. 3, 345.
2. Edwards, *Noted Guerrillas*, 230, 234.
3. Ibid., 231.
4. Frank Smith MS; Edwards, *Noted Guerrillas*, 283.
5. Eakin, *Recollections of Quantrill's Guerrillas*, 50–51.
6. Sylvester Akers, interview with William Elsey Connelley, August 20–21, 1909, McCain Library and Archives, University of Southern Mississippi, M243, box 1, folder 22.
7. *Blue and Grey Chronicle* 7, no. 5 (June 2004): 3.
8. *Confederate Veteran Magazine*, 1913.
9. Edwards, *Noted Guerrillas*, 234, 307.
10. *Boone's Lick Heritage*, 6, no. 1 (March 1998).
11. *OR*, ser. 1, vol. 41, pt. 3, 31.
12. Wilcox, *Jackson County Pioneers*, 369–70.
13. Frank Smith MS; Edwards, *Noted Guerrillas*, 234–35.
14. Trow, *Quantrell*, 207.
15. Missouri Historical Company, *History of Saline County*, 304.
16. *OR*, ser. 1, vol. 41, pt. 2, 623.
17. Watts, *Babe of the Company*, 14–19.
18. *Lawrence (KS) Journal World*, February 18, 1961.
19. Gene Owen, "Boonslick Sketches," *Boonville (MO) Standard*; Lilburn Kingsbury, "Way Back Yonder," *Cooper County (MO) Record*; McCorkle, *Three Years with Quantrill*, 118; Edwards, *Noted Guerrillas*, 309.

20. *Confederate Veteran Magazine*, 1913.
21. *Kansas City Post*, August 21, 1909; Lothrop, *History of the First Regiment Iowa Cavalry*, 188.
22. "Quantrill Raiders Recognized by Texas as a Confederate Unit," *Kansas City Star*, October 8, 1949.
23. *Confederate Veteran Magazine*, 1913.
24. "Quantrill Raiders Recognized by Texas as a Confederate Unit," *Kansas City Star*, October 8, 1949.
25. Edwards, *Noted Guerrillas*, 310.
26. Edwards, *Shelby and His Men*, 383.
27. Jones, *Rebel War Clerk's Diary*, 2:307; OR, ser. 1, vol. 41, pt. 4, 1069.
28. OR, ser. 1, vol. 41, pt. 4, 1069.
29. Boswell, *Quantrill's Raiders in Texas*, 166.
30. OR, ser. 1, vol. 41, pt. 1, 430–31.
31. National Historical Company, *History of Howard and Cooper Counties*, 285.
32. Kemper, "Civil War Reminiscences," 314–20.
33. Connelley, *Quantrill and the Border Wars*, 455; *Kansas City World*, September 11, 1898.
34. Edmund Kirby Smith to Sterling Price, August 4, 1864, in OR, vol. 41, pt. 2, 1040–41.
35. Foote, *Civil War: Red River to Appomattox*.
36. OR, ser. 1, vol. 41, pt. 4, 1069, 625–40.
37. Gilmore, *Civil War on the Missouri-Kansas Border*, 284.
38. Sylvester Akers, interview with William Elsey Connelley, August 20–21, 1909, McCain Library and Archives, University of Southern Mississippi, M243, box 1, folder 22.
39. Trow, *Quantrell*, 223.
40. *Kansas City Times*, September 9, 1965, Kansas City Public Library, Missouri Valley Room, Special Collections.
41. Kentuckytown Baptist Church Records, 106, Lucas Collection.
42. McCain Library and Archives, University of Southern Mississippi, M243, box 1, folder 22.
43. Trow, *Quantrell*, 223–25.
44. Hibbs, *Nelson County*, 121.
45. Kentuckytown Baptist Church Records, 107, Lucas Collection.
46. OR, ser. 1, vol. 26, pt. 2, 389.
47. *Kansas City Star*, May 23, 1926.
48. McCorkle, *Three Years with Quantrill*, 187.
49. Bartels, *Man Who Wouldn't Surrender*.
50. McCorkle, *Three Years with Quantrill*, 207; McCain Library and Archives, University of Southern Mississippi, M243, box 1, folder 22.
51. Quantrill Collection, Kansas Collection, University of Kansas Libraries, RH MS E170, vol. 1.

52. *Topeka Capital*, February 24, 1889.
53. George, *The Georges*, 3:786.
54. Fannin County, box 1, file 22, Lucas Collection; *OR*, ser. 1, vol. 34, pt. 3, 814.
55. Connelley, *Quantrill and the Border Wars*, 445.

CHAPTER 7: HEADING HOME

1. Elias Cornelius Boudinot to Stand Watie, Shreveport, LA, May 11, 1865, in Watie, "Some Letters of General Stand Watie," 55.
2. *OR*, ser. 1, vol. 41, pt. 4, 1312–13.
3. Smith to Sprague, May 30, 1865, Reynolds Memorandum to the Marshall Conference, May 10, 1865, *OR*, ser. 1, vol. 48, pt. 1, 191.
4. *Blue and Grey Chronicle* 6, no. 1 (October 2002): 1.
5. Edwards, *Noted Guerrillas*, 456.
6. Trow, *Quantrell*, 234.
7. Ancestral Trails Historical Society, Inc. 29, no. 3 (Fall 2004): 1–2.
8. Lucas and Hall, *History of Grayson County*; Steele, "Jesse James," 12–14; *Sherman Democrat*, August 11, 1916; Martha Hill Davis (great-great-granddaughter of Woot Hill) to Paul R. Petersen.
9. *McKinney Examiner*, April 25, 1931; *McKinney Daily Courier-Gazette*, August 7, 1933, and March 30, 1934; Martha Hill Davis (great-great-granddaughter of Woot Hill) to Paul R. Petersen.
10. *Wichita Falls Daily Times*, June 23, 1908.
11. "Reminiscences of John S. Kritser," 11–13.
12. Trow, *Quantrell*, 258.
13. *Sherman Democrat*, September 8, 1966.
14. Landrum and Smith, *Illustrated History of Grayson County*; Gunn, *First United Methodist Church, Sherman*; Tony Swindell Archives Collection; Texas Department of State Health Services; *Sherman Democrat*, May 16, 1951.
15. Lucas Collection.
16. CSA Archives, chap. 5, file no. 110, 16.
17. *Kansas City Star*, August 29, 1920.

EPILOGUE

1. T. U. Taylor, "The Lee Peacock Feud," Lucas Collection.
2. Warren, *Jefferson Davis Gets His Citizenship Back*, 93–94.

Selected Bibliography

Anderson, Ed H. *History and Business Guide of Sherman and Grayson, Co. Texas*. N.p.: n.p., 1947.

Anderson, John Q. *Campaigning with Parson's Brigade*. Hillsboro, TX: Hill Junior College Press, 1967.

Anderson, Mabel Washbourne. "General Stand Watie." *Chronicles of Oklahoma* 10, no. 4 (December 1932).

Appler, Augustus C. *The Younger Brothers: Their Life and Character*. 1876. Reprint, New York: Fell, 1955.

Baker, T. Lindsay, and Julie P. Baker, eds. *The WPA Oklahoma Slave Narratives*. Norman: University of Oklahoma Press, 1996.

Bailey, Anne J. *Between the Enemy and Texas: Parson's Texas Cavalry in the Civil War*. Fort Worth: Texas Christian University Press, 1989.

Bartels, Carolyn M. *The Man Who Wouldn't Surrender, Even in Death: General Jo Shelby*. Independence, MO: Two Trails, 1999.

Bevier, R. S. *First and Second Missouri Confederate Brigades*. St. Louis: Bryan, Brand & Co., 1879.

Biographical Souvenir of the States of Georgia and Florida. Chicago: F. A. Battery & Co., 1889.

Bonnewitz, Roberta L., and Lois T. Allen. *Raytown Remembers: The Story of a Santa Fe Trail Town*. Clinton, MO: Raytown Historical Society, 1975.

Boswell, Evault. *Quantrill's Raiders in Texas*. Austin, TX: Eakin Press, 2003.

Burns, Erin. "Illinois, the Railroads, and the Civil War." *Illinois History* (February 1994).

Castel, Albert E. *A Frontier State at War: Kansas 1861–1865*. 1958. Reprint, Westport, CT: Greenwood Press, 1979).

———. *General Sterling Price and the Civil War in the West*. Baton Rouge: Louisiana State University Press, 1968.

———. *William Clarke Quantrill: His Life and Times*. 1962. Reprint, Norman: University of Oklahoma, 1999.

Cave, Lillian L. "The Biography of Benjamin Potter." *Westport Historical Quarterly*, 8, no. 2 (September 1972).

Chumbley, Joe W. *Kentucky Town and Its Baptist Church*. Houston: Armstrong, 1975.

Connelley, William Elsey. *Quantrill and the Border Wars*. 1910. Reprint, New York: Pageant, 1956.

Eakin, Joanne Chiles. *Recollections of Quantrill's Guerrillas, as Told by A. J. Walker of Weatherford, Texas to Victor E. Martin in 1910*. Independence, MO: Two Trails, 1996.

————. *Tears and Turmoil: Order #11*. Independence, MO: Eakin, 1996.

————. "Will the Real Jim Crow Chiles Please Stand Up?" June 17, 1995.

————, and Donald R. Hale. *Branded as Rebels: A List of Bushwackers, Guerrillas, Partisan Rangers, Confederates and Southern Sympathizers*. Lee's Summit, MO: Donald R. Hale, 1993.

Edwards, John Newman. *Noted Guerrillas*. 1877. Reprint, Dayton, OH: Morningside, 1976.

————. *Shelby and His Men, or The War in the West*. Cincinnati: Miami Printing and Publishing Co., 1867.

Farber, James. *Fort Worth in the Civil War, as Published in the Fort Worth Star-Telegram*. Belton, TX: Peter Hansbrough Bell Press, 1960.

Foote, Shelby. *The Civil War: Red River to Appomattox*. New York: Random House, 1986.

Ford, John S. *Rip Ford's Texas*. Edited by Stephen B. Oates. Austin: University of Texas Press, 1963.

Gallaway, B. P., ed. *Texas, the Dark Corner of the Confederacy: Contemporary Accounts of the Lone Star State in the Civil War*. 3rd ed. Lincoln: University of Nebraska Press, 1994.

George, B. James, Sr. *The Georges: Pioneers and Rebels, David C. George and Nancy E. George, Their Life and Times*. 2 vols. Independence, MO: Jackson County Historical Society, n.d.

Gilmore, Donald L. *Civil War on the Missouri-Kansas Border*. Gretna, LA: Pelican, 2006.

Grayson County Frontier Village. *History of Grayson County, Texas*. 2 vols. Winston-Salem, NC: Hunter, 1979, 1981.

Gunn, Lois Sanders. *First United Methodist Church, Sherman, Texas, 1859–1984*. Wolfe City, TX: Hennington Publishing, 1993.

Hall, Roy F., and Helen Gibbard Hall. *Collin County: Pioneering in North Texas*. Quanah, TX: Nortex Press, 1975.

Hefan, Le Roy Reuben. *The Overland Mail, 1849–1869: Promoter of Settlement, Precursor of Railroads*. Cleveland: A. H. Clark, 1926.

Heidler, Jeanne T. "'Embarrassing Situation': David E. Twiggs and the Surrender of the United States Forces in Texas, 1861." *Military Affairs* (April 1984).

Hibbs, Dixie. *Nelson County: A Portrait of the Civil War*. Charleston, SC: Arcadia/Tempus, 1999.

Hicks, Hannah. "The Diary of Hanny Hicks." *American Scene* 13 (1972).

History of Vernon County, Missouri. St. Louis: Brown and Co., 1887.

Hoffman, David R., and Frances Hoffman. "The McKee's Move to Texas." *Missouri Historical Review* 97, no. 4 (July 2002): 296.

Jones, John B. *A Rebel War Clerk's Diary at the Confederate States Capital*. 2 vols. Philadelphia: Lippincott, 1866.

Kansas. Adjutant General's Office. *Report of the Adjutant General of the State of Kansas . . . 1861–1865*. 1867–70. Reprint, Salem, MA: Higginson Book Co., 1998.

Kemper, Mary Lee. "Civil War Reminiscences at Danville Female Academy." *Missouri Historical Review* 62, no. 3 (April 1968).

Landrum, Graham, and Allen Smith. *An Illustrated History of Grayson County, Texas*. 2nd ed. Fort Worth, TX: Historical Publishers, 1967.

Larkin, Lew. *Bingham: Fighting Artist; The Story of Missouri's Immortal Painter, Patriot, Soldier, and Statesman*. Kansas City, MO: Burton, 1954.

Lindberg, Kip, and Matt Matthews. "'It Haunts Me Night and Day': The Baxter Springs Massacre." *North and South Magazine* 4, no. 5 (June 2001): 42–53.

Lothrop, Charles H. *A History of the First Regiment Iowa Cavalry Veteran Volunteers, from Its Organization in 1861 to Its Muster Out of the United States Service in 1866*. Lyons, IA: Beers and Eaton, 1890.

Lucas, Mattie Davis, and Mita Holsapple Hall. *A History of Grayson County, Texas*. Sherman, TX: Scruggs, 1936.

McCorkle, John. *Three Years with Quantrill: A True Story Told by His Scout, John McCorkle*. 1914. Reprint, Norman: University of Oklahoma Press, 1992.

Maddox, George T. *Hard Trials and Tribulations of an Old Confederate Soldier*. Van Buren, AR: Argus, 1897.

Mansfield, J. B., comp. *The History of Tuscarawas County, Ohio*. Chicago: Warner, Beers and Co., 1884.

Masterson, V. V. *The Katy Railroad and the Last Frontier*. Norman: University of Oklahoma Press, 1992.

Missouri Historical Company. *History of Saline County, Missouri*. St. Louis: Missouri Historical Co., 1881.

Moore, John C. *Missouri in the Civil War*. Vol. 9, *Confederate Military History*. Edited by Clement A. Evans. 12 vols. Atlanta: Confederate Publishing Co., 1899.

National Historical Company. *History of Clay and Platte County, Missouri*. St. Louis: National Historical Co., 1885.

National Historical Company. *History of Howard and Cooper Counties, Missouri*. St. Louis: National Historical Co., 1883.

Norton, Richard L., ed. *Behind Enemy Lines: The Memoirs and Writings of Brigadier General Sidney Drake Jackman, CSA*. N.p.: Oak Hills Publishing, n.d.

Palmer, Jacob Teaford. "A Jackson County Citizen Writes of the Time of Quantrill and the Jayhawkers." In *Tears and Turmoil: Order #11*, by Joanne Chiles Eakin. Independence, MO: Eakin, 1996.

Pickering, David, and Judy Falls. *Brush Men and Vigilantes: Civil War Dissent in Texas*. College Station: Texas A&M Press, 2000.

Rankin, Melinda. *Texas in 1850*. 1850. Reprint, Waco: Texian Press, 1966.

"Reminiscences of John S. Kritser, A Civil War Veteran Under the Command of William C. Quantrill's Confederacy." *Western Historical Quarterly* 9, no. 1 (June 1973).

Rhodes, James Ford. *History of the Civil War, 1861–1865*. New York: Macmillan, 1917.

Snead, Thomas L. *The Fight for Missouri from the Election of Lincoln to the Death of Lyon*. New York: Scribner, 1886.

————. "The First Year of the War in Missouri." In *Battles and Leaders of the Civil War: From Sumter to Shiloh*. Edited by Robert Underwood Johnson and Clarence Clough Buel. New York: Thomas Yoseloff, 1956.

Snyder, John F. "The Capture of Lexington." *Missouri Historical Review* 7, no. 1 (October 1912): 1–9.

Steele, Phillip W. "Jesse James: Brother-in-Law." *Quarterly of the National Association and Center for Outlaw and Lawman History*.

Thruston, Ethylene Ballard. *Echoes of the Past: A Nostalgic Look at Early Raytown and Jackson County*. Kansas City: Lowell Press, 1973.

Titchenal, Oliver R. *The Titchenal Saga: 350 Years of Faith and Hope and Family Life in America: The Genealogy and History of Thirteen Generations of the Tichenor and Titchenal Families, Coupled with American and Local History*. North Ridgeville, OH: Titchenal, 1995.

Trow, Harrison. *Charles W. Quantrell: A True History of His Guerrilla Warfare on the Missouri and Kansas Border During the Civil War of 1861–1865*. Kansas City: n.p., 1923.

United Daughters of the Confederacy, Missouri Division. *Reminiscences of the Women of Missouri During the Sixties*. Jefferson City, MO: Stephens, ca. 1913.

U.S. War Department. *The War of the Rebellion: A Compilation of the Official Records of the Union and Confederate Armies*. 128 vols. Washington, DC: Government Printing Office, 1880–1901.

————, Record and Pension Office. *Organization and Status of Missouri Troops, Union and Confederate, in Service During the Civil War*. Washington, DC: Government Printing Office, 1902

Van Gilder, Marvin L. *The Story of Barton County: A Complete History, 1855–1972*. N.p.: Reily Publication, n.d.

Voss, Stuart F. "Town Growth in Central Missouri." *Missouri Historical Review* 66, no. 2 (January 1970).

Ware, James W. "Indian Territory." In *The Western Territories in the Civil War*. Edited by Leroy H. Fischer. Manhattan, KS: Journal of the West, 1977.

Warren, Robert Penn. *Jefferson Davis Gets His Citizenship Back*. Lexington: University Press of Kentucky, 1980.

Watie, Stand. "Some Letters of General Stand Watie." *Chronicles of Oklahoma* 1, no. 1 (January 1921).

Watts, Hampton B. *The Babe of the Company: An Unfolded Leaf from the Forest of Never-To-Be Forgotten Years*. Fayette, MO: Democratic Leader Press, 1913.

White, Alexander White. *The Red River Valley, Then and Now: Stories of People and Events in the Red River Valley During the First Hundred Years of Its Settlement*. Paris, TX: North Texas Publishing Co., 1948.

Wilcox, Pearl. *Jackson County Pioneers*. 1975. Reprint, Independence, MO: Jackson County Historical Society, 1990.

Wood, Larry. "Harry Truman: Federal Bushwhacker." *Missouri Historical Review* 98, no. 3 (April 2004): 201–22.

Woodson, W. H. *History of Clay County*. Topeka and Indianapolis: History Publishing Co., 1920.

Wooster, Ralph A. *Texas and Texans in the Civil War*. Austin: Eakin Press, 1995.

Young, Bennett H. *Confederate Wizards of the Saddle*. 1914. Reprint, Columbus, OH: Ironclad Publishing, 1999.

Index